AN UNUSUAL RELATIONSHIP

THE GOLDSTEIN-GOREN SERIES
IN AMERICAN JEWISH HISTORY

General editor: Hasia R. Diner

We Remember with Reverence and Love: American Jews and the Myth of Silence after the Holocaust, 1945–1962
Hasia R. Diner

Is Diss a System? A Milt Gross Comic Reader
Edited by Ari Y. Kelman

All Together Different: Yiddish Socialists, Garment Workers, and the Labor Roots of Multiculturalism
Daniel Katz

Jews and Booze: Becoming American in the Age of Prohibition
Marni Davis

Jewish Radicals: A Documentary System
Edited by Tony Michels

An Unusual Relationship: Evangelical Christians and Jews
Yaakov Ariel

An Unusual Relationship

Evangelical Christians and Jews

Yaakov Ariel

NEW YORK UNIVERSITY PRESS

New York and London

NEW YORK UNIVERSITY PRESS
New York and London
www.nyupress.org

References to Internet websites (URLs) were accurate at the time of writing.
Neither the author nor New York University Press is responsible for URLs that
may have expired or changed since the manuscript was prepared.

Library of Congress Cataloging-in-Publication Data
Ariel, Yaakov.
An unusual relationship : Evangelical Christians and Jews / Yaakov Ariel.
pages cm. — (The Goldstein-Goren series in American Jewish history)
Includes bibliographical references and index.
ISBN 978-0-8147-7068-9 (cl: alk. paper)
1. Judaism—Relations—Evangelicalism. 2. Evangelicalism—Relations—Judaism.
3. Evangelicalism—United States. 4. Judaism—United States. 5. Antisemitism. I. Title.
BR1641.J83A76   2013
261.2'6—dc23   2012049428

New York University Press books are printed on acid-free paper, and their binding materials
are chosen for strength and durability. We strive to use environmentally responsible
suppliers and materials to the greatest extent possible in publishing our books.

Manufactured in the United States of America

10 9 8 7 6 5 4 3 2 1

For Rachel

CONTENTS

ACKNOWLEDGMENTS

This book would not have been possible without the support of numerous institutions and individuals. In carrying out the research and writing for this book, I received invaluable assistance from a number of foundations. The Louisville Institute and its director, James W. Lewis, deserve special mention for providing a generous research grant that enabled me to conduct much of the archival and field research. The Institute for the Arts and Humanities at the University of North Carolina offered a fellowship that enabled me to conduct a semester of research. The Simon Dubnow Institute at the University of Leipzig provided a number of summer grants that allowed me to work in an engaging intellectual atmosphere. The institute's director, Dan Diner, also offered many inspiring ideas. Deputy directors, Susanne Zepp and Jörg Deventer, also offered valuable help. The University of North Carolina and the Department of Religious Studies provided me with a semester of leave to carry on my research and writing. Chairs, deans, and departmental administrators have shown support and goodwill. Malachi Hacohen and Julie Mell initiated an ongoing Duke-Carolina seminar that created an intellectual atmosphere congenial to discussions on the relationship between Christians and Jews.

I also owe thanks to a number of colleagues who shared knowledge or insights: Kelvin Crombie, Brantley Gasaway, Shalom Goldman, Gershon Greenberg, David Halperin, Motti Inbari, Jonathan Kaplan, Ruth Kark, Mark Kinzer, Anke Költsch, Shanny Luft, James Lutzweiler, Joel Marcus, Paul Merkley, Terry Muck, Gershon Nerel, David Pileggy, Mark Pinsky, Leonard Prager, Jorge Quiñónez, Richard Robinson, Alifa

ACKNOWLEDGMENTS

Saadya, Tsvi Sadan, Dirk Sadowski, Grit Schorch, Jim Sibley, Stephen Spector, Wes Taber, Grant Wacker, Donald Wagner, and Robert Wistrich. Lori Osborne, Matt Hotham, Stephanie Gaskill, and Stan Thayne provided valuable editorial assistance. Ben Zeller very graciously read the manuscript in its early stages. Hasia Diner and Jennifer Hammer offered guidelines and advice that helped turn the manuscript into a book. Finally, my wife, Rachel, to whom this book is dedicated, provided a highly vital ingredient: trust in my abilities, as well as the invaluable services of a highly skilled librarian.

In 2002, the American government released a 1972 recording of a conversation that Richard Nixon, one of America's most controversial presidents, conducted with Billy Graham, America's most respectable evangelist in the second half of the twentieth century. The content of the audiocassette shocked many Americans. The transcripts revealed that Graham and Nixon expressed negative opinions of Jews, blaming them for the ills of the age and echoing stereotypical images of Jews as subversive liberals whose aim was to undermine Christian values and institutions.[1] Many had already been aware of Nixon's prejudices against Jews but were surprised that Graham shared the disgraced president's opinions.

Remarkably, Graham's conversation with Nixon took place in the same year that the evangelist produced a movie, *His Land*, that portrayed the state of Israel in very favorable terms. Israel's prime minister at the time, Golda Meir, was a guest of honor at the film's opening night. The movie was not an isolated endeavor. Graham spoke and wrote many times in favor of Israel, viewing it as playing a significant role in the unfolding of prophecy as well as regarding it as an ally in the global war against the Soviet bloc.[2] In the late 1960s and throughout the 1970s, American Jewry supported Israel almost unanimously and judged pro-Israeli stands as indications of friendliness toward the Jewish people. In addition to his expressed pro-Israel sympathies, Graham spoke about Jews and Christians as overcoming prejudices together, a gesture that Jewish organizations particularly appreciated.[3] Until the recording was made public, Jewish leaders generally looked upon Graham as a devoted friend. In 1969, the Anti-Defamation League, one of the central Jewish organizations in America, awarded Graham the Torch of Liberty Plaque; and in 1977 the American Jewish Committee, another major Jewish group, awarded him its first Inter-Religious Award.

Other evangelical leaders were, at times, less careful than Graham, openly expressing long-held cultural stereotypes of Jews, often unaware of the sensitivities that their remarks could potentially stir. Such evangelists usually did not see any contradiction between long-held negative Christian opinions of Jews and an appreciative understanding, to which they often subscribed, of the place of the Jewish people in history. Graham's patron and mentor, William Riley, for example, condemned the Jews for their alleged destructive political leanings at the same time that he expressed hopes for the well-being of the Jews and for their rejuvenation as a nation.[4]

That Graham apologized in 2002 for the things he had said thirty years earlier and stated that he did not hold such views anymore illustrates that evangelical attitudes toward the Jews did not remain static, instead going through major changes and developments, especially in the late twentieth century.[5] In general, such opinions have improved over the years, both in response to political and cultural developments and following actual encounters between evangelicals and Jews.

Making Sense of a Complex Relationship

Graham's remarks on the negative impact of the Jews on American culture, juxtaposed with his friendly statements about Jews and support of Israel, highlight the complexity of evangelical attitudes toward the Jews. To outside observers such attitudes have seemed contradictory, but they make sense if one examines the history of evangelical-Jewish relations and evangelical theology, including the eschatological faith to which many conservative evangelicals have adhered. These attitudes have been the product of a particular kind of Christian theology and its understanding of the role of the Jews in history, coupled with long-standing Christian theological and cultural opinions about Judaism and the Jewish people. The varied and complex encounters between evangelicals and Jews have carried to an extreme the already complicated nature of traditional Christian attitudes toward the Jews, bringing to the forefront, as never before, highly mixed Christian ideas about Jews. Demonstrating unprecedented devotion toward the Jews as God's chosen people and as heirs and continuers of historical Israel, and offering extensive assistance to Jews as individuals and as a community, evangelicals have also criticized Jewish ways and manners that in their opinion have resulted from the Jews' nonacceptance of the Christian faith. For the most part, evangelicals have rejected Jewish religious liturgy, piety, and biblical exegeses, except as a means to keep the Jews oriented toward the eventual arrival of the Messiah, and they have remained confident that the Jews will eventually come to recognize Jesus as their Lord and savior.

Wishing to become involved in Jewish life and to reshape Jewish priorities, evangelicals set out to evangelize the Jews, hoping that at least some Jews would adopt the Christian faith and pietistic-evangelical values. However, propagating the Christian gospel among the Jews has involved not merely bringing the Jews to convert but also instructing the Jews as to their true identity and mission in history and teaching them what to expect when this era comes to an end and the apocalyptic stage of history unfolds. In conservative evangelical minds, evangelizing the Jews has meant helping to prepare humanity for the arrival of the Messiah. Missionary work among the Jews has also offered a means of interacting with them, getting acquainted with their culture, and ultimately influencing their destiny. The extensive and energetic missionary network that developed in the nineteenth and twentieth centuries has aimed at spreading the evangelical Christian message among the Jews, regardless of the immediate numerical results in terms of actual converts.[6] In contrast to the common Jewish perception, evangelical missionaries have viewed themselves as friends of the Jews and have often acted as their defenders. They have denounced discrimination against Jews in different parts of the world, and they have, like evangelicals holding to the messianic faith in general, lent support to Jewish causes that have seemed to them pertinent to the advancement of history, such as the return of the Jews to Palestine.

The complications in evangelical-Jewish relations go further than inherent theological and cultural ambivalences. In evaluating evangelical-Jewish relations, one must keep in mind that evangelical Christianity is not united or uniform. While there are features that most evangelicals share, evangelical Christianity is composed of numerous denominations, as well as thousands of independent churches. In a number of denominations, evangelicals are but one segment within churches that do not fully share their views. Different evangelical groups have inherited or developed varied ecclesiastical, liturgical, and theological traditions. There are noted divisions over such matters as baptism and the Lord's Supper, as well as over electionism versus predestination. Likewise, there are regional and national variations and ethnic divides even within the same geographical areas.[7] An important line of division among evangelical Christians in the past decades has run between charismatics and noncharismatics. Evangelicals also differ in their accommodations to or critiques of the general culture. Evangelical institutions of higher learning, such as Wheaton College, Liberty University, and Bob Jones University, differ from one another not only in their academic standards but in their codes of behavior as well.[8] Although most evangelicals throughout the twentieth century and into the twenty-first have adopted conservative social and political worldviews, some have been more progressive. Such variations play a role in evangelical attitudes toward the Jews: ironically, the more conservative elements have shown greater interest in and dedication to the Jews. At the same time, some theological perceptions are shared by almost all self-defined evangelical Christians. In fact, many evangelicals view their various differences and divisions as secondary in comparison to what they consider the essential elements of the evangelical Christian faith.[9]

Evangelical theology focuses on the redemption that Jesus's sacrifice on the cross offers individuals who accept him as their savior, through inner, spiritually and morally transforming conversion experiences. Evangelicals believe that all human beings need to undergo these experiences of conversion or being born again, in which they establish personal relationships with Jesus of Nazareth and adopt him as their personal savior. In the evangelical view, only those who have undergone such conversion experiences can obtain justification and be morally transformed, "saved," and promised eternal life. Evangelicals are therefore committed to spreading the Christian message and to persuading the unconverted of the need to accept Jesus as their personal savior. Evangelicals also view the Christian Bible, both the Old and New Testaments, as God's message to humanity and insist on the authenticity and integrity of the sacred Christian texts. Taking a more literal reading of the Christian sacred scriptures than liberal Christians, many evangelicals adhere to a messianic faith, expecting the second coming of Jesus to earth to occur in the near future. These theological principles—the emphasis on the need to accept Jesus as a personal savior, the commitment to universal evangelism, the more literal reading of the Christian Bible, and the messianic premillennialist faith, which expects the imminent arrival of Jesus to establish the kingdom of God on earth—have played important roles in shaping evangelical attitudes toward the Jews.

A comparative examination of different Christian groups and opinions points to a more literal reading of the Bible and to the evangelical messianic faith as the most decisive factors forming evangelical opinions on the Jews. Evangelicals do not always embrace a premillennialist messianic faith, and some of them hold to traditional Christian understandings of Judaism and its relation to Christianity. Yet messianically oriented evangelicals, who expect the imminent return of Jesus, have exercised ideological and political influences far beyond their numbers, often shaping much of the evangelical agenda toward Jews.[10] Since the late nineteenth century, most leading evangelists and popular evangelical pastors, from Charles Spurgeon and Dwight Moody to Billy Graham and Jerry Falwell, have adhered to a premillennialist messianic faith—that is, one that expects not only a Second Coming but also Jesus's literal and physical presence on earth during a thousand-year reign—and have helped to spread it within the larger evangelical community. Evangelical Christians with premillennialist leanings have departed from the traditional Christian claim that Christianity is the "true Israel" and the object of God's promises to that people. Believing that the covenant God established with Abraham is still valid, even if temporarily suspended, they view the Jews as heirs and continuers of the children of Israel and as the object of biblical prophecies about a restored kingdom of David. At the same time those evangelical Christians have insisted that the Jews, like all other people, have to accept Jesus as their savior in order to be redeemed and to gain sound moral and spiritual ground. This outlook has created a paradox. Evangelical Christians, who ardently believe that only those who have accepted Jesus as their savior are redeemed, have constructed an understanding of the Jews as a people in covenant with God who are about to resume their ancient position as God's first nation. This complicated, double-edged theological perception stands at the heart of the evangelical relation to the Jews and has given rise to an amazing relationship between the two communities.

Some of the details of evangelical-Jewish relations have been surprising. Evangelicals called for the restoration of the Jews in Palestine and devised political initiatives for the creation of a Jewish commonwealth in Palestine even before the rise of Jewish national movements in the later decades of the nineteenth century. Evangelicals supported the Zionist movement from its inception, showing much enthusiasm for the program of Jewish settlement in Palestine. Evangelical Christians reacted with approval to the establishment of the state of Israel in 1948, and with particular enthusiasm to the outcome of the war between Israel and its Arab neighbors in June 1967.

The War of 1967 enhanced the evangelical faith that the Jews were indeed preparing the ground for the events of the end times. Evangelicals have increasingly lent support to Israel, establishing a number of organizations intended to muster political and material support for the country and its people. Missions to the Jews have, likewise, become agencies for promoting pro-Israeli sentiments and organizing trips to that country. Millions of evangelicals, mostly from North, Central, or South America, have visited Israel as pilgrims.[11] Tens of thousands of young evangelicals have gone as volunteers to work at kibbutzim or archaeological digs. Thousands have settled in the country. Evangelicals have also developed networks of material support for needy Israeli Jews, becoming major sponsors of welfare programs in Israel. Since the nineteenth century, Israel, Jews, and the Holy Land have come to play central roles in evangelical preaching, conferences, theological tracts, historical studies, political analyses, novels, historical dramas and feature films, documentaries, TV programs, songs, and hymns.

Of special interest to many premillennialist evangelicals has been the prospect of rebuilding the Temple in Jerusalem. A number of evangelical writers and activists have considered the rebuilding of a Jewish temple to be an essential development of the apocalyptic era. Since the 1980s, conservative evangelicals and traditionalist Jews have begun unprecedented cooperation over preparations for such a project. This joint agenda has given rise to the almost surreal circumstance of evangelical Christians offering financial aid and moral support to groups of observant Jews, some of them ultra-Orthodox, intent on rebuilding the Temple.[12]

Such unprecedented encounters have brought members of both groups to amend their opinions of each other. Evangelical attitudes toward Jews as people have changed, with old stereotypes beginning to erode. Improvement in the image of the Jews within evangelical culture forms the background to another development that would have been unfathomable just a few decades earlier: the rise of an assertive community of Jewish evangelicals. Since the early 1970s, large numbers of Jews have converted to Christianity in its evangelical interpretation, yet have chosen to openly maintain their ethnic and cultural identities as Jews, combining Jewish rites and customs with faith in Jesus as Savior. This community, in its turn, has further influenced evangelical attitudes toward the Jews, becoming a lobby within the larger evangelical camp that argues for keeping causes such as missions to the Jews and goodwill toward that people high on the evangelical agenda. As a rule, these Jewish evangelicals adhere to a premillennialist understanding of the role of the Jews in God's plans for humanity and have adopted a pro-Israeli view of Middle East politics.

Jews have not remained indifferent to evangelical overtures. Their early encounter with evangelical culture came by way of the extensive missionary networks that evangelicals began establishing in the nineteenth century. Jews did not always react happily to attempts to evangelize them, although numerous Jews took advantage, as individuals, of the services the missions offered.[13] Jewish, especially Zionist, leaders welcomed evangelical supporters as early as the nineteenth century; often they were unaware of the details of Christian evangelical theology, which differed in important ways from Jewish visions of the future of the Jews, and they ignored the missionary efforts.[14] Those differences notwithstanding, a symbiosis developed between groups of Jews and evangelical Christians, with both communities, somewhat unwittingly, encouraging each other by offering each other reassurances that history was on their side.

The new evangelical-Jewish love affair has not been left on its own to proceed in peace without interference from grudging relatives and neighbors. The involvement of other religious groups, including liberal Christians and both Christian and Muslim Arabs, and the criticisms they have expressed are important for understanding the full meaning of evangelical-Jewish relations and for highlighting the uniqueness of conservative evangelical attitudes toward Jews. It demonstrates how different messianic visions and readings of the Bible have created various and at times diametrically opposed understandings of contemporary political and cultural realities as well as sharply different views of the Jews and their role in history. Liberal Protestants, especially since 1967, have come to view Israeli policies critically, and many nonevangelical Christians have reacted negatively to what they have considered a preferential evangelical treatment of the Jews, especially in relation to the Arab-Israeli conflict.[15] Liberal and Middle Eastern Christian writers have viewed evangelical support of Israel as resulting from misguided reading of the Bible, with some Christians taking exception to the evangelical departure from traditional Christian doctrines, especially replacement theology, the idea that Christians have superseded the Jews as God's chosen people.[16] Arabs and Palestinian sympathizers have become angry observers of the Jewish-evangelical relationship, preferring the company of liberal Christians or progressive evangelicals.[17]

The full picture of evangelical-Jewish relations has also been complicated by the voicing of dissenting views within the evangelical and

Jewish communities. Progressive evangelicals, a minority group within the evangelical network, differ from their more conservative brothers and sisters over their vision of how the kingdom of God on earth is about to materialize and consequently take exception to much of the social and political agendas of the conservatives, including the conservatives' position on the Israeli-Arab conflict.[18] Jews too have become divided in their reaction to the evangelical outpouring of interest in and support for them and for Israel. Liberal Jews have, at times, felt uncomfortable with the close relationship and cooperation that has developed between conservative Christians and Jews. Such Christians, they have asserted, promote values that go against the spirit of an open, progressive society.[19] Traditional and Zionist Jews, on the other hand, have often embraced the evangelical overtures.

This Book and Its Agenda

Until the 1970s, many saw conservative evangelicals as a secondary force in Christendom. Consequently, scholars have paid much more attention to the relations of Catholics, Greek Orthodox, or mainstream Protestants to the Jews.[20] Virtually no histories of Zionism, Israel, and the Arab-Israeli conflict have paid much attention to evangelical support of the advancement of the Zionist plan and the Israeli state.[21] Evangelical writers have often concentrated on missionaries and Jewish converts.[22] In recent years, however, journalists, academics, and the larger public have begun taking more interest in the evangelical involvement in the conflict in the Middle East and have noted the political alliances that have developed between evangelical Christians and Jews.[23] Until recently, writers have paid more attention to the British evangelical interest in the Holy Land. David Katz's seminal work on the Puritans and their understanding of the Jews and their role in history, and Eitan Bar-Yosef's study of the Holy Land in the English mind, provide excellent background for understanding British evangelicals' biblical imagery and the views they promoted toward Jews and the Holy Land.[24] Shalom Goldman and Paul Merkley have similarly explored the cultural and religious background of the American fascination with the Holy Land and Zionism, while David Rausch was one of the first to trace the American evangelical involvement in the early history of Zionism.[25] The books of Stephen Spector, Victoria Clark, and Motti Inbari have illuminated the dynamics of evangelical-Israeli relations and the larger political implications of evangelical support for Israel.[26] Writing from a concerned Christian perspective, Timothy Weber and Stephen Sizer have also published important studies of evangelical attitudes toward the Jews and Middle East politics, placing such elements within the larger context of the evangelical premillennialist faith.[27] In the last decades ethnographers such as Carol Harris-Shapiro and Shoshanah Feher have paid attention to the rise of Jewish evangelicals and their congregational life, adding important insights to this movement, while Gershon Nerel, Leonard Prager, and Jorge Quiñónez have paid attention to the literary expressions of evangelical Jewish culture.[28]

This book does not set out to dispute previous scholarly work. Appreciating and often referring to other studies, it promotes a somewhat different agenda. The volume explores the broad range of evangelical interest in the Jews and evangelical efforts to influence the course of Jewish history and the consequences of such endeavors in a number of realms. While it draws on previous studies, it explores additional aspects of evangelical-Jewish relations, as well as drawing some overarching conclusions. The book points to the power of messianic faith, theological perceptions, and understanding of sacred scriptures to shape the attitudes and policies of members of one community of faith toward another and to affect their opinions on political and social developments relevant to the other group.

At the same time the book also demonstrates the power of an ongoing relationship between two communities, evangelicals and Jews, to influence and reshape, in its turn, opinions and attitudes. While evangelicals began interacting with Jews armed with certain hopes and assumptions, their encounters stirred a set of reactions and exchanges that in their turn affected evangelical agents' thought and actions and by extension those of the evangelical community at large. Often unwittingly, evangelical and Jewish attitudes and exchanges have changed and developed, at times taking unexpected forms. They have created at times borderland cultures, communities, and alliances that neither evangelicals nor Jews could have envisioned when they first set eyes on each other.

The book deals mostly with evangelical Christians who have shown interest in and set out to interact with the Jews, many of them holding a messianic faith. It focuses particularly on American evangelicals, who since the late nineteenth century have become the larger and more dynamic segment of the evangelical movement, influencing the course and character of evangelicalism worldwide. The book pays attention to pietist and evangelical precedents and parallels in other lands. But it views America as the hub of evangelical ideas and activities and as the place where it is exercising the greatest political and cultural influence, often affecting the country's agenda. At the same time, there are global aspects to the evangelical-Jewish encounter. The focus of much of the evangelical interest in Jews is related to a territory on the eastern shores of the Mediterranean, and the involvement of the evangelicals with Jewish life has spread all over the globe, both in missionary activities and in fighting anti-Jewish persecution. In evaluating Zionism, and Israel, evangelicals have constantly paid attention to other countries and political developments around the globe. As students of prophecy and believers in the imminent second arrival of Jesus, many evangelicals have been busy studying world politics and incorporating their observations into their prophetic expectations. For example, much of the resurgence of evangelical interest in Israel took place during the cold war era, and evangelicals combined their opposition to the Soviet Union and communism with their support of Israel.[29]

The relationship between evangelical Christians and Jews has given rise in the late modern era to unprecedented political, cultural, literary, communal, spiritual, and theological initiatives that have revolutionized the historical dynamics of Christian-Jewish relationships, creating new and unexpected meeting points between the two communities of faith. Evangelical involvements with the Jews and the Jewish responses to evangelical overtures have in their turn affected the interaction between the two communities, both bringing about unprecedented alliances and projects and amending long-held opinions and assumptions. This book sets these innovative and unexpected encounters and initiatives within a larger historical perspective and examines their effect on developing new attitudes and interconnections as it furthers its argument that the evangelical-Jewish relationship has given birth to varied exchanges, alliances, literary venues, and even a borderland culture. It explores the beliefs, messages, language, literatures, and communities, as well as political agendas, agencies, and means, that evangelicals have created to affect the future of the Jews.

The chapters of the book follow the history, theology, literatures, institutions, and political and missionary efforts that are relevant to the understanding of evangelical-Jewish relations. The volume starts with a historical survey that provides the background for understanding the special evangelical relationship with Jews. The first chapter traces the history of Protestant interest in the Jews in the modern era and especially the precedents and inspirations that have offered a model for evangelical interaction with the Jews, while the second chapter examines the messianic faith that has served as the theological basis for, and the driving force behind, the evangelicals' relationships with the Jews. Chapter 3 follows the thoughts and works of major evangelical writers, scholars, thinkers, conferences, publications, and institutions that have played an important part in shaping evangelical opinions of Jews. Chapter 4 deals with evangelical initiatives for the restoration of the Jews to Palestine and the building of a Jewish commonwealth there, as well as the relationships that developed between evangelical Christians and the emerging Jewish Zionist movement. Chapter 5 recounts the stories of evangelicals who built their homes in Palestine, trying to help the Jews settle there as well as positively affect the Jews' opinions and agendas. Chapter 6 explores the extensive missionary efforts that have been a major venue for evangelicals to establish contact with and approach the Jews as well as to instruct the Jews about what they have considered to be the Jews' true mission in history and about what to expect when this era comes to an end and the apocalyptic stage of history unfolds. The book analyzes the extensive literatures that evangelicals have produced about and for the Jews, whether attempting to approach them or to propagate their understanding of the role of the Jews in history among fellow Christians. These writings include, as chapter 7 points out, a prolific, yet almost unknown, Yiddish evangelical literature, which evangelicals, both Jewish and non-Jewish, produced throughout the nineteenth and twentieth centuries. Chapter 8 deals with an important segment of evangelical publications on the Jews from the 1910s through the 1930s that amalgamated evangelical messianic thought, global conspiracy theories, and cultural stereotypes of Jews. The chapter explains the rise and decline of such literature within the larger context of evangelical attitudes and worldviews. Chapter 9 explores the evangelical literature on the Holocaust, much of which has lately taken the form of romance novels, the genre of choice for evangelical readers in the last two decades.[30] Examining these diverse bodies of literature offers many insights into the development of the evangelical perceptions of the Jews in the last generation. Chapter 10 concerns evangelical interaction with the state of Israel, a country evangelicals have come to view as playing a major role in history. Evangelical activists have established a number of organizations intended to muster political and material support for Israel and its people, and evangelical missions have become agencies for promoting pro-Israeli sentiments and organizing trips to that country. The next chapter is devoted to the almost unimaginable cooperation that has developed between evangelicals and Jews around the prospect of rebuilding the Temple. This task has been of special interest to many premillennialist evangelicals, especially since the 1980s. A number of evangelical writers and activists have considered the rebuilding of a Jewish temple to be an essential event of the apocalyptic era. The 1980s saw the beginnings of efforts to prepare for that project, with conservative evangelicals offering financial aid and moral support to groups of observant Jews, some of them ultra-Orthodox, intent on rebuilding the Temple. These encounters brought both groups to amend some of their opinions of each other. The attempt to rebuild the Temple on the Temple Mount, where its former ruins are said to be located, necessarily affects Muslims, who also have an interest in the site, so the chapter explores evangelical attitudes toward them and highlights Arab attitudes toward evangelical-Jewish rapport. The final chapter examines a development that would have also been unfathomable just a few decades ago: the rise of a vibrant and innovative community of Jewish evangelicals. While few expected to see communities of Jewish evangelicals come about in the late modern era, their creation has been a logical outcome of the relentless evangelical attempts to influence the Jewish understanding of history, as well as the new attitudes that evangelicals had developed toward the Jews. These Jewish Christian groups, in their turn, have made their mark on evangelical attitudes toward the Jews and have produced extensive literatures, which, among other goals, have helped create a new identity that is both evangelical Christian and Jewish.

* * *

This book as a whole offers a comprehensive analysis of the roots, manifestations, and consequences of the evangelical interest in the Jews and the ways evangelicals have offered alternatives to the more conventional historical interactions between Christians and Jews, as well as the Jewish and non-Jewish reactions to these developments. The best place to begin that story is with the innovative attitudes toward the Jews brought about by the predecessors of evangelicals within the Protestant camp.

1

The Roots and Early Beginnings of the Evangelical-Jewish Relationship

The evangelicals' interest in the Jews, the role they ascribe to that people in history, and their understanding of the relationship between Judaism and Christianity have roots that go back as far as the early generations of Christianity. Evangelical relations to the Jews, however, have also departed in meaningful ways from more traditional Christian perceptions of who the Jews are and what that people's position is in God's plans for humanity. One should look for the beginnings of evangelical attitudes toward the Jews among Protestant groups in the sixteenth and seventeenth centuries that emphasized a literal reading of the Christian Bible and advocated a new understanding of the Jews and their role in history. Some of the parameters of the evangelical-Jewish relationship were spelled out at that time.

The Protestant reformers reevaluated the Christian position toward the Jews, at times following traditional Christian perceptions and at other times questioning them, making up their minds anew on Judaism and its position vis-à-vis Christianity, as well as on Jews as sojourners in Christian societies. They took a renewed interest in the Jews and in the Hebrew Bible: a number of them, including Martin Luther himself, participated, at least to some degree, in the Hebraist tradition of the Renaissance and at times developed an appreciation of postbiblical Jewish texts.

While Protestants adopted the Roman Bible, both the Old and New Testaments, as their sacred scriptures, they produced their own translations and interpretations of the biblical texts and gradually gave up on parts of the Catholic sacred canon. By the eighteenth century the Protestant Old Testament came to resemble the Jewish Tanakh, since most

Protestants had removed from this first part of their sacred canon the books that the Jews had not included in their canon, such as the books of Judith or the Maccabees.[1] This would prove significant for evangelical-Jewish relations, since, when approaching Jews, evangelical Christians would point to a mutual sacred text as a basis for a theological discussion.

Likewise, Protestants gave up on the adoration of Mary and the saints, whom they saw as redundant mediating elements, and eliminated much of the traditional iconography and priestly vestments. They turned the Roman Eucharist, in which the sacrifice of Jesus had been reenacted, into the more symbolic Lord's Supper. Theologically, the boldest Protestant move was to give up on the idea of the priesthood and the sacramental system as necessary mediating elements between God and the faithful, replacing it with the idea that Christians could be justified before God on their own with no need for the mediating role of the church.[2] Likewise, Protestants declared that Scripture alone was authoritative, denying the authority of institutions and traditions that had developed throughout the Middle Ages. These new choices and understandings also enabled evangelicals to present their theology, liturgy, and environment as Jewish-friendly and compatible with Jewish understandings and styles.

However, the Protestant cultural heritage was that of Western Christian societies of the Middle Ages and the early modern era. The cultural baggage from those times strongly affected the initial evangelical relation to the Jews. While some Protestant and later evangelical theological attitudes were innovative, Protestant feelings toward the Jews were often shaped by traditional Christian teachings and popular Christian European images that portrayed the Jews as greedy, cowardly, dangerous, and diabolical.[3] Evangelical thinkers would change their theological positions on the Jews, developing more appreciative understandings of the Jewish people and their role in history, but as an examination of their opinions of Jews would show, this did not necessarily mean giving up all at once on the cultural Christian stereotypes of Jews that had endured for many generations.

While many Protestants continued to agree with the traditional Christian claim that Christianity had inherited God's covenant with Israel, many did not. It was within the ranks of Protestantism, both in the radical left wing of the Reformation and among a number of mainline thinkers, that a new appreciation developed toward the Jews. While their perspective retained some elements of anger and bitterness, such Protestants often looked upon the Jews of their generation as heirs to the covenant between God and Israel and as objects of biblical prophecies about a restored Davidic kingdom in the Land of Israel. In their relation to the Jews, these segments of the Reformation served as the forerunners of contemporary evangelical Christians.

In general, Reformed, pietist, and Puritan thinkers who were forerunners of evangelicals developed mixed feelings toward the Jews: both anger and appreciation, both hopes for the national revival of the Jews and claims that the Jews, by their refusal to accept Jesus, had halted the redemption of humanity. Even thinkers who on the whole expressed positive opinions on Jews found it difficult to shake off commonly held stereotypes. Such conflicting expressions would characterize the writings of evangelical thinkers well into the twenty-first century. Their attitudes have been too complex to be classified in the simple categories that late nineteenth-century thinkers established, such as "anti-Semitic" and "philo-Semitic." In general Judaism and Jews have been more important to Protestant thinkers than to exponents of other brands of Christianity in the modern era. Protestants related to the Jews in strong terms, their understanding of their own tradition depending on defining the role and place of Jews in God's plans for humanity. For their part, Jews paid attention to Protestant claims: the theological elites of both traditions were well informed about each others' opinions and publications. The lively exchanges that have taken place between Protestants and Jews have helped both communities define their feelings toward each other, as well as determine the character of their own communities.

Evangelicals have often referred to Martin Luther (1483-1546), the reformer who led much of the early protest against the Roman Church, as a forerunner of a new approach toward the Jews. Luther indeed set

some of the parameters of evangelical attitudes. He embodied in his
early thought the complex and ambivalent attitudes that would often
characterize the initial evangelical relation to the Jews. In the early stages
of his career as a reformer, he invested efforts and hopes in inviting Jewish conversions to Christianity and absorbing interested Jewish inquirers
into the newly created Protestant society. Luther was initially inspired by
Paul's letter to the Romans, in which the apostle predicted the redemption of the Jews in the fullness of time. He believed that the Jews had
been justified in refusing, over the centuries, to convert to Christianity,
since the Christian religion they had previously encountered was a cor-
rupted form. He was hopeful that the Jews would join his Protestant
Church, which he believed went back to the origins of Christianity, and
he looked upon the Hebrew Bible as one of its major sources of authority
and inspiration.[4] Many evangelical missionaries would adopt Luther's
attitude, insisting that there was really no reason for Jews not to accept
their version of Christianity.

Jews took notice of the Reformation and its innovations and were
actually impressed, although not with the results Luther hoped for.
Especially in areas where Protestants were minority groups, Jews were
sympathetic to the new community of faith and saw Protestantism as
a faith closer to Judaism, and liberated from what they considered to
be pagan elements prevailing in other forms of Christianity. Pietist and
evangelical missions to the Jews would promote the notion that Protestantism was a purer and friendlier version of Christianity, closer to Judaism. However, as a rule, Jews as a group did not see a reason to adopt
Protestantism, and Luther's attitudes turned hostile when he realized
that no major movement of Jewish converts to Protestant Christianity
was under way. In his negative sentiments, Luther was not original. Such
attitudes reflected Christian European understandings of Jews and Judaism at the time. While pietist and evangelical Protestant thinkers and
groups developed more friendly and appreciative attitudes toward the
Jews, they too would not be able to free themselves entirely from traditional negative images. As a rule, evangelical Christians would follow
in the footsteps of the younger Luther: while often disappointed over

the choices Jews had made throughout history, they would invest time, resources, and hope in attempts to approach them and convince them of the truth of the Gospel.

Luther's opinions were not the only Lutheran ones to affect the way evangelicals would approach the Jews. Some reformers, such as Andreas Osiander (1498-1552), defended the Jews, writing tracts denouncing the "blood libel," the accusation, originating in western and central Europe in the late Middle Ages, that Jews murdered Christian children to use their blood in rituals.[5] Denouncing such charges would become routine for evangelicals writing on the Jews. Evangelicals had developed their own complaints about the Jews, but they fought bigotry and discrimination that seemed to them to be based on unsubstantiated defamation. Like evangelicals in years to come, thinkers such as Osiander and Philip Melancthon had to contend with accusations that Protestants were "Judaizing" Christianity, and the need to combat the label *Judaizing* would occasionally affect evangelical writings as this segment of Protestantism struggled to create an environment that would be inviting to Jews.

In general, the Reformation did not bring about an immediate transformation in popular attitudes toward the Jews. Well until the late twentieth century, most Protestant churches held to replacement theology, the traditional Christian theological understanding that Christians had superseded the Jews as heirs to the covenant between God and Israel and that Jews were cast out on account of their refusal to accept Jesus as their Lord and savior. According to that view, the role of the commandments had come to an end with the sacrifice of Jesus on the cross and his atonement for human sins. Only through faith in Jesus Christ could humans attain justification and salvation. Only if Jews joined the Christian Church and accepted the faith in Jesus they would be morally and spiritually redeemed. While evangelicals would reject replacement theology, they would agree with the traditional Protestant understanding of the purposelessness of the commandments and the need for Jews to accept Jesus as their Lord and savior.

The Reformed tradition, which had developed alongside but separately from the Lutheran tradition, ultimately had a powerful impact on evangelical positions toward the Jews. Reformers of that school, such as Johannes Oecolampadius (1482-1531), Huldrych Zwingli (1484-1531), Martin Bucer (1491-1551), John Calvin (1509-64), and Theodore Beza (1519-1605), developed a more appreciative attitude toward the Jews. Leaders of the Reformed tradition put an even greater emphasis on the Old Testament than Lutheran reformers, viewing it as equal in importance to the New Testament. Their reading of the Hebrew Bible strongly influenced their view of the Jewish people and the role of that people in history, ultimately creating goodwill toward the Jews.[6]

John Calvin, who became the most well-known Reformed theologian, wrote commentaries on a number of books or chapters in the Hebrew Bible, taking special interest in the biblical codices of law as well as in psalms with messianic overtones.[7] Like Luther's, Calvin's thoughts about the Jews vacillated between rejection and appreciation, anger and sympathy. When it suited his arguments, he related to Jewish regulations based on biblical commandments as adequate and commendable, as when he discussed the Sabbath or the prohibition on images.[8] Less than pleased with the Jewish refusal to accept the Christian tenets of faith, Calvin nonetheless argued that when the Bible spoke about the sinfulness of the Jews it referred to that nation as symbolizing all people. Not only Jews but all humanity stood guilty before the Lord, and what happened to the Jews, he warned his readers, could also happen to the Christians.[9] Unlike Luther, who believed that the role of the Jewish people, as an entity separate from Christianity, had come to an end, Calvin believed that although God was angry at the Jews they could still be redeemed as a nation.[10] This idea would become a cornerstone of evangelical attitudes. At the same time, Calvin, like other Protestants, was influenced by the historical dispute between Christianity and Judaism. He wrote a dialogue in which he argued with a (probably imaginary) Jewish polemicist. Theodore Beza, Calvin's heir and continuer in Geneva, expressed more sympathy for the Jews. Like Luther in his early days as a reformer, Beza blamed the Christians for the Jewish refusal to accept the Christian faith. While holding the view that the Jews had been rightly punished by God through their exile and scattering and their subsequent tribulations, he was praying daily for the redemption of that people.

By the seventeenth century, a number of Reformed thinkers developed the understanding that the Jews were not cast out by God but were still, in principle, heirs and continuers of biblical Israel, destined to play an important role in the unfolding of the divine plan of salvation. While often mixed and ambivalent, Reformed attitudes toward the Jews were more positive than traditional Christian understandings of the Jews at the time and marked an improvement in the relation of Christians toward the Jews. For the most part it would be Reformed thinkers in England, Holland, France, and Switzerland, as well as in those parts of the New World where Reformed theology would gain influence, who would express hope for the Jews' prospect of national restoration and conversion to Christianity.[11] A number of Reformed theologians took special interest in the Jews, viewing them as the chosen people, and followed closely developments such as the rise of a large Jewish messianic movement in the mid-seventeenth century, stirred by Shabattai Zvi's claim to be the Messiah.[12]

Puritans and the Jews

The Reformation in England in the sixteenth century gave rise to groups and ideas that promoted a new outlook on the Jews. Expelled from that country in 1290, Jews lived on in English imagery despite their physical absence. Echoes of long-held negative images would persist for centuries and would eventually play a part in early evangelical conceptions of Jews.[13] However, the impact of the Reformation, and especially the Reformed tradition, and the Puritan and later on the evangelical messianic faith, would eventually counterbalance the traditional understanding of the Jews and their character. The translation of the Bible into the vernacular had a strong effect on the English Protestant mind, as well as on the English language.[14] The Christian sacred scriptures stirred new eschatological expectations, which became especially prevalent among those influenced by the Reformed tradition. While some thinkers identified the English with Israel and believed that Jerusalem could be built in England, many also paid attention to the prospect of the return of the Jews to Palestine and their conversion to Christianity.[15] Such attitudes began in the late sixteenth century but became more prevalent in the seventeenth century. Thomas Brightman, rector of Hawnes, predicted the conversion of the Jews to Christianity and their restoration to Palestine. Earthly Jerusalem, he believed, would become the center of the universe as well as the center of a world-dominant Christianity.[16] Giles Fletcher, fellow of King's College, Cambridge, and ambassador of Queen Elizabeth to Russia, expressed his belief in Israel's future restoration and conversion. Fletcher, who was considered an expert on Russian matters, believed the Tartars to be the ten lost tribes of Israel and included them in his vision for Israel's conversion. The lawyer Henry Finch published in 1621 *The Calling of the Jews*, which stirred much attention. Like other Protestants adhering to a Christian messianic faith, Finch insisted that the biblical references to Israel, Judah, Zion, and Jerusalem should be read literally and that the Old Testament prophecies that spoke about the return of Israel to its land were therefore meant for the descendants of Abraham, whom he identified with the Jews of his time.[17] Evangelicals would be strongly influenced by English Reformed theology as well as by the New England Puritan understanding of the Jews.

Premillennialist messianic convictions were popular among the first generations of English settlers in what was to become the United States.[18] The New England Puritans were committed to building a perfect Christian polity in the new land, "a city built upon a hill," and saw themselves as having entered into a covenant with God, based on their perfect Christian faith and saintly membership.[19] Strongly impressed by the Old Testament narratives and identifying with the biblical Children of Israel, they often referred to their experiences in their new environment in biblical terms, similar to those used in the sacred Jewish and Christian scriptures to describe the Israelites entering Canaan. While they worked to build the kingdom of God in America, their messianic hopes included the conversion of the Jews to Christianity and the restoration of that people to Palestine.[20] Similar aims and hopes would be evident in later years among the evangelicals. Increase Mather, a Con-gregationalist pastor in Boston and a leader of the Massachusetts Bay Colony, claimed that the conversion of the Jews and their restoration to Zion would come as a prelude to the millennial age. The title of his book *The Mystery of Israel's Salvation,* a best seller by the standards of the time, which he published in 1669, bore witness to his convictions regarding the future of the Jews. An associate of Mather who shared his hopes was the Congregationalist minister John Davenport, who endorsed Mather's opinions in the preface to *The Mystery of Israel's Salvation.*[21] Another supporter of the hope for the conversion of the Jews to Christianity and their return to Palestine was William Hooke, a colleague of Davenport in New Haven, who returned to England to serve as chaplain to Oliver Cromwell. He expressed his views on the matter in an additional preface to Mather's book.[22]

The civil war that began in England in 1642 gave further rise in the Puritan camp to groups and individuals that anticipated the imminent return of Jesus. Their eschatological hopes often included the prospect of the Jewish conversion to Christianity and restoration to Zion as a precursor for the arrival of Jesus. Puritan thinkers called for the cancel-lation of the Expulsion Act of 1290 and for the readmission of the Jews to England. On the basis of Deuteronomy 28:64, "The Lord shall scatter thee among one end of the earth even unto the other," some proponents of the readmission of the Jews argued that for the Messiah to come, the Jews had first to be scattered to all corners of the earth, including England. Others argued that the readmission of the Jews to England would make them more available to efforts aimed at their conversion to Christianity.[23] Some voices in the Puritan camp even suggested that England should take it upon herself to ship the Jews back to Palestine. In December 1655, Oliver Cromwell, the Lord Protector, summoned the Whitehall Conference, where he and others reiterated some of the aforementioned arguments. The conference did not produce a resolu-tion allowing free Jewish immigration to England, but it did assert that there was no legal bar against it. In actuality, Cromwell allowed Jews to settle in the country. This did not mean that all Protestants welcomed

Jews wholeheartedly. While some Protestant groups expressed a new, more appreciative, interpretation of the role of the Jews in God's plans for humanity, many of them still subscribed to deep-rooted negative ideas. They held a hopeful vision for the future of that people when they would be rehabilitated as God's chosen nation. But the Jews had not yet accepted Christianity, and as non-Christians they were morally and spiritually deprived.

Pietism and the Jews

The influence of millennial hopes declined in England and its colonies in the eighteenth century. Theologians such as Jonathan Edwards, leader of the First Great Awakening, asserted that the millennium would be ushered in through human perfection.[24] According to that belief, the arrival of Jesus would take place after humanity built the kingdom of God on earth on its own. The Jews, they believed, would convert to Christianity before that ominous arrival.[25]

However, at the turn of the eighteenth century, Christian pietist groups constructed new ideas about Jews that would strongly influence evangelical opinions and modes of action toward the Jews a few decades later. One of the branches of pietism that influenced Protestant attitudes toward the Jews most appeared in central Germany in the seventeenth century. Pietists advocated the need to live, on both personal and communal levels, a committed Christian life, to read the Bible literally, and to engage in international evangelism. Messianically inclined pietist thinkers were convinced that the Jews would again play a central role as God's chosen people.[26] Like their Puritan counterparts in the English-speaking world, they took special interest in the prospect of the conversion of the Jews, considering it to be an essential step toward the advancement of the messianic times.

Within the Protestant camp, pietists were pioneers of missions in general, and, like the evangelical missionaries who came after them, they gave priority to the evangelization of the Jews. Their first missionary field was India, and the mission to the Jews came next. In 1721, a group of pietist thinkers headed by Johann Callenberg (1694–1760) founded the Institutum Judaicum, a mission to the Jews in the Prussian city of Halle, the hub of German pietist activity and the home of pietist educational and missionary centers. They were not the first Protestants to attempt to bring the Gospel to the Jews. Such efforts began with Martin Luther and his contemporaries. A few years before the pietists started the Institutum Judaicum, Lutherans established a house in Hamburg for the assistance of Jewish converts, which turned into a mission in its own right. Puritan ministers had also been eager to convert Jews, but they had never institutionalized their efforts, and they did not study the culture of the Jews. The pietists were the first to systematize evangelism among the Jews, and their literature and attitudes influenced evangelical missions to the Jews for generations, as evangelicals often copied or emulated pietist pioneering methods in that realm.

Training its missionaries systematically, the pietist Institutum Judaicum offered its evangelists knowledge of Jewish culture, including Jewish languages.[27] The mission collected an impressive library, by the standards of the time, on Jewish themes and set out to publish books for the propagation of Christianity among the Jews as well as for disseminating knowledge on Judaism and Jews among Christian supporters and interested laypersons.[28] Christian theology and Christian popular opinion had often looked upon the Jews as a people frozen in time, practicing a uniformed and static tradition all around the globe. Few took notice of Jewish inner divisions or paid attention to the actual daily life of the Jews. Likewise, holding an image of the Jews as wealthy people, few Christians had any desire to engage in welfare work among the Jews. Missionaries affiliated with the Institutum Judaicum departed from such long-held attitudes, thereby setting an example for nineteenth- and twentieth-century evangelicals. Venturing to study the Jews and their living conditions, pietists discovered rampant poverty and need among that people in both Germany and Poland. They believed that Jews would appreciate Christian material assistance and set out to offer Jews examples of Christian charity. Assisting the Jews was also a means of connecting with them and gaining access to their lives and culture. Missionaries working on behalf of the institute took tours of Jewish communities, visiting with Jews, engaging in conversations, and encountering actual customs and hardships.[29] The pietist and later on evangelical methods of evangelism did not always correspond with twenty-first-century standards of openness to other people's faiths. Moving from one community to the next, missionaries used aggressive tactics, knocking on Jewish doors and entering Jewish public spaces, including synagogues during services. Missionaries did not shy away from making provocative statements, engaging Jews in debates on the appropriate manner of reading sacred texts, and arguing about whether the Messiah had already come once before. These modes of encounter, not always welcomed and not always civil, would become characteristic of many evangelical missionaries as they tried to instruct and evangelize the Jews.

The institute in Halle published a series of books to acquaint Christians with Jewish life, culture, and languages. These books show a systematizing of missionary efforts and a keen interest in the Jews, their cultures, and the effective means to approach them. The institute's catalog of such works, first published in 1733, then republished in 1736 and 1748, testifies to its success in attracting Protestant interest. The publications' users included not only the institute's people but other members of the community, as well as members of other pietist and evangelical missionary groups that began proliferating in the early nineteenth century.

One of the works published by the institute was a manual for the study of Yiddish.[30] Christians had written manuals for the study of Yiddish before, mostly to assist merchants who wished to trade with Jews, but this was the first one intended to help in the evangelization of Jews. It served as a precursor for a long line of evangelical manuals that would come to promote the knowledge of Jewish languages among Christians wishing to evangelize them. The University of Halle, which the pietists established in 1698, was the first in history to include courses on Yiddish in its curriculum. Significantly, evangelical institutions would become the first in the English-speaking world to teach Yiddish. Secular or liberal institutions of higher learning would include the teaching of Yiddish in their curricula only in the later years of the twentieth century.

As the institute's titles point out, the pietists recognized that Jewish languages had different local variations and literary expressions. An analysis of the various catalogs of books that the institute produced is revealing.[31] In its early years the institute also published books dealing with, or intended for, Muslims, but only a few in comparison to the growing number of publications relating to Jewish themes. The catalog for 1748 included a series of books about the Jews and their culture and a larger selection of books intended for Jews in Jewish languages. The latter included three books—the Epistle to the Romans, the Epistle to the Hebrews, and one other—in "the Syrian language" (i.e., Aramaic), "in Hebrew print," as well as forty-seven books in the German Jewish dialect, which eighteenth-century Jews in Germany still spoke.

The list of books in German Jewish dialect started with Jewish sacred texts, including what were titled "The Five Books of Moses." The title points to a Christian understanding of the text and its role. Other publications intended to appeal to Jewish culture and sentiments carried non-Christian titles for books in the Hebrew Bible. The book of Zion and the book of Solomon would awaken strong yearnings among Jews, as well as among pietists and evangelicals. The institute similarly published a compilation of the writings of the prophets Isaiah and Jeremiah, as well as the visions of Ezekiel and Daniel. These were not arbitrary selections. Pietist missionaries, and the evangelical missionaries who followed in their footsteps, considered the messianic hope to be a unifying meeting point between pietist hopes and Jewish yearnings for the realization of the messianic times. From this mutual point of view, the pietists set out to convince Jews that the Messiah had already come once before and was about to return rather than appear for the first time. They believed that shared Old Testament texts, which Jews knew and respected, particularly prophetic passages in the Hebrew Bible, such as those in Isaiah, would convince Jews that the pietists' messianic interpretation was correct. Evangelical writers would pursue this line of persuasion well into the twenty-first century.[32] In general, the institute's publications promoted Protestant Christianity as the proper continuation of the biblical faith and as a belief that would provide Jews with a secure, and even glorious, future.

Pietists and evangelicals would try to convince the Jews not only in the truth of the Trinity, or Christology, but in the idea that Jesus was about to arrive imminently for the second time. The list of publications included a tract on the role of Gog and Magog, the empires that in Christian messianic imagery were destined to play an important role in the battles of the end times.

A few works in the institute's list of publications in German-Jewish dialect were situated toward the end of the list, intended presumably for those potential converts who had read some or all of the earlier, more "elementary" tracts and would, so the missionaries hoped, be convinced by the Christian pietist reading of the prophetic biblical texts.[33] One was *The Ungodliness of the Talmud;* another was the Augsburg Confession, the classical text of the Protestant creed.

As dedicated as the pietists were to spreading the Christian faith among the Jews and learning the realities of Jewish life, they still held stereotypical images of that people. Contemporary historians who examine pietist opinions on Jews as a people are at times taken aback.[34] For example, the diaries of the institute's first director, Johann Callenberg, reveal some opinions on the Jews that are a far cry from twenty-first-century standards of tolerance. However, one should analyze such sentiments within the context of their time. Considering the Jews to be, in essence, God's first choice, who had been cast temporarily aside, pietists related to the Jews more appreciatively than other Christian thinkers of the period.[35] Mixed opinions and feelings on the Jews were another part of the pietists' heritage that evangelicals would inherit.

Pietism strongly affected the evangelical movement that came about in the English-speaking countries in the second part of the eighteenth century and the beginning of the nineteenth century. The roots of the evangelical wing of English-speaking Protestantism can be found in seventeenth-century Puritanism, in seventeenth- and eighteenth-century pietism, and in the American revivalist movement, which took shape during the mid-eighteenth and early nineteenth centuries. Like pietists, evangelical Protestants exemplified several diverse schools of thought that were not organized under one ecclesiastical roof but that shared a number of convictions and assumptions. Like pietists, evangelicals believed that formal baptism and church affiliation were not enough to define people as Christians. Like pietists, evangelical Christians also shared a deep commitment to the spreading of the Christian gospel. Like pietists, evangelical Christians emphasized the truth of the Christian sacred scriptures and viewed them as the messages of God to humanity, advocating a more literal reading of the Bible and opposing exegetical options that questioned the authenticity and accuracy of biblical texts. Like pietists, many evangelical Christians adhered to a messianic faith and understood biblical prophecies as relating to the restoration of Israel to its ancestral land.[36] Like the pietists, evangelicals found the mission an appropriate venue and a convenient institutional structure to express their interest in and be involved with the Jews.

Historians have paid little attention to favorable German and Scandinavian Protestant attitudes toward Jews.[37] However, pietist movements that promoted biblical-millennial faiths and related to the Jews as heirs and continuers of historical Israel existed in those countries, although they were more marginal within the larger culture than in English-speaking countries. Consequently, Christian Zionism, a movement of Christian supporters—mostly evangelicals or pietists—of Jewish restoration in Palestine, had fewer adherents, more limited standing and less social influence among Protestants in Germany and Scandinavia than in English-speaking countries, Holland, and Protestant France.

In the first half of the nineteenth century, in both Britain and America, evangelical influence in society grew considerably. The era also witnessed a revival of messianic expectations. The French Revolution, followed by Napoleon's wars, coupled with the Industrial Revolution, seemed to many to be indications that an era was ending and the apocalypse was about to begin.[38] Pietist and evangelical groups with premillennialist leanings adhered, at times, to different systems of biblical and eschatological exegesis. The prevalent premillennialist school in the eighteenth and nineteenth centuries has become known as "historical" or "historicist."[39] Certain that Jesus was about to return soon, adherents tried to find correlations between the political and environmental developments of their era and biblical passages that seemed to predict future events. Reading biblical passages, especially from Daniel in the Old Testament or the Revelation of John in the New Testament, they found in them references to occurrences in recent history. Dramatic developments, such as the French Revolution of 1789 and the exile of the pope from Rome in 1798, stirred the messianic imagination and served as the basis for calculations of when Jesus of Nazareth would come back to redeem humanity and establish his righteous kingdom on earth. Such messianic hope tended, at times, to lend itself to disappointments and to readjustments of predicted dates.[40]

During the nineteenth century, the historicist messianic faith was the prevalent choice among evangelicals in Britain, America, and other countries. Britain of the early and mid-nineteenth century turned into a hub of evangelical interest in the Jews and attempts to be involved in the life of that people. The leader of the evangelical movement in Britain in the 1840s and 1850s, the seventh Earl of Shaftesbury, promoted Jewish restoration to Palestine at the same time that he labored to evangelize the Jews and create centers of interaction with them. He, and others, attempted at times to bring the British cabinet to act on behalf of the establishment of a Jewish commonwealth in Palestine. Shaftesbury was not alone. Many British aristocrats, as well as members of the intelligentsia, took interest in the prospect of the imminent arrival of Jesus and discussed the role of the Jews in the events surrounding Jesus's return.

It was in this atmosphere of intensified eschatological expectations in Britain, and of a growing interest in the Jewish people and the prospect of their return to Palestine, that dispensationalism, a new school of belief in the second coming of Jesus, was born. In the 1820s and 1830s, the Plymouth Brethren, an urban, educated group of evangelicals, developed a new understanding of messianic expectations. They asserted that the first apocalyptic events were to happen in an imminent, but not precisely known, time in the near future, and they refrained from calculating exact dates. Their brand of messianic faith would therefore be labeled "futurist." The major futurist school of eschatology, dispensationalism, received its name from the view that history was divided into distinct eras, in each of which God had a different plan for humanity. Although it started in Britain, dispensationalism was to have a more influential role among American evangelicals than among the British. In the decades following the Civil War, much of the conservative evangelical elite in America became dispensational premillennialist. Adoption of the dispensationalist messianic faith as a philosophy of history and mode of biblical criticism caused a dramatic rise in interest, among American evangelicals, in the Jews, their fate, the prospect of their conversion to Christianity, and their national restoration in Palestine.[41]

Many adherents of the historical school of eschatology looked upon the Jews as heirs and continuers of biblical Israel, but not all. Dispensationalists, however, have been totally certain as to the necessary role of the Jews in helping to bring about the messianic age and have unequivocally pointed to the return of the Jews to their land as a precursor to the arrival of Jesus. In the United States and Canada, dispensationalism motivated a quest to be involved with the future of Jews, including intensified attempts to approach the Jews and acquaint them with the Christian gospel and the messianic hope. Noted evangelical leaders in America of the late nineteenth century and the early twentieth century, including William Blackstone, Arno Gaebelein, Reuben Torrey, William B. Riley, and James Gray, became proponents of both Christian Zionism and missionary work among the Jews. They promoted in their writings the expectation of the imminent second coming of Christ to usher in the kingdom of God on earth and the belief that, after recognizing Jesus as their true Messiah, the Jewish people would resume their place as the first nation of the Lord in the millennial kingdom.[42]

Conservative Evangelicals, Liberal Protestants, and Jews

Premillennialist-oriented evangelical Christians have not operated in a vacuum. They have often competed with other ideas and movements in the larger society and within Protestant Christianity in particular. In the later nineteenth century and early twentieth century, the evangelical position was strongly shaped by the "modernism versus fundamentalism" controversy that split the ranks of Protestantism in America.[43] Many evangelicals developed a reinforced conservative point of view, insisting on the need to preserve "the fundamentals of faith," in which they included the understanding that "no one can enter the kingdom of God unless Born Again."[44] For a few decades, fundamentalism was almost synonymous with conservative evangelicalism. It included an emphasis on the importance of evangelism and a belief in the prospect of the Jewish restoration in Palestine. When it became evident in 1925 that American public opinion, as a whole, did not accept the antimodernist opinions of the fundamentalists, they moved out of the limelight, although far from the public gaze they continued to evangelize and enlarge their ranks.[45] In the 1950s to 1970s, a more moderate and accommodating form of conservative evangelicalism emerged from within the fundamentalist camp and reentered American public life again with much vigor, replacing to a large degree the older fundamentalist culture. However, the liberal-versus-evangelical division still strongly affects evangelical culture and consciousness and shapes the character of American religion in general.[46]

The liberals stand in the background to the history of the interaction between evangelicals and Jews.[47] They present alternatives to the kind of attitudes and encounters that evangelicals and Jews developed with each other. Liberal Protestants have actively reacted to the special relationships that developed between evangelicals and Jews, often taking exception to evangelical attitudes and objecting to the alliances and projects evangelicals have initiated. The liberals have been committed to principles different from those of the conservatives. They have seen themselves as children of the Enlightenment and progressive political thought. Yet mainstream Protestantism as a whole did not necessarily become more accepting of Jews, at least not immediately. Liberal thinkers often denied the validity of the Hebrew biblical narratives, and Protestant intellectuals were split in their opinions on the integration of the Jews into Western societies.[48] The long-term effects of liberal notions, especially in the English-speaking world, eventually included interfaith dialogue and the beginning of a recognition of Judaism as a valid religious option alongside Christianity. For the most part, liberals were also more critical of Zionist and Israeli agendas.

Evangelicals would not be immune to the larger trends. They too would address the question of what kind of human beings the Jews were, and until the late twentieth century their answers to that question were mostly mixed. Evangelical writers who were trying to promote the investment of time and money in evangelizing the Jews used, at times, debates over the productivity and honesty of the Jews and their ability to become well-integrated and productive citizens to persuade their audiences, some of them leaning toward liberal opinions, of the necessity of missions, which they claimed would help reform and transform the Jews.[49] But whatever they thought of the Jews as members of contemporary societies, evangelical premillennialists were certain that when the messianic age arrived the Jews would become exemplary citizens and would recognize Jesus as their messiah.

The Jewish relationship with liberal Protestants had also its complications. Jewish scholars were impressed by liberal Protestant academic methodologies. However, they also noticed that liberal Protestant scholars related very differently to the Jewish sacred texts and epic narratives than to their own.[50] Jewish scholars often saw themselves as defenders of a defamed tradition, producing scholarship that validated the legitimacy and authenticity of Judaism over and against attacks by Protestant scholars, whom, they believed, underrated Judaism while exalting and exonerating Christianity. At times, Jewish defenders of the faith, such as the Reform leader Isaac M. Wise, directed anger at both liberal Protestant scholars and conservative evangelical missionaries.[51]

During the same decades, evangelical thinkers were busy writing theological tracts of a different nature, in which they incorporated a premillennialist messianic faith into a larger conservative Christian worldview. They too would try to defend the authenticity and integrity of the Bible against what they considered to be the liberal undermining of the sources of Christian authority and validity. Such attempts at defending biblical narratives did not bring about a united evangelical-Jewish front. While often resentful of liberal attitudes, Jewish scholars were divided in their relation to the higher criticism of the Bible, and many were more open to modernist modes of biblical criticism than conservative evangelicals. During the late decades of the nineteenth century, when evangelical leaders embraced the dispensationalist eschatological faith and worldview, this new belief affected their understanding of the Jews and their role in God's plan for the messianic times. They expressed their new exegesis in a series of sermons, conferences, and publications that would transform evangelical opinions of the Jews.

2

The Evangelical Messianic Faith and the Jews

Historical Background

The evangelical messianic vision, in which the Jews play a central role, draws on a long Christian eschatological tradition.[1] Christianity started as a messianic movement, its early texts speaking about apocalyptic times and the near coming of the kingdom of God on earth.[2] After Jesus's death, his disciples expected his imminent return and the beginning of a long-sought righteous divine reign. However, in the fourth and fifth centuries, when Christianity became the established religion of the Roman Empire, mainline Christianity became mostly amillennial in character. Christian thinkers such as Augustine, bishop of Hippo, postponed the materialization of the messianic era to a remote time.[3] Their vision has become the prevalent outlook among the major branches of Christianity. However, like a subterranean river, messianic yearnings for an imminent return of Jesus persisted and found expression in the writings of a number of Christian thinkers and communities. Arising periodically within Western Christianity, messianic movements often demonstrated nonconformist attitudes toward the church hierarchies and teachings.[4]

The Reformation of the sixteenth century gave rise to groups and individuals who expected the messianic times to arrive imminently. These included thinkers within mainstream Protestant churches, such as Martin Luther, as well as within the more radical, "left-wing" groups of the Reformation. In the seventeenth century, Puritan and pietist groups within English and German Christianity adopted premillennialist messianic understandings of the course of human history. A resurgence of interest in eschatology and the prospect of the imminent arrival of the Messiah took place in England during the revolutionary era of the 1640s and 1650s.[5] Puritans who were drawn to this premillennialism took an interest in the fate of the Jews and the prospect of their restoration to Palestine.[6]

As noted, a large wave of expectation of the return of Jesus took place in Europe and America at the turn of the nineteenth century. Historicist premillennialism, which thrived at that time, was not exclusively evangelical, and forms of premillennialism were also popular among groups that seceded from Protestantism and turned into independent movements, such as the Adventists. However, especially in Britain, the "historicist" line of messianic hope strongly influenced evangelical attitudes toward the Jews.[7] It inspired support for Jewish restoration in Palestine and motivated extensive missionary activities among the Jews.[8]

A good example of the effect of the historicist school on evangelical attitudes toward the Jews can be seen in the views and attitudes of Charles H. Spurgeon, pastor of the Metropolitan Tabernacle in London and the most influential British evangelist of the nineteenth century. Spurgeon, whose sermons are still in circulation in America, repeatedly expressed his opinion on the Jews, their role in history, and their eventual restoration and redemption.[9] Far from being a promoter of ecumenical approaches, he lashed out mercilessly at the "papal" Catholic Church, equating it with Antichrist and Babylon. Jews were a different category altogether. Viewing the Jews as historical Israel and calling upon Christians to treat them respectfully, the Baptist minister visited a major London synagogue during services and met on friendly terms with Rabbi Nathan Adler, Britain's chief Ashkenazi rabbi, at that time.[10] Like the young Luther, Spurgeon commended the Jews for not having joined the ranks of the Catholic Church. Evangelical Protestantism, he believed, was a different matter, and the Jews should accept Jesus as their savior under the auspices of evangelical Christianity.

> Let the true Christian church think lovingly of the Jew and, with respectful earnestness, tell him the true gospel. Let her sweep away superstition and set before him the one gracious God in the Trinity of His divine Unity. And the day shall yet come when the Jews, who were . . . the first

missionaries to us who were afar off, shall be gathered in again. Until that
time, the fullness of the church's glory can never come. . . . Let not the
chosen race be denied their peculiar share of whatever promise Holy Writ
has recorded with a special view to them.[11]

Spurgeon was not devoid of anger toward the Jews and asserted that
their condition of exile was God's punishment for their sins. Like many
evangelical thinkers holding to a premillennialist faith, Spurgeon was
committed to evangelizing the Jews and served as one of the leaders of
the British Society for the Propagation of the Gospel among the Jews.
British members of "Dissenting" churches, as they were known at the
time, including the Baptists, founded the society after concluding that
they could not labor to evangelize the Jews with the representatives of
the established Church of England. Like other evangelicals who have
considered the Jews to be the chosen people, Spurgeon saw Jewish restoration as a prerequisite to the materialization of the kingdom of Christ
on earth.[12] "For when the Jews are restored, then the fullness of the Gentiles shall be gathered in; and as soon as they return, then Jesus will
come upon Mount Zion to reign with his ancients [Jewish ancestors]
gloriously."[13]

The Rise of Dispensationalism

Spurgeon subscribed to historicist premillennialism. However, in the
early decades of the nineteenth century another school of messianic
expectations, dispensationalism, developed that would become widely
accepted in America, and consequently in other parts of the globe,
strongly influencing evangelical attitudes toward the Jews.[14]

Eschatological Christian doctrines that divide human history into different ages or eras can be traced to Christian texts as early as the *Epistle
of Barnabas*, a tract from the turn of the second century CE.[15] One of the
first proponents in post-Reformation Europe of this currently Protestant
evangelical school of premillennialism was, ironically, a Jesuit priest,
Francisco Ribera, who, attempting to defend the papacy from Protestant

accusations, suggested in 1590 that Antichrist could appear only after this age ended.[16] However, the modern eschatological belief known as dispensationalism crystallized in Britain in the 1820s and 1830s under the influence of John Nelson Darby and the group he led, the Plymouth Brethren.[17] It was Darby and the Plymouth Brethren who turned futurism into a popular eschatological belief that competed successfully with the predominant historicist school. When William Miller's prophecy seemed to have failed in 1844, the historicist school of premillennialism received a severe blow. The evangelical ground was clear for Darby and others to propagate futurist ideas. Darby did not construct dispensationalism out of thin air; he drew heavily on earlier ideas concerning the second coming of Jesus. Darby's teachings, however, differed on some major points from earlier historicist premillennialist convictions. Both schools predicted the arrival of Jesus to occur in the near future. However, while historicists believed that most eschatological events had happened in the past, futurists asserted that the messianic happenings had not yet begun. The latter often found signs that the present age (or dispensation) was terminating and that the eschatological events were to start very soon, but according to their understanding these had not yet happened.[18]

Darby was born in London in 1800 and grew up in Ireland, where he studied law at Trinity College, Dublin.[19] A conversion experience in 1825 caused him to abandon his profession and accept a position of curate in the Church of England (called the Church of Ireland in Ireland). In 1827, he resigned his ecclesiastical post as a consequence of his disappointment with the established church. He aimed at a more apostolic environment, similar to what he considered to be that of the early church. "The careful reading of Acts," he wrote, "afforded me a practical picture of the early church which made me feel deeply the contrast with its actual present state."[20] Darby then developed a theory that was to serve as a cornerstone for evangelicals worldwide. According to this view, "The Church of God, as He considers it, was composed only of those who were so united to Christ, whereas Christendom, as seen externally, was really the world and could not be considered as 'the Church.'"[21] For Darby, only true Christian believers, evangelical and pietist Protestants who underwent inner experiences of conversion and established personal relationships with Jesus of Nazareth, composed "the church," the body of the true believers that would be saved and united with Christ. Consequently Darby advocated congregational devotional gatherings devoid of vestments, ornaments, choirs, and musical instruments, as well as ordained clergy.

The former Anglican priest found in Dublin other persons who held views similar to his own. They began to meet regularly for prayer, Bible study, and discussions. Similar groups emerged in a few more cities in Britain, among them London, Bristol, and Plymouth. In 1831, the group in Plymouth invited Darby to join them. Darby was a man of great energy, and he embarked on successful campaigns of evangelism not only in the English-speaking world but in other countries as well. In Britain the Plymouth Brethren remained small and elitist, often preoccupied with internal struggles and splits, and its ideas did not become influential, as dispensationalism was to become in the United States.[22]

Darby introduced to futurist-dispensationalist premillennialism a new theory that was to give dispensationalism one of its main characteristics, namely the idea of the secret, any-moment rapture of the church.[23] According to this belief, the descent of Jesus to earth would occur in two phases. In the first, Jesus would not reach earth itself and would not yet begin his salvific mission. He would meet, in the air, the church, the body of true believers who had undergone personal experiences of conversion. These genuine believers, both the living and the dead, would be instantly snatched from earth—an event that would come about when the apocalyptic moment began. "But the true Church which is not of the night, being watchful and prayerful, will be accounted worthy to escape it, by the Rapture."[24] Thus the church, the body of the true believers, would be spared the turmoil and misery that those who remained on earth, Jews and non-Jews, would encounter during those tumultuous years.[25] In the second and final phase, Jesus would come with his saints (those previously snatched from earth), defeat Antichrist, and begin his reign on earth for a thousand years. In contrast to historicist interpreters of the end of time, dispensationalists usually refrained from predicting a particular time for the appearance of Jesus. They asserted that the rapture of the saints would occur very soon but that one could not know the exact time.

Evangelical Christians holding to a dispensational premillennialist faith have occasionally differed as to where to place the Rapture in the course of eschatological events, whether it will occur prior to, in the middle, or at the end of the Great Tribulation, the harsh apocalyptic period between this era and the next. Most evangelicals holding to a dispensationalist premillennialist faith have adopted the theory that the Rapture will occur before the Great Tribulation. The rapture of the church is one feature of their teachings that dispensationalists claim to base not merely on the Bible (1 Thess. 4:17) but also on a private revelation.[26] Darby also claimed that the rapture of the church correlated with its nature as a heavenly, spiritual entity.[27] However, Darby and many evangelicals since have seen the Rapture as a vehicle to take the believers out of the earth before the turmoils and horrors of the Great Tribulation begin.

Another salient feature of dispensationalist teachings has been the place ascribed to the Jewish people in the course of human history. Dispensationalists have differentiated sharply between Israel and the church. In contrast to the traditional Christian understanding that identifies the church with biblical Israel, they view the Jewish people as the heirs of Old Testament Israel. According to their view, God's covenants with Israel are still valid. They point to the covenant in which God promised to make Abraham the father of a great nation (Gen. 12:2-3); the covenant between God and the whole nation of Israel (Ex. 19-20); and the covenant in which God promised to keep David's royal house forever (2 Sam. 7:4-17). The Israelites in the Old Testament failed, at times, to honor their obligation under the Mosaic covenant. However, the prophets foresaw the rejuvenation of the covenants between God and his nation when the Messiah, who would be descended from David, would reign over a restored Israel in its own land (e.g., Jer. 31:21-34, 33:15-16).[28]

In a manner that accords with Jewish messianic expectations, the Messiah, in the evangelical narrative, is expected to redeem humanity at large and establish justice and peace on earth at the same time that he will serve as king of the Jews. According to the dispensationalist premillennialist view, the church came into being because the Jews refused to recognize Jesus as their savior when he appeared for the first time, and the kingdom could not materialize and was delayed.[29] The current age, "the time of the Gentiles," is thus a parenthesis in the development of the ages.

> The Messiah, instead of being received, is cut off. . . . In place of ascending the throne of David, He goes to the Cross. . . . God signified His sense of this act, by suspending for a time His dispensational dealings with Israel. The course of time is interrupted . . . and all the time since the death of the Messiah has been an unnoticed interval—a break or parenthesis, during which Christ has been hidden in the heavens, and the Holy Ghost has been working on earth in forming the body of Christ, the Church, the heavenly bride.[30]

Between the rejection of Jesus and the beginning of the Great Tribulation, there is this parenthesis, and history has in some ways taken a break.[31]

According to this school of eschatological expectations, in the current dispensation the Jewish people do not serve any constructive function except when they help prepare for the next stage in history. However, their role has not ended. In the next dispensation, the millennium, the Jews will return to their position as God's first nation and will assume a leading role in Jesus's kingdom, the role the Jews would have played had they accepted Jesus in his first coming. Thus, although dispensationalist thinkers have anticipated a great future for that nation, they have also expressed a certain amount of bitterness concerning the ancient Jewish refusal to accept Jesus, since it has caused the delay in the advancement of the ages and the materialization of the messianic kingdom.

Dispensationalists consider the Bible to be the word of God, which reveals God's plans for humanity, both for the present and for future dispensations. According to this view, God did not leave humanity in the dark: he provides in the Bible clear guidance for humanity as well as

exact descriptions of its future. Like other evangelicals, dispensationalists claim that they have built their predictions of the events of the end
times on biblical texts, which they claim to read literally. Emphasis on
accepting what is conceived to be the "literal," "no nonsense" meaning
of the Bible stands at the core of their reasoning. Particularly in the later
nineteenth century and early twentieth century, conservative evangelicals, with dispensationalists taking the lead, vehemently rejected the
higher criticism of the Bible as an erroneous teaching that stripped the
Bible of its divine message and turned it into a profane book.[32]

Although dispensational premillennialist hermeneutics of the Bible
is sometimes challenged as exceeding the simple literal meaning of certain biblical passages, it can indeed be evaluated as more "literal" in its
approach than other systems of biblical exegesis.[33] The dispensationalist
interpretation of "the Land of Israel" and "Zion" could be regarded as
more literal than that of other Christian groups. This mode of reading
biblical texts influenced conservative evangelical attitudes toward the
Jewish people, Zionism, Israel, and the Holy Land. Most evangelicals
consider the Jews to be heirs and continuers of ancient biblical Israel.
Similarly, they recognize earthly Jerusalem and the land of Israel as the
actual places where the messianic events will take place.

Dispensationalism has provided large segments of conservative evangelical Christians with their philosophy of history. History, according
to this view, develops in a predictable line, divided into stages or ages.
God has a different plan, or "economy," for humanity in each age, and
humans are expected to obey God in a different manner in each of the
different eras or dispensations.[34] Most evangelicals holding to a premillennialist faith divide human history into seven such periods. Though
there are variations on the theme, all would agree that the last dispensation is the millennium and the current age is the penultimate one, nearing its end.[35] History, then, has a definite and predetermined course that
has been decided by God and recorded in Scripture. It culminates with
the apocalyptic events and the messianic age.

The Eschatological Hope and the Future of the Jews

According to the dispensationalist understanding, God has designed different plans for three different categories of human beings: the uncon-verted, the Jews, and the "church," that is, true Christian believers who have converted and accepted Jesus as their savior. The rapture of the church will mark the beginning of a period known as the Great Tribu-lation, which will stand between the end of the current dispensation and the beginning of the kingdom of God on earth.[36] Most dispensa-tional premillennialists expect the Great Tribulation to last for seven years, although some, like Cyrus Scofield, have suggested three and a half years.[37]

All dispensationalists agree on its substance: "There will be in it a period of unequalled trial, sorrow, and calamity (Daniel 12:1; Matthew 24:21), spiritual darkness and open wickedness (Luke 18:7; Peter 3:2-4). It is the night of the world (John 9:41; Luke 17:34)." For the Jews it will be "the time of Jacob's trouble."[38] At the beginning of the Great Tribula-tion, 144,000 Jews (12,000 persons from each tribe), will recognize the events that will occur at that time as proceeding according to the pre-dictions they have heard from missionaries or read in premillennialist evangelical tracts and will accept Jesus as their savior. These Jews will become apostles of the Christian message among those "left behind" who will remain on earth after the Rapture.[39] According to the dispen-sationalist apocalyptic scenario, the Jewish evangelists and the converts they make will be persecuted by Antichrist's evil government, and some of them will be martyred. By that time, the Jews will have returned to their ancient homeland "in unbelief," without having accepted Jesus as their savior, and will establish a commonwealth there. But this will not yet be the righteous kingdom to which the biblical prophecies have referred. The Jews will rebuild the Temple in Jerusalem and will reestab-lish the sacrificial service there. Antichrist, an impostor and charlatan, will appear, present himself as the true Messiah, and become the ruler of Israel as well as other parts of the planet.[40] In most evangelical tracts until recently it was assumed that, because he would be counterfeiting

Jesus as much as possible, he would be a Jew. Antichrist will reinforce his rule by terror, which together with famine, plagues, wars, and natural disasters will cause deaths in unprecedented numbers. Only one-third of humanity will survive these times, while the rest will perish. Armies of four empires from all corners of the earth—east, west, north, and south—will invade the Land of Israel. Especially since the Bolshevik Revolution of October 1917, evangelicals have identified the northern empire with Russia.[41] After the fall of the Soviet Union in 1988-90, some of them considered other possible options, such as Saddam Hussein's Iraq, Assad's Syria, and Ahmadinejad's Iran.

The dire circumstances of the Great Tribulation will terminate in the Battle of Armageddon (Har Megiddo), a site in northern Israel. Jesus will come with his saints (the truly converted) to the Mount of Olives and will proceed quickly to destroy the forces of evil. "Then the Lord shall come with His saints down to the earth and destroy this lawless Antichrist, deliver Israel, who will then look upon 'Him they have pierced.' . . . He will judge the living nations and establish His millennial kingdom."[42] Satan will then be bound for a thousand years, and the millennium will begin, with Jesus serving as the king and ruler of the world, installing peace and justice. The world will be organized in nations, with Jerusalem the capital of Jesus's global government. The Jews who survive the Great Tribulation will recognize Jesus as their Lord and savior. They will turn into a nation of evangelists, spreading the Gospel among the inhabitants of the earth. There is no basis to the claim that the millennium will have a Jewish character.[43] Evangelicals holding to the messianic view often appreciate, grudgingly, observant forms of Judaism, which, they believe, have kept Jews waiting for the Messiah and for their return to their ancient homeland. However, in the dispensationalist view of the millennium, rabbinical Judaism will cease to exist, and the postbiblical religious and cultural heritage of the Jews will be largely abandoned.

The righteous and peaceful reign of Jesus on earth will last for a thousand years. At the end of this time planet Earth will again go through a dramatic metamorphosis. Satan will be released and will rebel, but Jesus will crush Satan and his followers, who will be defeated forever. Cosmic changes will then take place, and there will be "a new heaven and a new earth." Jesus will present his kingdom to God the Father for mutual governing. God, Father and Son, will pass judgment upon all living souls, including the unconverted dead, who will be resurrected to appear in this divine court. The eternal kingdom of God will thus be ushered in, this time for evermore.

Analysis of the dispensationalist eschatological faith reveals unmistakably that the Jewish people are essential for many of the events of the end times to get going, especially during and after the Great Tribulation. Evangelical Christians have therefore taken special interest in the fate of the Jews and in the developments in the life of that nation and have often interpreted these events in light of their eschatological convictions. Since they predicted the return of the Jews to their land "in unbelief," prior to the arrival of Jesus, it is no wonder that evangelicals saw in the rise of Zionism, and in the large Jewish immigration to Palestine since the late nineteenth century, a fulfillment of biblical prophecies. It has also been no wonder that they lent their support to Jewish resettlement in the Land of Israel, as well as to spreading the knowledge of Jesus's messiahship among the Jews.

The Jews in the evangelical view have been more special than Greeks, Burmese, or Swedes. This does not mean that all facets of evangelical theology place the Jews on a pedestal. In the current era the Jews as a whole are separated from Christ and as such have been deprived of the spiritual comfort and eternal salvation he can offer. Judaism, on its own, cannot provide Jews with atonement for their sins or reconcile them with God. Such spiritual benefits can be obtained only through faith in Jesus as a savior. According to that view, the sacrifice of Jesus on the cross opened a new epoch in history that made Jewish laws and rituals lose their purpose. Only the acceptance of Jesus will redeem the Jews, personally and nationally. This understanding of the position of the Jews has given evangelical Christians a dual view of that people as errant in the present era and as a privileged nation in the next. Influenced by the dispensationalist eschatological hope, many evangelical Christians have come to believe that they have the duty to educate the Jews as to their role in history and help them amend their relationship with God. Consequently, the position of the Jews in evangelical minds has been mixed, inviting both scorn and appreciation, anger and hope. Most importantly, the place of Jews in evangelical theology has stirred evangelicals to take active interest in that people and to invest time, money, energy, and dedication in the prospect of converting Jews to Christianity and helping bring about their return to their ancestral homeland in Palestine. Such ideas made their way, in the nineteenth century, into the center of evangelical thought and messages, bringing with them a transformation of attitudes toward the Jews. Evangelical theologians holding to a dispensationalist faith have given expression to their ideas and hopes in a long series of theological tracts, biblical exegesis, sermons, popular novels, movies, radio and TV broadcasts, and videos and DVDs. Likewise, evangelical schools have often included messianic teachings in their curriculum. Tens of millions of evangelical Christians have heard of or read about the evangelical messianic dispensationalist premillennialist hope through one venue or another. While many have not fully adopted that particular faith, they have internalized, at least partially, theological and cultural premillennialist perceptions and have familiarized themselves with eschatological terminology. In that manner, many evangelicals have acquired a dispensationalist messianic understanding of global realities, including the position of Jews and their role in the advancement of history.

The Messianic Faith and the Jews in Evangelical Novels

An especially important recent venue for disseminating evangelical premillennialist ideas and values has been the novel series Left Behind. From the 1980s up to the present, novels became a particularly popular genre of literature in the evangelical community and a major means for evangelical theologians to disseminate opinions and sentiments. Longtime theologians such as Tim LaHaye and Grant Jeffrey, who previously expressed themselves via theological tracts, switched to writing novels. Tim LaHaye helped to found or direct several prominent evangelical groups, including the influential Moral Majority, which played an important role in advocating conservative causes in America in the 1970s and 1980s. Leaders of the group, the most noted of them Jerry Falwell, were also ardent supporters of Israel.[44] LaHaye was also a founder in 1981 of the conservative evangelical group Council for National Policy and served as its first president. This organization, too, has viewed the developments in the Middle East through premillennialist ideas similar to the ones later expressed in the Left Behind series.[45] The Left Behind series sold tens of millions of copies and was translated into dozens of languages. Evangelical producers turned the early parts of the series into films and Internet games. The publishers have adapted the series for young readers. The novels have acquired a broad readership, most of it not necessarily convinced evangelicals, and are aimed at bringing them closer to the faith, including its premillennialist dimension. Relating to timely issues, the novels are easy and pleasant to read. Such messianic-oriented fiction provides an interpretation of current political, economic, social, and cultural developments and an assurance that true Christian believers will survive the turmoils and not be "left behind."

In the Left Behind series as well as other novels dealing with the Rapture and its aftermath, Jews stand at the center of the stormy developments. Likewise, some of the significant political and spiritual events of the apocalyptic era take place in the Holy Land. The novels relate to the state of Israel as a stepping-stone in the advancement of the messianic timetable, signifying that attempts to destroy it are therefore futile. *Left Behind* introduces its readers even in the first pages to a Jewish protagonist and to the state of Israel and its economic and political issues. The characterization of Jewish people is revealing. Chosen by a major journal as its "man of the year," Chaim Rosenzweig is a naive scientist-wizard whose secret formula has helped turn Israel into a thriving nation.[46] His name and profession recall Chaim Weizman, Israel's first president, and he fits into the more positive stereotype of Jews as groundbreaking scientists. Just when a journalist for the *Global Weekly* interviews Rosenzweig, a major Russian attack on Israel is launched. But while potentially highly destructive, the attack proves to be miraculously futile. After the Rapture takes place, Rosenzweig emerges as an international figure.[47] Initially he finds Nicolae Carpathia, the charming emerging Antichrist, persuasive, and Orthodox Jews look to Carpathia's international government as an ally in building the desired Temple. At the same time, Jewish evangelists appear near the Wailing Wall and preach the Christian message relentlessly to the people of Israel. Antichrist eventually shows his real intentions, and as the Left Behind series proceeds, Jews join the underground opposition to his tyrannical reign.

Israel is presented as more than an ordinary country. It plays a crucial role in the unfolding of the eschatological drama and attracts vicious enemies as well as dedicated evangelists. While LaHaye and Jenkins try not to present hostile stereotypes of Jews, the Jews in the novels serve as archetypes. They stand for entire groups of Jews and come to represent the premillennialist evangelicals' expectations of that people and their role in history. Rosenzweig, for example, stands for a certain image of the Jews: they have great abilities and potentials, and a good character, but they lack a reliable spiritual compass. An inherently decent person, Rosenzweig is destined to become an instrument of Antichrist, since he cannot differentiate between the real savior, Jesus of Nazareth, and an impostor. Although Rosenzweig is portrayed sympathetically, ultimately he is a victim of his own inability to accept Jesus and the truth of the Gospel, and by extension he characterizes what the authors view as the unfortunate consequences of the Jewish refusal to accept the true Messiah.

The choice of the names Moshe and Eli for the two miraculous preachers is also not accidental. It points to their being protected by God while passing the word of the true Savior to the people of Israel. Moshe and Eli follow in the footsteps of two central biblical prophets: Moses and Elijah. Both prophets fought against idolatrous tendencies among the Israelites. Moses reintroduced the children of Israel to their God, serving as an intermediary between God and his people. "Eli," a popular Israeli abbreviation of Elijah, stands for the great "crusader" against Baal and his worshippers who was also a forerunner of Jesus in his ascension to heaven.

Tsion Ben Judah also carries a significant name: Zion, Son of Judah. Ben Judah is a rabbinical scholar who interprets correctly the developments of the Great Tribulation and turns into a Christian underground leader and preacher.[48] Tsion exemplifies the Jews who see the light, accept Jesus, and turn into virtuous Christian believers and admirable and articulate evangelists. Zion, Son of Judah, signifies the "completed" Jews who have discovered their true role and mission in history. In drawing the character of Tsion Ben Judah LaHaye and Jenkins have revealed the evangelical understanding of Jewish converts to Christianity. In evangelical eyes, they are "fulfilled" or "completed" Jews who have obtained salvation, inner peace, and eternal life, as well as exemplifying the completion of Judaism in Christianity.

The name and character of David Hasid, another righteous convert, follow in that vein. Hasid means "pious," "merciful," and "a follower of the rightful path." Some groups of ultra-Orthodox Jews call themselves "Hasids." But LaHaye and Jenkins assert that the Orthodox "Hasids" are not really the pious ones—rather, the pious are those who follow Jesus and dedicate themselves to his mission. The delineation of another character as an ardent Christian Jordanian believer is also not accidental: Arabs are acceptable when they follow the right path. Some parts of Jordan sit on lands that, according to biblical narrative, were part of David's kingdom but not the heart of the land of Israel, the Promised Land, thus signaling that Jordan can serve as a legitimate Arab country, while Israel must be first and foremost Jewish.

An important aspect of evangelical interest in Israel is the prospect of the rebuilt Temple, which has come to symbolize the advancement of the millennial kingdom.[49] In *Left Behind* the rebuilding of the Temple becomes a mutual interest of Antichrist and Orthodox Jews, and the orchestration of the removal of the Temple Mount mosques and the building of the house of worship is part of Antichrist's agenda.[50] One of Antichrist's "schemes" is the removal of the mosques and their transfer to New Babylon. The novel, however, is oblivious to the history of Christian evangelical–Jewish Orthodox cooperation over the prospect of rebuilding the Temple and the proactive attitude that many evangelical

Christians have shown toward the idea that Jews prepare for the rebuilding of the Temple. The building of the Temple in the Left Behind series
becomes an obsessive Jewish cause, one that brings Jews of many walks
of life to support Antichrist.

Although Tim LaHaye and Jerry Jenkins have presented Jews somewhat stereotypically, they made a crucial gesture in their refusal to
depict Antichrist as a Jew. From the early nineteenth century until
the publication of *Left Behind,* premillennialist evangelical writers had
routinely characterized Antichrist as a Jew. LaHaye and Jenkins, in
contrast, tried to reassure the Jews that they were not being identified with Antichrist. At the same time they did not want to write a
Catholic-Protestant polemic and scare away potential Catholic readers,
so they did not readopt the old Protestant claim that the pope was the
Antichrist. Some awkward qualifications notwithstanding, evangelical
Christians in the past generation avoided attacking Roman Catholi-
cism or describing Roman Catholics as non-Christians. Following in
that line, LaHaye and Jenkins made a gesture toward Roman Catholics,
declaring the pope among the true Christians snatched from earth.
LaHaye and Jenkins skillfully came up with an Antichrist who would
not be Roman Catholic but would still be a Roman: a Roman(ian).
Since Protestants had not pointed historically to an Orthodox Christian leader as Antichrist and had not been engaged in a war of defamation with that segment of Christianity, Orthodox Christians, the
authors concluded, would not be very offended, as a Romanian Antichrist would not touch on sensitive historical nerves.[51] LaHaye and
Jenkins were not the only ones who modified the classical Christian
messianic scheme in deference to the new atmosphere of evangelical-
Jewish friendship. Responding to input from Jewish activists who had
been working with Christians toward the rebuilding of the Temple, and
who wondered about their dubious role as laborers in the service of the
Antichrist, evangelical writers such as Randall Price reassured them
that premillennialist Christians expected the Temple to survive the rule
of Antichrist and to function gloriously in the millennial kingdom and
not only in the period that preceded it.[52]

The novels point to the complex attitudes of the authors toward the Jews and Israel both in their current situation and in a prophesied future when Jews are "left behind." Evangelical writers have given much thought to the subject, at times making their own choices as to how to present the Jews and their special mission in history. The Jews in the novels stand at the forefront of cosmic events, and it is not surprising that the series has stirred strong reactions. A number of scholars of American policy toward the Middle East have taken exception to the novels,[53] while right-wing Christian groups that do not share the authors' views of Israel and the Jews have suggested that Jews are not so central to the end times developments.[54]

The Left Behind books are then not necessarily about the future. They serve as an excellent source to reveal evangelical attitudes toward many aspects of contemporary culture and world order, from abortions to the United Nations. They show the evangelical understanding of Israel and the Jews as a misguided nation, yet one that is destined to return to its biblically promised position as God's first nation. LaHaye and Jenkins have little appreciation for the Jewish faith, which, in their novels, keeps Jews fanatically hostile to Jesus and the Christian gospel. Yet the Jewish community has given rise to extraordinary figures and serves as a nursery for future evangelists and leaders of the true faith. The Left Behind series has been marked by a deliberate wish to convey a sympathetic understanding of the Jews, avoiding bitter or defamatory representations that have characterized, often unwittingly, evangelical writings on Jews. Some cultural stereotypes have, however, persisted, and the series is, in the last analysis, an improved, sympathetic version of the evangelical premillennialist representation of the Jews. The novels thus reflect a new development in evangelical-Jewish relations, an outcome of the intensive involvement of evangelicals with Jews and Israel from the 1970s to the 2010s. Giving expression to eschatological perceptions, evangelical best sellers have shaped views on the Jews among a new generation of conservative Christians.[55] Some novels have been published on their own, some as trilogies, others in longer series. Maintaining some long-held Christian stereotypes of Jews, the novels also introduce and popularize new or modified images of the Jews. The representation of Jews in evangelical novels gives evidence to expectations and hopes, as well as frustrations. In general, Jews in contemporary evangelical novels are shown as errant but not evil people and as potentially righteous beings, which they will come to be when they finally recognize their true savior. Novels such as the also very popular Zion series convey evangelical values and cultural agendas as well as dispensationalist messianic theology. The Jews, according to that view, are a special category. The Left Behind series emphasizes the centrality of the Rapture, which many premillennialist evangelicals consider to be the end of this era and the opening moment of eschatological events and a harsh life for those "left behind."

However, contemporary evangelical writers such as Tim LaHaye and Jerry Jenkins are not the only evangelical novelists to write about Jews and the end times. They are heirs and continuers of a long chain of writers who have promoted the Christian messianic faith, connecting it with a larger evangelical worldview. During the nineteenth century, a number of British and American evangelical writers, including Edwin Wallace, author of *Ben Hur,* came out with novels on Jewish themes. George Eliot, while not an evangelical herself, wrote on both evangelical and Jewish themes, and her *Daniel Deronda* centers on Jewish attempts at restoration to Zion.[56] Such writers promoted the idea that Jews should go back to their ancient homeland and reestablish a Jewish commonwealth there. In America, since the latter decades of the nineteenth century, there has been no shortage in writers and readers interested in the topic. Yet until recently most evangelical publications on Jews and Israel were in the form of biblical exegeses, theological explorations, travel journals, or political tracts.

Ironically, contemporary apocalyptic Christian novels resemble Jewish novels on historical themes, especially the struggle for nationhood in Palestine. The Jewish novels offering a heroic understanding of Jews and their struggles also began in the nineteenth century. Jewish authors in Germany wrote dozens of romantic novels, lionizing Jews throughout the ages and taking pride in their deeds and choices.[57] A similar genre of historical novels began in late nineteenth-century eastern Europe when Jews attempted to revive the Hebrew language as part of a larger program of national rejuvenation.[58] Like the evangelical novels, books such as *Ahavat Tsion (Love of Zion)* tended to differentiate between good and evils characters as representatives of larger forces. They too tended to point to an ideal past, presumably under righteous judges or kings in biblical times, as foreshadowing a future Jewish heroic era. Jewish historical, messianically oriented literature appeared in America, Israel, and Europe in the aftermath of World War II and the Israeli War of Independence. Leon Uris's *Exodus* was perhaps the most widely circulated novel that depicted both Jewish suffering and Jewish heroism and pointed to the creation of Israel as an ultimate stage in the advancement of the ages. Israeli popular literature of the 1950s and 1960s, especially novels intended for young readers, promoted similar outlooks.[59]

Such literature blossomed in the aftermath of the June 1967 War. *O Jerusalem* appeared at that time, offering a heroic understanding of the Jewish position in the struggle between Jews and Arabs over the creation of the state of Israel.[60] But by the 2010s such Jewish literature was almost gone. The seemingly never-ending Arab-Israeli war, new assessments of Zionism and its history, and the influence of postcolonial worldviews had caused many liberal Jews to abandon heroic, dualistic, and messianic understandings of Jewish history in general and of the development of Israel in particular. Ironically, Christian evangelical novelists have, at the turn of the twenty-first century, shown more enthusiasm about the Jewish struggles for Palestine. At this point, Christian evangelical writings often seem more Zionist than Jewish ones. Jews, and especially Zionists, show up as more heroic and righteous in Christian novels than in contemporary Jewish accounts of twentieth-century Jewish history. The only Jewish milieu where such literature is still in vogue is the settlers' community, with which evangelical Christians have built a friendly relationship.

Jews in Evangelical Historical Novels

Even more than Left Behind, Bodie and Brock Thoene's two popular series The Zion Covenant and The Zion Chronicles, point to a remarkable change in the evangelical portrayal of Jews. The authors of the Left Behind series removed some features of the evangelical messianic faith that would be objectionable to Jews, such as a Jewish Antichrist, replacing him with a Romanian one. Jews in the Left Behind series are not depicted negatively as vicious people, but they often fall into expected stereotypes, such as the naive, brilliant scientist or the newly converted tireless evangelist. Such protagonists fit well into the dispensationalist premillennialist understanding of the Jews and their actions during apocalyptic times.

The authors of the two Zion series have gone a few steps further, creating a very different set of characters. The Jews depicted in the Zion Chronicles and Zion Covenant series are reminiscent of those in American novels and movies on World War II: they are good guys, dignified and heroic, who bravely and resourcefully take part in the Allies' efforts to defeat the Nazis. The novels emphasize that Arabs in the Middle East supported the hostile Axis. In both periods, Jews appear not as regular people but as heroic "others." As a whole, contemporary novels demonstrate the influence of premillennialist theology, which entails both romanticization of the Jews as a unique people with a special role in history and a touch of bitterness over the Jewish rejection of Christianity. The authors of the Left Behind series have strikingly claimed that "Jews hate Jesus."[61] Such perceptions are even more apparent in evangelical fiction about Jews in the early years of Christianity. The *Cup of Courage* describes the Jews of the first century as united in their hatred of Jesus's disciples, although often novellas in the same anthology treat Jews much more appreciatively once the time period moves to the late modern era.

The Chalice of Israel, a collection of four romance novellas, demonstrates the characteristics of this genre.[62] While the stories oppose the persecution of Jews and express support for the Jewish national revival of the twentieth century, they blame Jews for having allegedly persecuted

Christians. The events of *Cup of Courage,* one of the stories in the anthology, take place around the year 50 CE, a time between the crucifixion of Jesus and the failed Jewish rebellion against the Romans. The major protagonist, a Jewish Christian, finds himself between the devil and the deep sea, as he is harassed and threatened by both pagan Romans and mainstream Jews.[63] Jews, according to the novella, resented the early Christians vehemently and were out to get them. In some respects the story follows traditional Christian narratives, beginning in the medieval period, that have found expressions in passion plays as well as in other literary forms. It portrays Christianity of the first century as an embattled minority movement and Judaism as a united monolithic faith, overlooking the large number of Jewish groups and factions during that period. The role of Jews reverses, however, in *Cup of Honor,* a short story by Marilou Flinkman. In this novella Jews are a persecuted albeit heroic minority, many of whom are determined to reach Palestine and build a homeland there. However, a true rehabilitation of that people, the story tells us, will not take place until they establish a faith in Jesus. Being wise and righteous, the Israelis are starting to understand that and are beginning to change their attitudes. Like the Left Behind series, *Cup of Honor* reflects the dramatic effect of the June 1967 War on evangelical attitudes toward Israel and Jews in renewing their fascination with the Jews and spurring a commitment to both assist and evangelize them.

Since the 1970s, millions of evangelical Christians, including evangelists such as Tim LaHaye, have visited Israel, often turning it into a home away from home. The growing familiarity of evangelical Christians with Israel, its people and its issues, is reflected in the novels. Both the Left Behind and the Zion Covenant series, for example, convey good working knowledge of the country, its topography, and its social structure.[64] The Left Behind series also conveys an acquaintance with Israeli officials. Not only have Tim LaHaye and other writers visited Israel frequently, but they have met with public figures and government representatives.

The novels also represent an evangelical understanding of Jewish thought, suffering, and the unpleasant aspects of Christian-Jewish encounters. Many evangelical Christians believe that Jews have been responsible, at least partially, for their own unhappy history. Had they been willing to accept their true savior, they would have been spared the turmoil and miseries that they have undergone. At the same time such writers have exonerated their own tradition from maltreatment of Jews. They have asserted that true Christians, those who have undergone genuine experiences of conversion and have accepted Jesus as their savior, have neither hated Jews nor harmed them. Even if the perpetrators of acts against Jews were nominally members of Christian churches, in essence they were non-Christians. This outlook has been adopted by the authors of the Left Behind and the Zion Covenant series and of *The Cup of Courage*. Evangelical writings have asserted that true Christians treat Jews with goodwill, even though Jews have not always treated Christians appropriately. They claim that the suffering that at times characterized Jewish existence during the Middle Ages and the modern era did not derive from Christian instigation; rather, it was the outcome of ignorance and non-Christian behavior. Murderous regimes and senseless acts of brutality in general represented an alienation from God, although harming the Jews was particularly wrong, since it was directed toward God's first nation.[65] From an evangelical viewpoint, maltreatment and brutalization of Jews are, first and foremost, a chapter in the Jewish and non-Jewish encounter with, or alienation from, Christ. The more Jews and non-Jews accept the values of evangelical Christianity, the less chance there is of such brutalities repeating themselves.

For the most part, evangelical Christians have not joined in the movement of interfaith dialogue. Some evangelicals have occasionally held dialogues or conversations with Jews, as well as with members of other communities of faith.[66] However, as a rule, they have insisted that the only means of spiritual salvation and moral righteousness is the acceptance of Jesus of Nazareth as Lord and Savior. Religious systems that are advocating anything else are ultimately misleading their followers; creating a nonevangelical universal religion, as Antichrist attempts to do in the Left Behind series, is a diabolic idea. The proper "dialogue" to have with Jews, or for that matter members of any other religious group, is the missionary one of educating the unconverted to take the right spiritual path. As the Left Behind series shows, in the evangelical premillennialist understanding the evangelization of Jews is important not so much for the benefit of those who can be convinced before the Rapture takes place as for those Jews "left behind." Some of them will recognize the unprecedented apocalyptic developments as correlating with the predicted scenarios they have heard about from Christian evangelists. While previously such Jews have not taken such prophecies as seriously as they should, after the Rapture takes place they will realize their mistake. As the Great Tribulation takes its course, 144,000 Jews will convert instantly and become evangelists, spreading the knowledge of God among the people of the earth even as Antichrist and his cronies try to stop them.[67] The Left Behind books offer lively descriptions of such Jewish evangelists and their determination to carry out their mission against all odds.

3

Evangelical Theologians, Institutions, and Publications and the Jews

Leading evangelists, major Protestant publications, popular prophetic conferences, and new teaching institutions were instrumental in spreading and shaping the dispensationalist messianic hope in America and beyond. They turned the dispensational view of the Jewish people into part of the creed of millions of evangelicals, often connecting it with their understanding of America and its role in world history. Dispensationalism reached America in the 1860s. John Darby, who helped crystallize the new messianic faith in Britain, visited America to disseminate his ideas. From 1862 to 1878 he made seven trips to the United States and Canada, lecturing, meeting ministers, and teaching in small groups. Though Darby established groups of Plymouth Brethren in the country, his main achievement was the impact of his teachings on members of established Protestant denominations. In its early years in America, dispensationalism attracted some Episcopalians and occasionally Lutherans. But this would become an exception to the rule. Dispensational premillennialism found its adherents mostly among members of denominations that were shaped by the Reformed tradition, as well as by nineteenth-century revivalism: Presbyterians, Baptists, Methodists, Congregationalists, Disciples of Christ, members of Holiness churches and later on Bible churches and megachurches, Pentecostals, and charismatics. In America, converts to the dispensationalist messianic faith usually remained active members of their denominations, and this faith became a belief held by conservative members of mainstream Protestant churches.

Dispensationalism has become important for American evangelicals, as it has become part of a larger view of history and of contemporary society. It has served as a philosophy of history for conservative Christians, explaining the course of history, offering a picture of the future, and providing hope and reassurance over troubling political and cultural developments. For example, it provided an explanation and a sense of comfort in the face of one of the greatest fears of the cold war (from the late 1940s to the late 1980s), the atomic bomb.[1] Likewise, it has meshed well with a pessimistic outlook on current culture and the ability of humanity to reform its institutions and solve its difficult problems on its own. It also agrees with the conservative evangelical sense of righteousness in face of evil and the special role of America in history.

In its first decades, dispensationalism did not become a mass dramatic premillennialist movement of the kind William Miller had succeeded in gathering in the early 1840s. The progress of dispensationalism was slower, but it gathered strength and became a conviction accepted by many in America and later by many evangelicals around the globe, and its impact on the evangelical mind has lasted for over a century. Proponents of the new eschatological school struggled, among other things, to convince their audiences in the special role of the Jews in the end times. It was not an easy task.

James H. Brookes and the Niagara Conferences

One of the early converts to dispensationalism in America was James H. Brookes, an influential Presbyterian minister from St. Louis, Missouri, who was impressed by Darby's teachings, although he and other Americans did not merely follow in Darby's footsteps. Only a limited number of evangelicals read Darby, but many more read Brookes and other American proponents of the faith who adapted the British ideas to the American scene. Brookes published a series of books that came to popularize the belief in the imminent second coming of Jesus and make it part of the accepted conservative evangelical creed. The most widely circulated was *Maranatha: Or the Lord Cometh* (1874). In *Maranatha*, Brookes spent 545 pages elaborating the dispensationalist belief, its scriptural hermeneutics, its eschatological scheme, and its understanding of the course of human history. He devoted a long chapter to describing what he considered to be the role of the Jews in the drama of the end times. Brookes saw it necessary to convince his readers of the continuing validity of God's promises to the Jewish people and of the glorified future that awaited that nation.[2] He made numerous references to the Scriptures, insisting that Christians read those passages literally.

Brookes also wrote another popular, shorter, book on the second coming of Jesus: *"I Am Coming."*[3] It included a chapter dedicated to the understanding of the past and future of the Jewish people in relation to the events that would precede and follow Jesus's return to earth. "From Moses to Malachi, and from Matthew to Revelation, there is abundant and unvarying testimony that the literal descendants of the literal Abraham and Isaac, and Jacob, shall be literally scattered among all nations, as a punishment for their sins, and in the last days, shall be literally restored to their own land, and rejoice once more in the covenant relations to Jehovah, as the head of the millennial nations."[4] Using "literal" and "literally" repeatedly, this short passage provided an indication of the connection that Brookes, and other premillennialist evangelicals, made between their reading of the Bible and their understanding of the role of the Jews in history. The passage also offers an example of what would become a common theme in evangelical writings: a defense of the Jews that expressed hope for their eventual redemption and was at the same time coupled with a traditional Christian understanding of the course of Jewish history. There was no doubt in Brookes's mind, as well as that of many other evangelical leaders, that the Jews had been punished "for their sins."

In 1875, Brookes started an evangelical dispensationalist periodical, *The Truth*. Editing the journal and writing a large part of its content, the Presbyterian minister included articles that expressed his opinion on the fate of the Jewish people.[5] Arguing against the long-standing traditional Christian position that the Christian Church had superseded the Jews as heirs to the covenant between God and Abraham, Brookes relied on a literal reading of the biblical promises to Israel to convince his audience; he claimed that "along with the promise of Christ's second Advent comes the clear, explicit, unconditional and often repeated promise of Israel's return to their lands."[6] Like other evangelical leaders who adopted the dispensationalist premillennialist faith, Brookes linked the promise of the imminent arrival of Jesus to the return of the Jews to the central stage of history. And like other evangelical preachers, Brookes saw himself as an enemy of anti-Jewish sentiments, advocating greater appreciation for the Jews and their historical role. "Thus if we remember that God's revelation came to the Jews . . . surely this fact should be sufficient to rebuke the contempt and hatred, which is so commonly manifested toward them by professing gentile Christians who do not follow the divine command 'Pray for the peace of Jerusalem: they shall prosper all that love thee, PSCXXII: six.'"[7]

Like other evangelical Christians who adopted the dispensationalist faith, Brookes took special interest in the evangelization of Jews and believed that premillennialist evangelicals were particularly suited to preach the Gospel to the Jews: "No man is fit to preach to the Jews unless he believes in the personal coming of the Messiah. He must go to them with the message, 'Behold, the days come, saith the Lord, that I will raise unto David a righteous branch.'"[8] Brookes also asserted that Jews who accepted Jesus as their Lord and savior should not be asked to assimilate into the general "Gentile" community and turn their backs on the Jewish heritage, and he praised missions to the Jews that he thought were implementing his principles.[9] He marveled at Joseph Rabinowitz's Christian synagogue in Kishinev, Russia, and looked favorably at Arno C. Gaebelein and Ernst Stroeter's attempt to establish a congregation of Christian Jews in the Lower East Side of New York.[10]

Brookes criticized the hostile attitude of Christians toward Jews and called for an appreciative and amicable approach toward them, but he himself held some prejudices against that people.[11] The following passage, in which he both defends the Jews and expresses negative stereotypes, demonstrates his ambivalence: "It is probable that if our ancestors had been banished and expelled, kicked, robbed and murdered for centuries the world over, we too would feel like raising our hand against every man. The Gentiles in view of the past, and what they ought to know of themselves at present, should be slow to speak of the meanness of the Jews."[12] Brookes would have considered his words to embody positive thoughts about the Jews.

The Presbyterian minister was the living spirit and leader of a series of meetings known as the Niagara conferences. Gatherings devoted to the study of Bible and prophecy served as a means for conservative evangelicals to establish their own movement within contemporary Protestantism. Speakers differentiated themselves from their liberal Protestant brethren, adopted a separate philosophy of history, and promoted a more literate system of biblical hermeneutics that meshed with their critique of current culture and society.[13] The Bible and Prophecy conferences helped turn dispensationalism into a prevailing faith acceptable to the theological elite of evangelicals in America.

The first Niagara conference, the Believers' Meeting for Bible Study, as it was officially called in the early years, was a small gathering held in New York City in 1868.[14] Reacting negatively to the rise of a modernist trend within Protestantism, in 1875 the proponents of conservative evangelicalism summoned a conference in Chicago, which thereafter met annually for one or two weeks. From 1883 to 1897, the conferences met at Niagara, Ontario, from where they derived their name. In 1878, Brookes drew up fourteen articles of "fundamentals of faith," which were to serve as the common ground upon which all conservative evangelical participants of the Bible study conferences, and, by extension, others too, would agree. In 1890, these fundamentals of faith were officially adopted by the Niagara conference as its creed. The document manifests close ties between the premillennialist messianic faith in the second coming of Jesus, including a belief in the restoration of Israel and a conservative Protestant worldview.

The document starts with a declaration of purpose, namely to combat the secular and liberal trends in contemporary culture, especially among Protestant Christians, who, in the authors' opinion, have taken a wrong path. Statements in the creed assert that the Bible is divinely inspired and reveals God's instructions to humanity. Another article declares that "no one can enter the kingdom of God unless born again."

The last article refers to eschatological times: "We believe that the world would not be converted during the present dispensation . . . and hence that the Lord Jesus will come in person to introduce the millennial age, when Israel shall be restored to their lands."[15] The place of the Jews in the plan of the ages is thus linked to a broader eschatological hope, which, in its turn, becomes part of the "fundamentals of faith" of the emerging conservative evangelical movement in its "fundamentalist" stage. In this segment of American Protestantism the dispensationalist hope found a home and the belief in the role of restored Israel in the messianic era received growing acceptance. The dispensationalist understanding of history and the role of the Jews in God's plans for the end times thus became part of a larger conservative Protestant worldview.

Dwight L. Moody and the Jewish People

The messianic hope associated itself with the revivalist tradition of the English-speaking world and received an enormous boost among evangelicals when Dwight L. Moody, the leading evangelist in America during the last quarter of the nineteenth century, adopted the premillennialist faith. Moody's career as a revivalist developed throughout the 1860s and 1870s. Together with his brother-in-law, the gospel singer Ira Sankey, he held revivals larger than America had seen before and helped turn the revival into an urban phenomenon.[16] Revivals were intended, in the spiritual sphere, to bring the lost sheep to their savior, Jesus. On a more practical level, they were meant to bring the unchurched to join Protestant churches. Revival sermons aimed, first, at making individuals in the audience recognize their existential sinfulness, their hopeless spiritual condition, and the eternal damnation that awaited them. The sermons then moved to present the promise embodied in Jesus's atonement on the cross, open to all who repented and sought salvation through the acceptance of Jesus as their Lord and savior. Many who attended revival meetings underwent deep emotional and spiritual metamorphoses culminating in a moment of conversion, a recognition that Jesus had died on the cross for their individual sins.[17] They should now be justified before the Lord, join a church, and lead a righteous and productive life.

Moody met John Nelson Darby, the leader of the Plymouth Brethren, several times. Like his British evangelist counterpart, Charles Spurgeon, Moody never became an "orthodox" dispensationalist believer.[18] However, his acceptance of the belief in the imminent return of Jesus added strength and prestige to that faith. Moody invited dispensationalist thinkers to a series of Bible conferences that he organized in Northfield, Massachusetts, thus offering them another forum to express their ideas. He was also instrumental in establishing the Bible School in Chicago, which became a major center for training activists of conservative evangelicalism holding to the premillennialist faith and served as a model for more schools of its kind. Moody also incorporated dispensationalist themes into his messages, and the millennial faith added a sense of purpose to his work.[19] In one of his sermons, Moody asserted: "I look on this world as a wrecked vessel. God has given me a lifeboat and said to me: 'Moody, save all you can.'" Moody and other evangelists thus connected the coming end of this era with the urgency of evangelism.[20] Indeed, since the turn of the twentieth century, the eschatological messianic hope has been an essential part of the message of most American evangelists.

Moody referred extensively to the Jewish people in his preaching. His thoughts concerning that nation represented many common stereotypes of Jews, as well as the influence of the dispensationalist messianic belief, which worked to modify and complicate former perceptions. In Moody's view, the Jews were the sinning sons of Israel who had disobeyed God.[21] They were the people who had failed to help their neighbor in the parable of the Good Samaritan.[22] They were the vicious crowd that preferred the execution of Jesus to that of Bar-Aba, humiliated Jesus on his last journey, along the Via Dolorosa, and cried, "Let his blood be upon us and upon our children."[23] The destruction of Jerusalem and the Temple, in 70 CE, came as a prophesied punishment for the wickedness of the Jews.[24] The Jews' worst transgression was their unwillingness to recognize Jesus as their Lord and savior.[25] This stubbornness earned

them their position as outcasts.[26] Moody also held to the popular Western stereotype of the Jews as greedy and materialistic. Preaching on the
theme of the Good Samaritan, he said: "You know, a Jew must have a
very poor opinion of a man if he will not do business with him when
there is a prospect of making something out of him."[27] When Moody
was in need of an example of a rich man, he used Rothschild, an affluent European Jewish family, not one of America's financial magnates.[28]
Moody was not original in his criticism of the Jews, and he followed
stereotypes shared by many in Protestant culture at the time. In a manner typical of that culture, he had very little knowledge of postbiblical
Judaism or of the actual socioeconomic position of the Jews. At the same
time, his representation of the Jews included elements of appreciation
and hope, and unlike some preachers in Germany of the time he never
launched an attack against the Jews or blamed them for any of America's
troubles or faults.

Jewish activists noted statements made by evangelists regarding the
Jews. In the winter of 1875-76, Jewish leaders protested angrily Moody's
accusation that in 1873 Jews in Paris had boasted over the killing of
Jesus.[29] Alarmed by Moody's remarks, Isaac Mayer Wise, a prominent
Reform rabbi, asked Moody to debate the deicide charge with him,
but to no avail.[30] Moody later claimed that he had been misquoted and
added that he respected Jews.[31] Public criticism approached Moody
again in 1893 when he invited Adolf Stoecker (1855-1909), a German
preacher and anti-Jewish agitator, to carry out evangelistic work with
him in Chicago.[32] Moody rejected the newspaper's accusations against
Stoecker: "We give you a warm welcome. . . . We don't believe the newspapers. We believe the Bible. We have confidence in you. We love you."[33]
Moody might have believed in good faith that Stoecker was innocent
and was undertaking, in Germany, the same kind of work Moody was
doing in America. But for Jews, Moody's welcome to Stoecker meant an
endorsement of his views, and they became suspicious of Moody.[34]

Moody's thoughts on the Jews were more complicated than Jewish
leaders assumed. He had hopes for the Jews to be restored to Palestine
and to regain their old position as the nation of God. On a few occasions,

Moody predicted Israel's future: "When Christ returns, he will not be treated as he was before. There will be room for him at Bethlehem. He will be welcomed in Jerusalem. He will reveal himself as Joseph revealed himself to his brethren. He will say to the Jews, 'I am Jesus,' and they will reply: 'Blessed is he that cometh in the name of the Lord' and the Jews will then be that nation that shall be born in a day."[35] While discussing God's promises to Abraham (Gen. 22:17-18), Moody expressed his appreciation for the long endurance and achievements of the Jewish nation. "Hasn't that prophecy been fulfilled? Hasn't God made that a great and mighty nation? Where is there any nation that has ever produced such men as have come from the seed of Abraham? There is no nation that has or can produce such men. . . . That promise was made 4000 years ago, and even now you can see that the Jews are a separate and distinct nation." "When I meet a Jew," he declared, "I can't help having a profound respect for them, for they are God's people."[36] Moody spoke further on the future of the Jewish people: "I have an idea that they are a nation that are to be born in a day, and when they are converted and brought back to Christ, what a mighty power they will be in the land, what missionaries to carry the glad tidings around the world."[37] This last idea is central to the premillennialist evangelical understanding of the role of the Jews in the millennial era. Moody promoted the idea that true Christians should devote time and energy to the evangelization of the Jews.[38] He claimed that Jesus, when he was on the cross, had sent his disciples back to Jerusalem "to preach the gospel to the men who had crucified him."[39] It was Christ's "command" that his message be preached first and foremost "to those Jerusalem sinners."[40]

Moody saw no contradiction between his sometimes unpleasant opinions on Jews and his hopes for their return to Palestine and their rebirth as God's favored nation. In his view, though the Jews might have treated Jesus viciously and rejected him, Jesus himself did not abandon hope for them. As wicked as they might have been in the past, and as greedy as they might be in the present, in the future the Jews would assume a new role, restored to their glory. When they recognized their savior, God would keep his promises to them.

In the Bible conferences Moody initiated in Northfield, Massachusetts, the speakers often read papers on the Jews and their role in history.
George Needham expressed an opinion similar to that of Moody. "In
opposition to their national degradation in the present age, the seed of
Jacob are to take precedence in the age to come," he declared. The Jewish
homeland, he promised, "shall be restored and extended to the limits of
the original grant to Abraham." Jerusalem, he believed, "shall become the
ecclesiastical center of the world. . . . Ten men shall take hold of one Jew
and say 'we will go with you, for we have heard that God is with you.'"[41]

In 1894, a visitor from Palestine, Florence Ben Oliel, spoke at the
Northfield conference. Florence was the daughter of Abraham Ben
Oliel, a North African Jew who had converted to Christianity around the
middle of the nineteenth century and had devoted his life to the evangelization of his brethren. In the 1890s, at the time of the conference,
he was working as a missionary among the Jews of Jerusalem, where
his daughter assisted him.[42] Ben Oliel's speech exhibited the emerging
role of converted Jews in the evangelical camp. Although her parents
had converted to Christianity, she retained the ethnic identity of a Jew
and looked favorably on the early beginnings of what she saw as Jewish
national restoration in Palestine.[43] Ben Oliel pleaded with her audience
to do their utmost to help missionary work among the Jews. Her terminology reflected the prevalent notion among premillennialist evangelical Christians that evangelizing among the Jews was an expression of
kindness toward that nation and the repayment of Christians' indebted-
ness to God's chosen people.[44]

Jews who have converted to evangelical Christianity have often
adopted premillennialist understandings of the course of history, and
some have decided to enter the field of missions to the Jews. The premillennialist reading of the Scriptures and its understanding of the course
of history offered them the opportunity to embrace Christianity and still
take pride in their Jewish roots.

The International Prophetic Conferences

One way that premillennialists integrated their messianic beliefs and modes of reading the Bible into the larger Christian evangelical world-view was through a series of what came to be known as international prophetic conferences. Held in big halls in major American and Canadian cities, and attracting large audiences, the conferences helped shape a more coherent and unified evangelical creed. They were also an opportunity for evangelicals to build contacts with their counterparts in other English-speaking countries and with pietists in Germany, Holland, Switzerland, and Scandinavian nations. The speeches delivered at the conferences reflected the growing centrality of the Jewish people and the prospect of their restoration to Zion in the evangelical understanding of history and world events.

The first conference convened in New York in 1878, at the initiative of the conveners of the Niagara conference. Although some premillennialists of the historical school also presented their opinions, members holding to a dispensationalist eschatological faith dominated the convention and largely shaped its pronouncements. Many of the speeches defended the validity of this version of the messianic premillennialist creed. Some pointed to the antiquity of the creed and its continuity throughout the ages.[45] William Nicholson, a bishop in the small Reformed Episcopal Church, delivered a speech on the Jewish role in the eschatological times. His extended presentation set forth virtually the entire dispensationalist creed. He claimed that the Bible prophesied "the gathering back of all the twelve tribes of Jacob from their dispersion . . . to their own covenanted land, Palestine, and the resettlement of them there as one nation."[46] Nicholson insisted that biblical prophecies referred specifically to the Jewish nation and the Land of Israel. He opposed symbolic or allegorical interpretations that rejected his own more literal one.

Nicholson claimed that many Jews would return to their land before accepting Jesus as their Lord: "They will be gathered back in their unconverted state. . . . It will be still as rejectors of Christ and rebellious to God, that they will occupy their land."[47] Jewish life in the Land

of Israel during apocalyptic times, before the return of Jesus, will not
be rosy: "The object of their gathering is ultimately their conversion,
but primarily, their chastisement and suffering. Their terrible suffering, when ended, will have reduced them to a remnant. 'The third part
shall be brought through the fire, and refined as silver is refined' (Zach.
13:9)."[48] Matters will change after the return of Jesus to the earth, when
the Jews "will look on him whom they have pierced. . . . They shall
mourn for their sins. . . . They will believe in the Lord Jesus Christ, and
they shall be not forgiven only, but accepted in all the preciousness of
that name, which they and their nation had rejected." As for the country
itself, Nicholson predicted, "In extent, it will be according to the covenant with Abraham. As to fertility and beauty . . . '. . . It shall blossom
abundantly' . . . (Isaiah 35)."[49]

In November 1886, conservative evangelicals convened a second
international prophetic conference, this time in Chicago, where speakers presented their understanding of the role of the Jewish people in the
drama of the end times. Nathaniel West, a Presbyterian minister from St.
Paul, Minnesota, and an evangelical leader, delivered a speech entitled
"Prophecy and Israel." West expressed in sharp terms a dispensationalist opinion that the nation of Israel was central to God's plans for the
redemption of humanity. "A predetermined plan lies at the foundation
of the whole evolution of the kingdom of God, in which Israel appears
as an abiding factor. The fortunes of the chosen people decide the fortunes of the world. . . . 'Salvation is from the Jews.' . . . At the end of this
present age, Israel shall form the historic basis of the New Testament
kingdom."[50] West saw an additional meaning in the travails of the Jewish people. They were those of the suffering servant, part of the troubles
any messenger of redemption undergoes when participating in the mission of salvation. Like many other evangelicals who dealt with the theme
of Israel in prophecy, the Presbyterian minister devoted a large portion
of his speech to counter prevailing Christian views that identified the
church with Israel and Canaan with Christendom.[51]

William Erdman, a Congregational minister and one of the leading propagators of a combatant conservative evangelical worldview,

presented an interpretation of Romans 11:25-27, in which Paul discusses the future of the Jewish nation. In Erdman's view, Paul's words "set forth the grounds of the mysterious dealings of God with Israel and the Gentiles in this present time." Erdman claimed that Paul's announcement of "this ministry" was intended, among other purposes, "to prevent the self-complacent conceit of believers from among the Gentiles that, because of the fall of Israel, there was for them as a nation no future of special blessing and preeminence." At the same time, Erdman spoke harshly about the Jewish unwillingness to accept Jesus's messiahship. His criticism of the Jews and his insistence on the place of the Jews as God's chosen people and the glorious future awaiting them were interwoven. "Israel, though now as a people smitten with judicious hardness of heart, shall again be restored to favor and blessing."[52]

In the third international prophetic conference in Allegheny, Pennsylvania, in 1895, Ernst Stroeter delivered an address that voiced the growing centrality of the Jewish nation in the evangelical understanding of God's plans. A German-born academician who had become a leader of the Hope of Israel mission in New York, Stroeter promoted the ideology of his mission, which was one of the first to encourage Jewish converts to maintain Jewish identity and customs. Both William Moorehead, a professor of the New Testament at a Presbyterian seminary in Ohio, and Edward Goodwin, pastor of the first Congregational Church of Chicago, emphasized the strong ties between the evangelicals' claim to biblical literalism and their perception of the Jews as God's chosen nation. Moorehead warned that "if we spiritualize Israel, then we may adjust it [the Bible] . . . to make it mean whatever we wish."[53]

The dispensationalist faith associated itself with the conservative elements in Protestantism, especially in America and in countries where American Protestant culture exercised influence. Dispensationalists were among the leaders of the emerging "fundamentalist" movement, combating modernist notions and insisting on the authoritative nature of the Bible and the understanding of the Christian sacred scriptures as a guide for a Christian society.[54] The conservatives' messianic faith offered an outlook on history very different from the progressive postmillennial view that reigned among liberal Christians at the turn of the twentieth century. The strong link that developed between dispensational premillennialism and conservative evangelical Protestantism helped spread the belief in the second coming of Jesus in its dispensationalist form. American evangelists have often tried to "sell" their audiences a package of beliefs that combines the promise of being born again in Christ with a more literal reading of the Bible, a belief in the imminent return of Jesus, and a conservative outlook on society and culture. The dispensationalist hope has often been accepted as part of a broader outlook that emphasizes the idea that the Christian sacred scriptures are divine and inerrant. It was as part of such a "package" that millions of Protestants who came to believe in the imminent return of Jesus also accepted the idea of the central role the Jews were to play in the millennial kingdom.

Along these lines, William Moorehead gave a speech at the 1886 prophetic conference that connected the Jewish people with the validity of the Christian evangelical premillennial faith: "If I were asked to furnish proof of the world's conversion, of evidence that God will one day bring this whole planet in subjection to himself, and fill it with his glory, as he has promised, I should unhesitatingly point to Israel, the chosen people, the center for blessing for the whole world."[55] Moorehead had little appreciation for Judaism, which in his view erroneously interpreted the Old Testament: "One of the striking things to be witnessed in modern Jews, no less than in those of remote times, is their inability to understand the Old Testament. They cannot see its truth, nor grasp its real meaning, for Christ is its key, and rejecting him, they have lost the key, and so their own Scriptures are to them an enigma."[56] Like many other evangelicals, Moorehead believed at the same time that Christians should show love and thankfulness toward the Jews and express it in the evangelization of that people. "We look in vain for any extensive and loving evangelization of the Jews," he declared. ". . . The darkest and saddest page of the Church's history is . . . not only obstinate neglect of the Jew, but contempt for him, and hatred and oppression and expulsion and attempted extermination by the so-called Christian nations."[57]

By the conference in 1914, evangelical leaders such as William Riley, a Baptist minister who later would establish the Northwestern Bible School and become Billy Graham's mentor, were commenting on the rise of the Zionist movement. Premillennialist evangelicals like Riley regarded it as a "sign of the time," indicating the imminent return of Jesus: "The Zionist movement of recent years has impressed profoundly many students of the Scriptures. It has looked to them like the beginnings of fulfillment for that great line of prophecies that point unmistakably to the return of the Jew to his native land, and the making of Jerusalem ready for Israel's King."[58] Conservative evangelical Christians were impressed by the events of World War I, including the unprecedented magnitude of its destructiveness and the resulting British conquest of Palestine. These developments fueled them with a sense of rightness concerning their interpretation of the course of history. They gave voice to their enthusiasm over what they considered to be the unfolding of God's plans for human history in two prophetic conferences in 1918. The first took place in Philadelphia in May, with participants discussing the prophetic meaning of the advancement of the Zionist movement and the British capture of Palestine. Albert Thompson, who had served as leader of the Christian and Missionary Alliance in Jerusalem, described the capture of Jerusalem by the British as a fulfillment of prophecy. He expressed the view that a Christian conquest of the City of the Great King meant that the end of its desolation was at hand.[59] The conference adopted a statement of faith, the fifth article of which read as follows: "We believe that there will be a gathering of Israel to her land in unbelief, and she will be afterwards converted by the appearance of Christ on her behalf."[60]

The last international prophetic conference took place in Carnegie Hall, New York, in November 1918. Two speakers, Rueben Torrey, dean of the Bible Institute of Los Angeles, and David Burrell, pastor of Marble Collegiate Church, New York, referred to the destruction that had accompanied World War I as a proof that, in contrast to liberal claims, humanity was not making progress. On the contrary, society was deteriorating. Arno Gaebelein, editor of the influential conservative evangelical journal *Our Hope,* and William Riley saw the capture of Jerusalem by the British as indicating that history had reached its eschatological phase. "To the Jews, it means that their hopes are about to be realized. For true Christian believers, it is a sign that the Times of the Gentiles are rapidly nearing their close," Gaebelein asserted.[61]

The addresses delivered at the international prophetic conferences revealed strong awareness on the part of the speakers of the relative novelty of dispensationalist eschatological theory in general and the role assigned to the Jews in particular. The speeches defended and promoted these beliefs and tried to show that they were rooted in early Christian doctrines and based on sound interpretation of Scripture. Throughout this period, evangelicals holding to the dispensationalist faith gained more confidence in their particular reading of the Bible and their understanding of the course of history. World War I helped validate their claim that the world situation was not improving, and the rise of the Zionist movement, the British takeover of Palestine, and the Balfour Declaration of 1917 seemed to them to verify that history was indeed proceeding in accordance with their predictions.

The Scofield Reference Bible and the Fundamentals

Prophetic conferences were not the only means conservative evangelicals used to express and promote their eschatological convictions, a critique the larger culture, and their understanding of the role of the Jews in history. Evangelists and theologians wrote books and pamphlets in which they propagated their newly acquired eschatological hopes. One of the publication most instrumental in spreading dispensationalism in America and beyond was the *Scofield Reference Bible,* named after its commentator and editor Cyrus Scofield.

Scofield had served as a soldier in the Confederate Army during the Civil War. Later he worked as a lawyer until, in 1879, a conversion experience made him adopt the dispensationalist messianic hope and mode of reading Scripture, and he decided to devote himself to spreading this premillennialist hope. He participated in the Niagara and Northfield

Bible conferences and in the international prophetic conferences and became one of the influential advocates of premillennialism and conservative evangelicalism of his time. In 1909, the newly established New York branch of Oxford University Press published its first reference book on American soil, the *Scofield Reference Bible*. It would become the press's most widely circulated publication, selling millions of copies.[62]

The original *Scofield Reference Bible* was the King James version of the Bible, edited and accompanied by notes and commentaries. Scofield's main means of disseminating his ideas was to give titles to the various chapters as well as subtitles to parts within them. The titles served as commentaries in and of themselves, offering interpretations of biblical chapters and paragraphs that supported the dispensationalist eschatological understanding of God's plans for humanity. The Scofield Bible also provided commentaries at the bottom of the pages. In some of the books, the editor's work was not particularly apparent. However, Scofield edited and commented much more aggressively in those books of the Bible that related to prophecy, such as Daniel and Revelation. His commentaries introduced the reader to such dispensationalist terms as "the Great Tribulation," "the time of Jacob's trouble," "the time of the Gentiles," and "the Rapture." Dispensationalist ideas on the future of the Jewish people were introduced to many homes in America and elsewhere through this commentary.

The rise of dispensational premillennialism to a position of influence among evangelicals was also partly due to another literary enterprise, *The Fundamentals*. In 1909, Lyman Stewart, an oil magnate from California and a conservative Protestant, decided to sponsor a publication that would combat the higher criticism of the Bible as well as other modernist liberal trends that in his view threatened to undermine Christian values. A series of evangelical leaders successively edited *The Fundamentals*: Amzi Dixon, pastor of Moody Church in Chicago and later Spurgeon's Metropolitan Tabernacle in London; Louis Meyer, a converted Jew who had abandoned the medical profession and become an evangelist; and Rueben Torrey, Moody's most noted disciple. Between 1910 and 1915, *The Fundamentals* appeared in twelve volumes, comprising dozens of essays, with three million copies distributed altogether. Articles focused on defending the authenticity and inerrancy of the Bible as God's message to humanity, as well as other elements of the Christian belief that the conservatives considered to be under attack by modernists, such as the virgin birth of Jesus. A whole volume was devoted to mission and evangelization. One article focused on promoting belief in the dispensationalist eschatological hope. Its author, Arno C. Gaebelein, presented the history of the Jewish nation as a proof of the absolute accuracy of the Bible. "These oracles of God, the holy Scriptures . . . are filled with a large number of predictions relating to their own history."[63]

The Bible Institutes

American conservative evangelicals created another vehicle to influence the Protestant community and spread their messages: Bible institutes. These schools of higher learning trained ministers, missionaries, Sunday school instructors, editors and writers of journals, and interested evangelical laypersons. They established publishing houses, periodicals, and radio stations that served as major pulpits for conservative evangelical views. The deans and presidents of these institutions became leaders, spokespersons, and theoreticians of conservative evangelicalism. In their writings they expressed ideas concerning the Jewish nation.

In 1886, a group of evangelical activists led by Dwight Moody established the Chicago Evangelization Society, which was renamed the Moody Bible Institute after Moody's death in 1899. Throughout the years this institute has instructed hundreds of thousands of men and women. The leaders of the Moody Bible Institute have taken special interest in the fate of the Jews, and the institute has invested resources in evangelizing that people. In 1917, it established a department, still in existence, to train missionaries to the Jews.

The school's magazine has published numerous articles on Jewish themes, such as missions to the Jews, and later the state of Israel and the Zionist movement. Reuben Torrey, the first superintendent of the institute, included the belief in the Jewish nation's central role in the return of Jesus to earth in instructional books and articles he wrote on the Bible and on Christian doctrine.[64] He requested that students at the institute study statements expressing these views. One of the aims of Christ's second coming, Torrey wrote, was "to deliver Israel in the day when his trials and suffering shall culminate. . . . Jesus Christ is coming again to gather together the outcasts of Israel from the East country and the West country and into Jerusalem. . . . At the Coming Again of Jesus Christ, divided Israel—Ephraim and Judah—shall be reunited into one nation under one king David—Jesus." He further asserted that "Israel shall be cleansed from all their filthiness and from all their idols, a new heart will be given them and a new spirit put within them, the stony heart shall be taken away from them and they will be given a heart of flesh," and "Israel shall be greatly exalted above the nations."[65] Torrey's opinion on the Jews and their role in history, like that of other evangelical leaders of his era, was a mixture of traditional Christian understanding of the Jews' "blindness" and "stony" hearts and a new evangelical premillennialist concept of the soon-to-be-reformed and exalted Jews.

From 1912 to 1925, Torrey served as dean of the Bible Institute of Los Angeles, where he promoted similar ideas. In *The Return of the Lord Jesus* he made the following bittersweet prediction about what the Jews would experience when Jesus returned: "As great as their joy shall be, it shall begin with a great mourning . . . especially over their former rejection of their king."[66] Torrey's successor as director of the Moody Bible Institute, James Gray, provides another example of the attitudes that characterized conservative evangelicals between the two world wars. Like many of his comrades, Gray believed that the Jews were God's chosen nation, whose covenant with God was still valid and effective.[67] He expressed appreciation for what he considered to be the merits and achievements of the Jews and their contribution to society and was convinced of the glorious future that awaited them in the millennial kingdom.[68] Gray responded enthusiastically to the Zionist movement, the Jewish immigration to Palestine, and the British takeover of Jerusalem.[69] It was under Gray's administration that the Moody Bible Institute established its program for training missions to the Jews, signaling the belief of this conservative evangelical school that the Jews were important to the unfolding of history. At the same time, Gray also held some traditional Christian views. Like other evangelical writers, such as Reuben Torrey, he believed that Israel in biblical times had failed "to be faithful witness to Jehovah before the other nations of the earth, and in consequence is suffering the dispersion and persecution, which, alas, we know about today."[70] Like other evangelical leaders, Gray spoke against the maltreatment of the Jews and at the same time expressed the opinion that the Old Testament prophets had worse things to say about the Jews than modern anti-Jewish agitators.[71]

Conservative evangelicals established Bible institutes in other cities in the United States, as well as Canada, Britain, and other nations. Among the more noted were the Bible Institute of Los Angeles (1903) and the Philadelphia School of the Bible (1914). Both schools opened departments for training missionaries to the Jews, and the heads of both institutions took a special interest in the Jews, the prospect of their conversion, and their eventual restoration. William L. Pettingill, first dean of the Philadelphia School of the Bible, authored a few books in which he discussed the place of the Jews in God's plans for humanity. One of his tracts, *Israel—Jehovah's Covenant People,* was aimed at distribution among Jews. Evangelical missionaries used the premillennialist understanding of the role of the Jews in history as a means of reassuring the Jews that evangelical Christianity was friendly to them and was a faith they should embrace willingly. The book described the glorified future that awaited the Jewish nation after its restoration to Palestine and the arrival of Jesus.[72] In other, nonmissionary, tracts, Pettingill described the future of the Jewish people in more complicated terms. He mentioned the treaty that the Jews would, according to his belief, make with Antichrist. "The wholesale return of Jehovah's chosen people to their land will be preceded by the return of a remnant in unbelief. I say, 'in unbelief,' because only unbelievers would be so deceived by the Beast king as to make a treaty with him."[73] He was not the only evangelical leader to express such mixed views.

William Blackstone: *Jesus Is Coming* and Jewish Restoration

In 1878, William Blackstone (1849-1935), a businessman from Oak Park, Illinois, published a tract that quickly became an evangelical best seller. *Jesus Is Coming* sold millions of copies in forty-two languages, including Yiddish and Hebrew. Blackstone strongly influenced the development of dispensationalism and the role of the Jews in conservative evangelical thought. A lay Methodist and a successful businessman, he became convinced of the truth of the dispensationalist messianic faith.[74] That belief gained popularity during the 1870s among the Protestant commercial classes in Chicago, and a number of friends of Blackstone also adopted it. Associating with leading evangelists, such as Dwight Moody, Blackstone become an evangelist for the Christian evangelical faith in its dispensational premillennialist form, traveled to Bible and prophecy conferences, and spent time, energy, and money on promoting both the faith and what he considered to be its implementation. He took a leading part in establishing organizations and producing publications that came to convince the Protestant community of the dispensationalist reading of Scripture as well as the need to educate Jews and non-Jews on what to expect in the years to come.[75]

Blackstone viewed contemporary Jews as heirs and continuers of the children of Israel.[76] He showed appreciation toward the Jews, as a people he considered to be chosen by God for a special role and mission in history, as well as warmth and goodwill toward a vulnerable people. At the same time he was critical of Jewish choices throughout history and believed in some of the long-held Christian stereotypes of the Jews. He considered the Jews' unwillingness as a people to accept Jesus as their messiah to have been a mistake of colossal proportions, one that had cost them "centuries of sorrow."[77] Moreover, that unwillingness had prevented the establishment of the desired kingdom of God on earth.[78] Blackstone also mentioned the Jewish maltreatment of Jesus, although he did not repeat that complaint often. In his understanding, in the current era the Jewish people played a passive role, overshadowed by the church, but the current age was merely a parenthesis in the advancement of the ages.[79] In the last period, the millennium, the Jews would resume their initial role in history as God's first nation. This turn of events, he believed, was beginning to unfold, manifested by the Jewish national revival that had begun in the late nineteenth century and the building of new Jewish settlements in Palestine.[80]

One can comprehend how a messianic vision of the kind Blackstone adopted and promoted would motivate a commitment to get involved in the life of Jews and try to prepare them for their role in history. He wanted the Jews to be able to recognize the true meaning of the developments of the Rapture and the Great Tribulation when these occurred. For that purpose, Blackstone had thousands of copies of *Jesus Is Coming,* in Hebrew and in other languages, stored in Petra in Trans-Jordan. His intention was that Jews who would flee there in the "time of Jacob's trouble" would be able to discover the truth, accept Christ, and save themselves. Blackstone, not surprisingly, became a central figure in the field of missions to Jews and in 1887 founded the Chicago Hebrew Mission. Supported initially by a number of Protestant denominations and leaders, the mission promoted a premillennialist understanding of the Jews' role in history. The mission's magazine, the *Jewish Era,* published articles on Jewish themes, expressing mixed views.[81] On the one hand, Blackstone and other writers believed that Judaism could not offer its adherents salvation and that only in Christianity could Jews find true meaning and spiritual delivery. On the other hand, the traditions, texts, laws, and rites of the Jewish people kept them waiting for the Messiah and for the reestablishment of their national home.

Blackstone opposed Reform Judaism as well as liberal, secular, and socialist Jewish options. Reform or secular Jews, in Blackstone's view, had turned their backs on their role and duty, since they would not participate in the Jewish national restoration, which served as a stepping-stone for the advancement of history.[82] As these groups of Jews were, at that time, largely resistant to evangelical missionary efforts and would not accept Jesus as their savior, they were errant twice over. Blackstone considered evangelical Christianity to be the only religious belief that could offer salvation to its believers. Heathens and non-Christians in general, as well as non-Protestant Christians and members of dissenting Protestant groups, like the Seventh-Day Adventists and the Mormons, were doomed.[83] Orthodox and Zionist Jews were in many ways exceptions to this rule, since they fulfilled a role in the advancement of God's plan for humanity.

Blackstone believed that the United States had a special role and mission in the divine economy. God had assigned it a task, to help prepare the way for Christ's return and assist in the Jewish restoration to Palestine.[84] This sense of America's historical mission became an accepted conviction among American evangelicals with a dispensationalist understanding of history, and one can find echoes of it in our time in the thought of such evangelists as John Hagee.[85] It has served as a basis for the political and financial support that conservative evangelicals have offered the Zionist movement, and later on Israel and its people, and for their advocacy that the United States offer such support. It has given expression to both evangelicals' messianic faith and their sense of American patriotism.

Blackstone was well aware that the new messianic faith departed radically from traditional Christian theological teachings as well as popular understandings of the position of Jews in society. He knew he would need to respond to possible objections. Blackstone appealed to a literal reading of the biblical verses to which conservative evangelicals have become committed. "Dear reader: have you not read the declarations of God's word about it? Surely nothing is more plainly stated in the scriptures," he declared.[86] To a large extent, he and his comrades were successful. Evangelical writers turned their eschatological faith and their understanding of the role of the Jews in history into part of the worldview of a large and influential religious movement. This new messianic faith stirred a renewed interest in the Jewish people and the prospect of their national restoration. Ironically, it was conservative, messianically oriented Christians who came to relate to the Jews as the authentic Israel and who looked on them as a potentially positive force in history. Analysis of the first two generations of American evangelicals influenced by premillennialist thought reveals how attitudes have since become more favorable while remaining at the same time highly complex. These early premillennialist evangelicals saw the Jews as the chosen people, God's first nation. However, their belief in the centrality of the Jewish people in God's plans for humanity did not fully eradicate their disappointment over the Jewish historical refusal to accept Jesus as Lord and Savior. Nor did it eradicate deep-rooted cultural stereotypes, although it did soften and improve overall conservative Protestant attitudes toward the Jews. These conservative Christians also tried to intervene in the life of the Jews and reshape the future of that people.

4

Evangelicals and Jewish Restoration

As early as the seventeenth century, Protestants holding to the premillennialist faith had followed the prospect of Jewish restoration to Zion and had promoted the idea that Christians should assist Jews in carrying out this project. In the early nineteenth century, with the rise of a large evangelical movement in English-speaking countries, evangelical Protestants took a renewed interest in the Jewish people and their fate, at times directing their energies to initiatives to restore the Jews to Palestine. Most such evangelical proto-Zionist initiatives were undertaken in the English-speaking world, although one could find proponents of Jewish restoration in other societies in which pietist or evangelical convictions held some influence. For the most part they had no immediate result, but they had long-lasting effects on the development of Zionism, creating sympathy for the movement and its aims in Christian societies and at times counterbalancing more negative views. They offered encouragement to Jewish proponents of national restoration, and at certain moments, such as in 1917, evangelical openness to the Zionist ideas influenced actual governmental policies.

Shaftesbury's Attempts

One early evangelical initiative to restore the Jews to Palestine was that of Lord Ashley Cooper, the seventh Earl of Shaftesbury, one of the more noted leaders of British evangelicalism from the 1830s to the 1850s. Like many British evangelicals of his era, he believed in the imminent arrival of the Messiah and the coming kingdom of God on earth. And like a number of evangelical leaders who were concerned with the fate of the Jews, he was involved both in evangelizing the Jews and in trying to restore them to their ancestral homeland. Utilizing the international crisis over the Egyptian invasion of Palestine in 1838–40, he took out a full-page advertisement in the *Times* of London calling on the monarchs of Europe to act on behalf of the Jews' restoration to Palestine. He also tried to persuade the British government to gain the support of the Ottoman Turks for the establishment of a Jewish commonwealth in Palestine. Wishing to offer a noneschatological justification for his plan, Shaftesbury argued in his petition to the Foreign Office that a Jewish homeland in Palestine would provide a buffer against future Egyptian incursion into Ottoman lands as well as increase the prosperity of the Ottoman Empire. Like other evangelical petitions that would follow it, the petition included a theological-biblical argument that "the Land of Palestine was bestowed by the Sovereign of the Universe upon the descendants of Abraham." Shaftesbury succeeded in convincing Lord Palmerston, who served as the minister of foreign affairs, to back his initiatives. The relationship between the two offers an example of the interaction between evangelical leaders and supportive politicians concerning the idea of Jewish restoration. Palmerston was not a convinced premillennialist, but he was one of the early statesmen in the English-speaking world who became open to evangelical suggestions concerning the return of Palestine to the Jews.[1]

Shaftesbury, like later evangelicals, claimed that the Jews themselves, being an industrious people, would be able to cover much of the expense involved in their voyage to Palestine and the rehabilitation of that land. He wrote to Lord Ponsonby at the British Foreign Office: "The Jews . . . should be induced to go and settle in Palestine, because the wealth and habits of order and industry which they would bring with them would tend greatly to increase the resources of the Turkish Empire and to promote the progress of civilization therein."[2]

Shaftesbury's initiative represented a larger movement in Britain of his time. Hundreds of upper- and middle-class members of British society expected the imminent return of Jesus and organized gatherings to discuss the details of the eschatological timetable.[3] In Britain, however, evangelicalism, premillennialism, and interest in the Jewish restoration in Palestine were not necessarily interconnected. Some evangelicals did not readily adopt a premillennialist vision of the future of the Jews. And among the ardent premillennialists there were, at times, nonevangelicals too. This being said, evangelical premillennialism had reached a zenith in British society during Shaftesbury's and Palmerston's years of advocacy for a Jewish restoration to Palestine.

Occasionally evangelical activists took more modest, yet practical, steps toward helping Jewish settlement in Palestine. In 1849, George Gawler (1795–1869), a retired officer and former governor of South Australia, accompanied Moses Montefiore to the Holy Land. An English Jewish businessman and leader who became a patron of the Jewish community in Palestine, Montefiore visited the country a number of times, attempting to improve the conditions of its small but growing Jewish population.[4] The encounter between Montefiore and Gawler was one of the first examples of Jews and evangelical Christians encouraging each other to take interest in helping the Jewish population of Palestine. Gawler, who had been an ardent evangelical since his recovery from being wounded in the Battle of Waterloo, wrote a series of books on the subject of Jewish restoration in light of biblical prophecy. "I should be truly rejoiced," he wrote, "to see in Palestine a strong guard of Jews established in flourishing agricultural settlements. . . . I can wish for nothing more glorious in my life than to have my share in helping them do so."[5]

The influence of the evangelical movement weakened in Britain in the second half of the nineteenth century and the early twentieth century, although British evangelical missionary work directed toward the Jews became most extensive at the turn of the twentieth century. Evangelicalism in America remained an influential movement, going through a new, urban phase in the decades following the Civil War, even as a rift began to develop between liberal and conservative American evangelicals in the industrial North. By that time, American evangelicals were busy building a large missionary infrastructure and a network of publications focusing on propagating the Christian gospel among the Jews, as well as on attempting to educate Christians on the centrality of the Jews in God's plans for humanity.

Like Shaftesbury, William Blackstone was an energetic missionary leader and a tireless advocate for the building of a Jewish commonwealth in Palestine.[6] In 1889 he visited Palestine, a country that for him, as well as other evangelical Christians, was the site of biblical events and the place where the more dramatic developments of the end times were about to happen. Blackstone was impressed by the communities of Jews who had come to Jerusalem during the nineteenth century for religious, often messianic reasons. He also noted that the first wave of Zionist immigration to a country that he considered to be underpopulated had resulted in the building of new Jewish neighborhoods, widespread agricultural resettlement, demographic growth, and growth of an economic infrastructure. The American evangelist viewed the expanding settlement of Jews in the country to be a "sign of the time," an indication that the current era was ending and that the events of the end times would occur very soon.[7] Blackstone's visit to Palestine strengthened his determination to take a proactive line and help bring about Jewish national restoration in Palestine.[8] His comment that Palestine was "a land without a people for a people without a land" echoed a claim by Shaftesbury half a century earlier that Palestine was "a country without a nation" for "a nation without a country," namely the Jews—although Blackstone had probably never read the British leader's diary.[9] This remark, coined by premillennialist evangelical Christians, was picked up a few years later by Theodor Herzl, founder of political Zionism, and became a motto for Jewish Zionists for decades to come, usually without awareness of its Christian evangelical origin.

In November 1890 Blackstone organized a conference in Chicago, to which he invited both Christian and Jewish religious leaders, to discuss the situation of Jews around the world. His aim was to reach a resolution that would demand international political action on behalf of the return of Palestine to the Jews. But the conference did not develop in that way. The Jewish participants were three Reform rabbis, while the Christian participants included both premillennialist and nonpremillennialist Protestant clergymen and professors in local theological seminaries.

Ironically, the Christians spoke favorably about Jewish restoration to Palestine while the Jewish representatives were not enthusiastic about that prospect. J. M. Caldwell, a Methodist minister, remarked: "I can have no doubt about the restoration of Israel. Not only does the Bible declare it, but the signs of the times all indicate that the realization is near at hand." Rabbi Emile G. Hirsch of Sinai Congregation in Chicago, a noted leader of the radical wing of Reform Judaism, expressed a very different opinion: "We modern Jews do not wish to be restored to Palestine. We have given up hope in the coming of a political personal Messiah."[10]

Despite disagreement on the question of the return of the Jews to Palestine, the members of the conference were united in their concern for the fate of Jews in Russia, who were living under severe legal restrictions as well as threat of pogroms. The conference issued a resolution that expressed "a disapprobation of all discrimination against the Jews 'as such'" and declared "sincere sympathy and commiseration to the oppressed Jews of Russia and the Balkans, the victims of injustice and outrage." It pleaded with the Jews' persecutors "to stay the hand of cruelty from this time-honored people, which have given them as well as us our Bible, our religion, and our knowledge of God." That Jews had a special role in history was a notion both Reform Jews and prophetically oriented evangelicals agreed on, although they interpreted its nature very differently.

The Blackstone Memorial

Encouraged by the resolution in favor of Russian Jews, Blackstone took it upon himself to petition the president of the United States, asking him to respond to the plight of the Jews in Russia by collaborating internationally to provide a haven for them in Palestine:

> What shall be done for the Russian Jews? . . . The Jews have lived as foreigners in [Russia's] dominions for centuries . . . and [Russia] is determined that they must go. . . . But where shall 2 million of such poor people go? . . . According to God's distribution of nations Palestine is their

home, an inalienable possession from which they were expelled by force. Under their cultivation it was a remarkably fruitful land . . . as well as a nation of great commercial importance—the center of civilization and religion. Why shall not the powers, which under the Treaty of Berlin in 1878 gave Bulgaria back to the Bulgarians and Serbia to the Serbians, now give Palestine back to the Jews . . . ?"[11]

Blackstone's motivation was based in Christian eschatology: he wished to see the Jews go back to their land and prepare the ground for the return of the Messiah. But in the petition he justified the initiative with a set of humanitarian, political, legal, and economic reasons. On the political and legal levels, he referred to precedents among the new states that came about in Europe, in the late nineteenth century, by means of international consent. He argued that world Jewry could help finance the settlement of "their suffering brethren in their time-honored habitation" and could compensate Turkey for "whatever vested rights by possession she had in Palestine." Presenting the memorial to President Benjamin Harrison, Blackstone stated, "Protests against Russia would make matters worse. . . . This memorial . . . does not come to antagonize Russia, but seeks peaceably to give Jews control of their home in Palestine." Blackstone's humanitarian call appealed to the American public who were concerned with the fate of Russian Jewry. In the 1880s and 1890s, the United States had intervened a few times on behalf of the Jews in Russia, and the U.S. Congress had discussed the condition of Russian Jews.[12] But although Blackstone was careful not to mention premillennial hopes in the petition and relied on nonmessianic arguments, his argument was firmly established on evangelical interpretations of the Bible: it based the Jewish claim to Palestine on "God's distribution of nations" and affirmed the duty of the Christian nations to "show kindness to Israel." The Christian-biblical appeal of the petition, which was endorsed by many notable Americans, reflected the impact of the Bible on Protestant America as well as a measure of sympathy toward the Jews and their condition. Four hundred and thirteen eminent citizens—politicians, clergymen, judges, journalists, editors and publishers of major newspapers, and prominent businessmen—signed the petition. Among them were Supreme Court chief justice Melville Fuller, congressman and later president William McKinley, the mayor of New York Hugh Grant, and the financial magnates J. Pierpont Morgan and John D. Rockefeller.

Blackstone's petition appeared five years before Theodor Herzl published *Der Judenstaat* and six years before Herzl convened the first Zionist congress in Basel. There are striking resemblances between Blackstone's and Herzl's proposals for a Jewish commonwealth in Palestine. Both men came forward with a plan for the establishment of a Jewish state by means of diplomacy and international consent. Both plans were based on a great amount of optimism and a messianic vision of sorts: one overtly Christian and biblical, the other seemingly modernist and secular but drawing on old religious yearnings. Both Blackstone and Herzl thought that the world powers would promote such a plan, that Turkey would consent to the creation of a Jewish commonwealth in its territories, and that the founding of a Jewish state would induce massive Jewish immigration to, and settlement in, Palestine. Both men assumed that all obstacles—political, economic, and communal—could be overcome by persuasion, proper planning, and cooperation. There was however, a major difference between Herzl, a secular Jew who wished to safeguard his people and turn them into a European nation, and Blackstone, who, while not lacking in warmth and goodwill, looked at the Jewish people from the outside, with an ulterior motive. In his mind, preparation for the second arrival of the Messiah could be combined with efforts to secure the well-being of the Jews. Although Blackstone's proposal preceded Herzl's by merely five years, he had probably no direct influence on the Jewish leader. However, such ideas and efforts as Blackstone's indirectly encouraged and legitimized Jewish hopes for the creation of a Jewish national entity in Palestine.[13]

Reactions to the Memorial

The petition provoked a stormy reaction in the American Jewish community, which manifested itself in an unprecedented debate within the pages of Jewish publications. Isaac M. Wise, editor of the *American Isra-elite,* the leading Reform periodical in the United States, took a sharply negative line. He feared that the establishment of a Jewish state would encourage countries in which the Jews "have achieved success to expel their Jews to Palestine." The weekly *Jewish Messenger* stated: "First, it revives the old approach of the anti-Semites that the Jews cannot be true patriots, if Palestine is their national home today. Secondly, it makes the Jews again a subject of newspaper comment, when such publicity does more harm than good." The *Menorah,* the official organ of the B'nai B'rith organization, partially endorsed Blackstone's petition. It favored the idea of Jewish settlement in Palestine but opposed the idea of a Jewish state.[14]

The *Reform Advocate* rejected Blackstone's plan. But although many in the Reform movement did not embrace Blackstone's initiative, some notable figures in the movement endorsed it, and some, such as Kaufmann Kohler and Bernhard Felsenthal, even signed the petition. Like most Reform leaders, Orthodox rabbis, as a rule, were not enthusiastic over Blackstone's petition. The fledgling American Jewish Orthodoxy of the late nineteenth century was mostly of the moderate non-Hasidic brand, and some Orthodox rabbis held pro-Zionist sentiments. Yet many Orthodox Jews were skeptical. Blackstone approached the Orthodox rabbi A. J. G. Lesser to ask him to validate the claim, which he had expressed in his petition, that the Jews had always been yearning to return to Zion and build their national home there. Lesser was afraid that such a statement from a rabbi would be used by anti-Jewish agitators to show that Jews were disloyal citizens because their hopes and aspirations lay elsewhere. He therefore wrote a tract *In the Last Days,* in which he claimed that Jews wished to remain in the countries in which they resided. Their hope for a national restoration was to be realized only in a remote and distant future.[15]

The small Zionist groups in America of that era welcomed Blackstone's initiative. *Ha Pisga,* the only Hebrew periodical at that time in America, endorsed the memorial warmly. Fully aware of Blackstone's Christian messianic motivations, its editor, Wolf Schur, took a utilitarian

Jewish-Zionist approach: "It is not their intention to bring us under the wings of Christianity in our time . . . but rather in the days to come after the battle of Gog and Magog. Let the Christians do whatever they can to help us in the resettlement of Palestine. As to the question of our faith, let that rest until Elijah returns and then we shall see whether or not their dream materializes."[16] While few future Zionist leaders would read either Blackstone's petition or *Ha Pisga*'s endorsement of it, Zionist and Israeli leaders would often embrace Schur's recommendation. They would be happy to receive evangelical support while ignoring the details of the messianic faith.

The U.S. government took some minor steps in response to the petition, such as asking for the opinion of diplomats. Selah Merrill, the American consul in Jerusalem, a nonevangelical, nonpremillennialist Protestant who opposed Jewish restoration to Palestine, wrote that "Turkey was not in the habit of giving away whole provinces for the asking."[17] On April 6, 1891, the American ambassador to Russia met with the Russian minister of foreign affairs and brought up the possibility of an international conference "to consider the conditions of the Israelites and the question of restoring Palestine to the hands of the people as the asylum . . . of their race." The Russian minister replied that if the United States would suggest such a conference, Russia would cooperate.[18] The United States, however, never convened such a conference, and there is no evidence that it intended to do so. In his third annual message to the Congress, in December 1891, President Harrison spoke at length on the fate of Russian Jewry,[19] but he did not refer to the Blackstone Memorial or to the idea of a Jewish restoration to Palestine. Yet although Blackstone's petition failed to bring the American government to take any meaningful action toward the organizing of such a conference, the petition reflected the warm support that the idea of the Jewish restoration to Palestine could receive among American Protestants. In later years this attitude would translate into more concrete actions.

Evangelical Christians and Zionist Leaders

The rise of political Zionism enhanced the cooperation between Jewish Zionist leaders and evangelical activists. Attempting to establish contacts with European Protestant political leaders, Theodor Herzl sought the advice and cooperation of William Hechler. Hechler bridged, in his convictions and career, continental pietism and English-speaking evangelicalism. A tutor at the court of the Grand Duke of Baden, Hechler encountered Protestant German pious aristocrats and royalty. Like other evangelical thinkers, he reacted strongly to news of massacres against Jews in Russia and published, in 1893, a major work in which he expanded upon his views on the role of the Jews in God's plans for humanity. In the *Restoration of the Jews to Palestine,* Hechler predicted that a breakthrough in the return of the Jews to Palestine would take place in 1897–98. When Herzl began his attempts to create a world Zionist movement, in 1896–97, Hechler looked upon it as a prophetic moment. He and Herzl met and were impressed by what they considered to be the other's merits and goodwill, with the result that Hechler became, in effect, Herzl's confidant and adviser in matters of European diplomacy.

Hechler, and consequently Herzl, hoped that the Reformed and pietist-leaning Prussian royal family would look favorably upon the Zionist attempts at returning the Jews to Palestine. In April 1896, Herzl, with Hechler's help, met with the Grand Duke of Baden, who expressed sympathy for Herzl's goals. Some of the characteristics of evangelical-Zionist cooperation took shape with that early encounter. Herzl did not take seriously Hechler's messianic faith and considered his Christian friend to be a naive visionary but nonetheless trusted him. Hechler, for his part, considered the Zionist project to be a very welcome development, one prophesied and predicted long in advance. However, while he saw Herzl as a decent, impressive person, he considered him to lack a realistic idea of the unfolding of history. Claude Duvernoy, a French Protestant theologian and historian, described the two as "the prince and the prophet."[20] Theirs was ultimately a marriage of convenience.

While they liked and appreciated each other, each saw the other as useful and helpful for the realization of different goals.

Another decisive moment of Zionist activists' and evangelical Christians' cooperation occurred in the midst of World War I over attempts to influence the American and British governments to support the creation of a Jewish homeland in Palestine. Historians have paid attention to evangelical influences on the British government's decision to issue the Balfour Declaration in 1917.[21] Few, however, have noted the role of evangelical Christians in influencing the American government to consent to the British issuing of the declaration. In this case too a lively cooperation developed between evangelical Christians and Zionist leaders. William Blackstone played again a central role. Not deterred by the lack of immediate results to his first petition, Blackstone organized a second petition in 1916, calling upon the president of the United States to help restore Palestine to the Jews. This time his efforts were carefully coordinated with those of the Zionist leadership and had more influence on the American government and its positions.[22]

The character of the Zionist movement changed dramatically between 1891 and 1916. Although the majority of Jews at that time did not take an interest in Zionism, the movement grew considerably from a few dozen members to a few thousand. American Zionist leaders such as Louis Brandeis, Nathan Straus, and Stephen Wise saw Blackstone's efforts as beneficial to the Zionist cause, expressed support for his actions, and maintained a friendly relationship with him. Blackstone did not keep his messianic premillennialist motivations secret from his Jewish friends. He sent them his published works and expressed his opinions in correspondence with them. He even entrusted Supreme Court justice Louis Brandeis with his "Rapture Will." His request was that Brandeis would take care of his earthly possessions when the Rapture took place and born-again Christians, such as himself, disappeared from the earth, while Jews, such as Brandeis, were left behind. The Zionist leaders were not bothered by Blackstone's prediction that great turmoils were awaiting the Jews in the events of the end times or by his belief that the Jews would eventually accept Jesus as their messiah. Not adhering to such

messianic faith, the Jewish leaders focused instead on the concrete support that Christians holding such convictions could give the Zionist
agenda.[23] As for evangelical premillennialists such as Blackstone and
Hechler, they did not fully endorse the Jewish Zionist agenda either.
They criticized the secular character of Zionism and were disappointed
that Jewish Zionists were unaware of the real significance of the Jewish
national awakening and resettlement of Palestine. But they supported
the Zionist endeavor, and their reports on what they saw as the achievements of Jewish immigrants in Palestine were reminiscent of those of
the more enthusiastic Jewish supporters of the Zionist cause. Their differences apart, both parties focused on Palestine and the necessity of
Jews to settle there and "rejuvenate" the land.

Whereas the petition of 1891 took its point of departure from the
plight of Russian Jewry, that of 1916 spoke more of "the persecuted Jews
of Europe," probably because between 1891 and 1916 almost two million
Jewish immigrants from eastern Europe had arrived in America. But it
emphasized that "the Jewish question is world-wide and demands an
international remedy." This time, precedents for the creation of national
states on former Turkish territory were omitted. Instead, Blackstone
hinted at his and other premillennialists' understanding that the First
World War would serve as a significant step in the advancement of the
ages. Blackstone tried for fewer signers than in 1891, this time collecting
only eighty-two signatures of prominent figures. As far as he was concerned, the idea of the restoration of Palestine to the Jews enjoyed strong
support among the American public.[24] More impressive than the number of signatures on the 1916 petition was the fact that major Protestant
groups endorsed it and presented it to President Wilson as their official
proposal for solving the problem of Jewish suffering around the globe.
On May 26, 1916, the General Assembly of the Presbyterian Church
U.S.A. adopted Blackstone's petition as its own resolution and presented
it as such to President Wilson, who accepted it "in a very kindly manner."[25] A series of Protestant groups in Los Angeles, then Blackstone's
hometown, endorsed and adopted his petition, including the Methodist
Ministers' Meeting of Southern California, the Presbyterian Ministerial

Association of Los Angeles, and the Los Angeles Baptist Ministers' Conference.[26] Blackstone organized a formal committee made up of distinguished Protestant churchmen to present his petition to President Wilson. They included J. W. Bashford, a bishop in the Methodist Church; F. M. North, president of the Federal Council of Churches of Christ in America; Robert Speer, secretary of the Presbyterian Board of Foreign Missions; and John Mott, general secretary of the International Committee of YMCA. All those men were pillars of mainstream American Protestantism. Bashford, in particular, identified with Blackstone's cause and was his confidant in all the negotiations concerning the petition.[27]

Although many of the church leaders who supported Blackstone were not dispensationalists, Blackstone's initiative apparently found more approving audiences among members of denominations that had a strong evangelical wing, as was the case with the Methodists, Presbyterians, and Baptists. Blackstone's good connections with leaders of mainstream Protestantism in America, and his ability to bring many of them to openly support the idea of a Jewish restoration in Palestine, manifest one difference between American evangelicals of 1916 and those of today. Although the modernist-conservative debate had already emerged, the boundaries between liberal and conservative Protestantism were not fully defined. Blackstone, himself a conservative and a premillennialist, was able to establish friendly relations with leaders of established mainstream Protestant churches and persuade them to work for his cause. After the modernist-conservative debate reached its dramatic climax in the mid-1920s with the Scopes trial, these boundaries became increasingly more pronounced, and it is doubtful if thereafter an evangelical activist could mobilize liberal denominations to act on behalf of advancing his eschatological hopes.

Blackstone was ready to have his petition presented to President Wilson by October 1916, but the Zionist leadership prevented him from doing so, claiming that the time was not ripe for a public presentation and that it should be formally delivered to Wilson when the president could give it full attention.[28] President Wilson not only knew about the petition but saw it informally a few times and received versions of it with the endorsements of the various religious groups mentioned above.[29] The official presentation of the petition, however, was constantly delayed and never actually took place.[30] Blackstone was willing to leave the matter of the public presentation of the petition to the Zionist leadership, claiming that he had "no personal ambition" and that his only concern was that "it may accomplish the best results for the Jewish people in all the world."[31]

It seems that Wilson was hesitant to accept Blackstone's petition publicly, but he did treat it seriously.[32] He suggested changes that he thought should be made in it.[33] Had he considered it an unimportant, eccentric document, he could easily have given his consent to its presentation. The president of the United States was used to accepting petitions on various matters, including many he cared little about. Harrison had accepted Blackstone's petition solemnly in March 1891, although he had no intention of carrying out its suggestions. One should note that the United States was not then in a state of war with Turkey, and given that Palestine was under Turkish rule, an official, ceremonious acceptance in the midst of the Great War of a public demand to deprive the Ottoman Empire of part of its territory seemed undesirable to Wilson as a potential endorsement of British colonial ambitions.[34] It was at this time (1916-17) that the president developed a favorable attitude toward the Zionist movement and the idea of a Jewish national home in Palestine, but he did not publicly state his support of Zionism until September 1918. His pro-Zionist sentiments were kept hidden from the American public in general and even from his secretary of state, Robert Lansing, who knew little about Wilson's attitude and his consent to the Balfour Declaration.[35] Although the petition was never formally presented, it nonetheless achieved its goal. It was intended, as far as both Blackstone and the Zionist leadership were concerned, to show President Wilson that Protestant America favored the idea of a Jewish restoration to Palestine. Endorsed as it was by the Presbyterian Church and other church bodies, it served this purpose well. By the summer of 1917, the Zionist leaders were convinced of Wilson's support for their cause and saw no need to embarrass the president by publicly presenting the petition.[36]

Woodrow Wilson was not a premillennialist,[37] but he was a committed Protestant, the son of a Presbyterian minister, who had grown up in an evangelical atmosphere. Daily reading of the Bible was part of his routine. The Presbyterian Church that had endorsed Blackstone's proposal was his own church. Wilson revealed his Christian feelings concerning the Jewish homeland in Palestine, though only in private. In a talk with Rabbi Stephen Wise in June 1917, for example, he remarked, "To think that I, the son of a manse [a Presbyterian minister's home], should be able to restore the Holy Land to its people."[38] However, perhaps because evangelical religious sentiments helped shape Wilson's favorable attitude toward Zionism, he was careful not to reveal the fact publicly.

Not all the voices of Protestant America favored a national Jewish home in Palestine. Nonpremillennialist, nonevangelical Protestant activists associated with the American-established Syrian Protestant College in Beirut organized a pro-Arab lobby. These Protestants were committed to Arab nationalism and favored the idea of an Arab state in "Greater Syria," including Palestine, and they considered the idea of a Jewish home in Palestine a threat. An energetic pro-Arab Protestant group lobbied at the Peace Conference in Paris.[39] One of its influential members, Cleveland Dodge, was a close associate of Wilson who had backed him financially in his election campaign. Blackstone took no steps to create a lobby to counterbalance the pro-Arab one, although he continued to write to the president and share his opinions with him. Perhaps he regarded the fulfillment of the Balfour Declaration and the establishment of a Jewish home in Palestine as a fait accompli and did not see a need to fight on its behalf. An examination of Blackstone's tactics reveals that he never tried to establish a lobby or a permanent organization. This attitude would change dramatically in the later decades of the twentieth century, when evangelicals would establish such lobbies.

Evangelical Reactions in the Aftermath of World War I

Following World War I, evangelicals with premillennialist leanings continued to take a profound interest in events in the life of the Jewish people, and especially in new developments in the Jewish community in Palestine. Leading evangelical journals, such as *Our Hope,* the *King's Business,* the *Moody Monthly,* and the Pentecostal *Evangel,* regularly published news on events such as the opening of the Hebrew University in Jerusalem in 1925, and of the new seaport in Haifa in 1932. They interpreted these events as signs that the Jews were energetically building a commonwealth in their ancient homeland and that the great events of the end times were to occur very soon.[40]

Likewise, news of clashes between Arabs and Jews in 1920-21 and in 1929 worried evangelicals. The Arab Revolt in Palestine in 1936-39 and the British "White Paper," which restricted Jewish immigration to Palestine, the buying of land there, and the building of new settlements, also stirred negative reactions. The editor of *Our Hope,* Arno Gaebelein, for example, lashed out at the British for restricting Jewish immigration and settlement and criticized the Arabs for their hostility toward the Zionist project and for their violence against the Jews. He considered attempts to block the building of a Jewish commonwealth in Palestine as equivalent to putting obstacles in the way of providence.[41]

British policies were not always adversarial to Christian Zionist aspirations. Some convinced premillennialist evangelicals served in the British administration in Palestine. Wyndham Deedes, the chief secretary of the British administration in Palestine from 1920 to 1922, was one such Christian Zionist, although he tried to relate to all sections of the local population fairly and promoted the creation of the Supreme Muslim Council as a counterbalance to the Jewish Agency.[42] Another striking example of a Christian Zionist within the British administration in Palestine was Orde Wingate, who grew up in a British military family associated with the Plymouth Brethren. Assigned to Palestine in 1936, Wingate saw his calling in organizing Jewish combat units to fight the Arab Palestinian rebellion. Several of his followers, including Yigal Alon and Moshe Dayan, became commanders in the Jewish military infrastructure of Palestine and adopted some of Wingate's tactics.[43] A number of evangelicals protested the British restrictions on Jewish immigration and purchase of land. But despite their resentment toward these policies, evangelicals did not mount any organized efforts to combat them, and few took their protests beyond the pages of newspapers or journals.

When Nazi policies against the Jews took effect in Germany in 1933, evangelical writers strongly condemned them, setting aside their own prejudices and complaints against the Jews. They considered the Nazi ideology to be a rebellion against God and a distortion of Christian theology and values. The Nazis, they complained, were "Aryanizing" Jesus and denying the validity of the Old Testament. They were also victimizing the Jews, and in so doing stirring God's anger.[44] But evangelicals did not establish an anti-Nazi front, perhaps because during the 1930s conservative evangelicals were generally not very active politically as a group. After the notorious Scopes trial in 1925, they withdrew for many years from the American public arena and their public influence weakened considerably. Their activities concentrated instead on evangelism and on the enlargement of their conservative educational infrastructure. Evangelical leaders did not see themselves as influential figures who would be heard by policy makers in Washington and could therefore advance a political agenda on the international level. They voiced their political opinions in their journals and expressed their relationship to the Jews in their extensive missionary activity. They also helped Jewish missionary workers and converts escape Nazi-occupied Europe. Those efforts were made on a one-on-one basis, but they cumulatively helped save hundreds of people. Since missions could not find visas to America for all of their protégés, they, at times, directed them to other countries, such as Argentina.[45]

The years in which evangelical interest in the Jews and their future did not translate into political action were the years of Nazi persecution and destruction of Jewish life in Europe. During those years liberal Christians became more involved politically in assisting Jewish emigration from Nazi-occupied Europe and mustering public support after the war for the establishing of a Jewish state.[46] A series of such organizations raised their voices during the deliberations and public debates that preceded the decision of the United Nations to partition Palestine and the decision of the American government to support the creation of a

Jewish state in Palestine. In the 1930s, mainstream Protestant activists established the Pro-Palestine Federation of America, which advocated for the rights and interests of the Jews in Palestine. Such Protestants did not, as a rule, hold to messianic premillennialist hopes and joined these organizations for political and humanitarian reasons. The liberal support had been a product of a specific time and atmosphere. Unlike evangelicals, liberal Protestants had no inherent theological motive to support the Zionist agenda or the creation of a Jewish state. They were divided on the merits of the establishment of a Jewish state:[47] some sided with the Arab claims, but many showed sympathy, in the late 1940s and throughout the 1950s and early 1960s, to Israel and some of its struggles. Since the 1967 War and the development of postcolonial ideologies, many of them have criticized Israel and especially its occupation of Palestinian territory.

In the 1970s and 1980s, a progressive evangelical faction, much smaller in size and influence, came into being in America. On issues such as personal morality, the progressives would side with the conservatives. Like other liberals, they showed goodwill toward their Jewish friends with whom they cooperated on social and political issues. However, they joined their liberal Protestant counterparts in criticizing Israel for what they saw as its unjust policies.[48] The difference here from conservative evangelicals points unmistakably to the influence of the premillennialist eschatological faith. Liberal Protestants, who lacked it, turned their attentions and energies to concerns far removed from those of conservative evangelicals. Premillennialist evangelicals, on the other hand, found special meaning both in the Jews and in Palestine and continued to take proactive steps to influence the fate of both.

5

Evangelicals and Jews in the Holy Land

William Blackstone was one of a long series of evangelical Christians who found meaning in the Holy Land. In principle, evangelical Protestants had not recognized the concept of holy sites, but during the nineteenth century Palestine became more accessible to evangelical Protestants than before, and their relation to that country came to resemble that of Catholic, Orthodox, and Monophysite Christians. They began traveling to Palestine, arriving as tourists, missionaries, explorers of the land, biblical scholars, archaeologists, and diplomats. They wished to obtain inspiration or solace, or to be at "ground zero" when the great events of the end times took place, or to help the Jews build the kingdom of God on earth. British evangelicals were particularly predominant in the early stages of evangelical visits and settlement, but by the late nineteenth century American evangelicals took the lead.

When Blackstone arrived in Palestine with his daughter in 1889, he encountered individuals and even vibrant communities of pietist and evangelical Protestants who had settled in the country. At that time many of them were from America and included personal friends of Blackstone. The evangelical community in Jerusalem started in the 1830s and 1840s when British evangelists and German pietists initiated the establishment of a Protestant bishopric, strong missionary stations, and consulates to protect Protestant missionary activity. James and Elizabeth Anne Finn, the British consulate and his wife, provide an example of evangelical Christians whose work in Jerusalem, motivated by a premillennialist understanding of the Jews, created meaningful exchanges between evangelicals and Jews. Elizabeth Finn was the daughter of Alexander McCaul, one of the more noted missionaries of the London Society for Promoting Christianity amongst the Jews.[1] Like McCaul, the Finns considered the Jews heirs and continuers of historical Israel and a people who were destined to revive their position in Palestine and resume their place as God's first nation. James Finn, who arrived in Jerusalem in 1845, used his position as British consul to protect Jews from maltreatment either by the authorities or by members of other religious communities. He even helped settle disputes within the Jewish (and Arab) communities. The Finns participated in, or encouraged, projects that aimed at helping Jews acquire skills, livelihood, and a solid position in the land.[2] One endeavor was facilitating the purchase of lands along the road from Jerusalem to Jaffa, where Jews established an agricultural village. Among Finn's initiatives was also the establishment in 1852 of a farm about a kilometer northwest of the city walls. Its name, Abraham's Vineyard, like that of other institutions established by evangelical Protestants in Palestine, demonstrated the understanding of the Jews as continuers of biblical Israel. The farm supplied dozens of Jews with steady jobs and a source of income and offered its employees training in such arts as stonemasonry.

The Finns were not alone. A series of evangelical Protestant writers, artists, explorers, missionaries, educators, and physicians holding to a biblical-messianic vision settled in the city, creating their own social-cultural and religious circle.[3] William Hunt, one of England's noted pre-Raphaelite painters, arrived in Jerusalem in 1854, living on the Prophets Road outside the city's walls. His Palestinian-era paintings gave expression to his biblical messianic outlook. One of Hunt's striking sets of paintings during that period focused on the scapegoat and its role in helping to bring about human redemption. The goat in Hunt's paintings represents Jesus, ready to be sacrificed in order to atone for the sins of humanity. The evangelical premillennialist artist used an actual goat as a model. In the pictures, the goat is white, symbolizing his total innocence. He is dignified, even regal, with a red imperial crown on his head, and he accepts his suffering without resentment. He is the true king of the Jews, and during the messianic age he will turn into the ruler of the entire planet.[4]

A noted group of evangelicals in Jerusalem were the representatives of the London Society for Promoting Christianity amongst the Jews. By that time, the Society was fully Anglican, although the mission's theology often represented the evangelical and premillennialist section in the church. One of the most outstanding members of the mission's staff was the German-Swiss architect and archaeologist Konrad Schick, who initially came to Jerusalem in 1850 as an emissary of the St. Chrischona Pilgrim Mission. The London Society allowed him ample time to pursue archaeological and architectural endeavors, and Schick designed a series of Protestant institutions: schools, orphanages, hospitals, and hospices. His style combined the local architectural tradition, including building with stone and the use of arches and round roofs, together with the German neo-Gothic, a synthesis that made his buildings exceptional. Blackstone took special interest in Schick's work. Schick, like Blackstone, had researched the topography of ancient Jerusalem and, among other projects, had built a model of the Temple.

In 1840, Britain and Prussia established a joined Protestant bishopric in Jerusalem, and the two nations took turns appointing bishops. This was a particular moment in time when the Prussian pietists and British evangelicals exercised influence on the ruling elites in their respective countries and were thus able to bring them to support the idea of evangelizing the Jews and the rejuvenation of Palestine. A similar exercise of influence would take place in America from the 1980s through the 2000s, when conservative evangelicals would be able, at least to some extent, to influence national policies toward the Middle East. The bishopric and the London Society established a compound near the Jaffa Gate in the old city of Jerusalem, as well as a hospital and school on the western slope of Mount Zion, outside the city walls.[5] Built in the 1840s with the help of Maltese masons, the chapel evidenced the attitudes of evangelical missionaries toward the Jews. Devoid of pictures of any kind, it was designed to resemble a synagogue. The audience sat facing the Temple Mount, and, as in Jewish synagogues, there were Hebrew inscriptions listing the Ten Commandments on wood tablets on the eastern wall that resembled the Ark of the Covenant.

Jerusalem in the later decades of the nineteenth century attracted a series of messianically oriented evangelical groups and individuals, many of them affiliated with particular missions or churches, with zeal to explore the country, propagate the Gospel, and, from their perspective, influence the course of history. Others came as individuals wishing to encounter biblical sites and experience future messianic moments. The term *Jerusalem syndrome* was not yet coined, but the symptoms were already apparent during this time.[6] The scientist, traveler, and author Ada Goodrich-Freer describes an almost surreal scene among evangelical Protestants in Jerusalem. Well versed in the biblical narratives, and often expecting the Messiah to arrive in Jerusalem, they would mistake themselves for biblical figures or would daily await the return of Jesus. She offers a colorful description:

> On the north of the Holy City is the settlement of the American Colony, commonly known from their founder Spaffordites, on the south that of the Templars or Hofmannites, both societies admirable for their order and their industry, if somewhat creative in theological opinions. On the west we have the immense ruin of the unfinished building in which, half a century ago, some wealthy lady . . . proposed to house the hundred and forty and four thousand. . . . To the east, we have the mount of Olives, geographically the rallying-place of an extraordinary variety of enthusiasts, including a worthy Englishwoman who is . . . in constant readiness to welcome our Lord's return thither with a cup of tea. . . . We have a colony profanely known as the Tishbites—English and American—presided over by "the prophet Elijah." Scarcely a year goes by without the arrival of someone who dares to assume a personality still more sacred.[7]

Such people added a sense of anticipation of messianic times to the atmosphere of the city. In this they were not much different from a number of Jewish groups and individuals who settled in the city in the nineteenth century.[8] Such evangelical groups also affected the economy and topography of Jerusalem. Of particular importance was the group of American evangelicals who became known as the "American Colony" and whom Goodrich-Freer calls the Spaffordites. Settling in Jerusalem, the Spaffords brought with them the American premillennial evangelicalism of their time. While the group started with a handful of families and individuals from Chicago, it grew within a few years into a major presence in Jerusalem, influencing the life and welfare of the city.[9]

Like William Blackstone, the first leader of the community, Horatio Spafford (1827-88) was a northeastern businessman who, after settling in Chicago, became an evangelist dedicated to urban revivalism. In 1861 he married the Norwegian-born Anna Lawson, and the couple built their home in an affluent neighborhood in northern Chicago. During the 1860s Horatio and Anna were among a number of evangelicals in the commercial classes in Chicago who had adopted the dispensational premillennialist faith and had become convinced of Jesus's imminent return.[10] The Spaffords also became followers of the Holiness movement, viewing the current era, the period preceding the messianic age, as a time of the "outpouring of the Holy Spirit." In addition to the conversion experiences necessary for salvation, Holiness followers sought a "second blessing," "complete sanctification," and "perfection," which the Holy Spirit would manifest in their lives.[11] The Spaffords encountered a tragedy in 1874. En route to vacation in Europe, Anna and the couple's four daughters sailed on the *Ville du Havre,* whose sinking was one of the major maritime accidents of the time, and the four children drowned. Horatio Spafford wrote the hymn "It Is Well with My Soul" to help reconcile himself to his loss.[12] After this tragedy, the Spaffords became even closer to Dwight Moody, who arranged for Anna to do welfare work in Chicago.

In 1880 the Spaffords' son, born after the *Ville du Havre* tragedy, died of scarlet fever. The bereaved couple came to believe in universal salvation, claiming that there was no hell and that children in particular would not suffer eternally. The Spaffords did not think that universalism contradicted their Christian evangelical messianic faith, but the Presbyterian Church decided to terminate their membership. The Spaffords gathered a small group of relatives and friends around them that became a religious community of its own and practiced Holiness and premillennialist evangelical teachings. These included Horatio's sister, Margaret Lee, who, for a while, received revelations and became an intermediary between the group and God, "giving us truth and telling us that this coming was the coming of Elias, or Christ coming as a thief."[13] The Spaffords considered their journey to Jerusalem in 1881 to be a pilgrimage, explained in spiritual, moral, and messianic terms.[14]

Like other evangelicals who came to Jerusalem, they hoped that the city where Jesus had taught and suffered, and to which they believed he would soon return, would have a profound effect on their moral and spiritual well-being, and they were convinced that they had a role to play in the millennial scheme.[15] Anna Spafford described the group's motivation: "We wished to go there when God brought the Jews back; we wanted to see the prophecies fulfilled."[16]

Upon their arrival in Jerusalem, the Spaffords and their friends decided to live a communal life similar to that described in Acts, with property held in common. At first they settled in the Muslim Quarter of the Old City and took daily walks to the Mount of Olives, where they expected Jesus and his saints to arrive imminently. The community also practiced sexual abstinence; men and women lived in separate quarters, and for over two decades there were no marriages in the group.[17] Ada Goodrich-Freer, who wrote about the group with much appreciation, explained its "condition of chastity as giving up on earthly love for the sake of the love of God."[18] Although new to the city, the Colony was the first community in Jerusalem to offer assistance to several hundred Jews who had departed Yemen as the result of messianic fervor, arriving destitute in Jerusalem in 1882. The Spaffordites provided the newcomers, who were living in open fields outside the city wall, with tents, medical care, and food. The arrival of the Yemenites furnished them with a "sign of the time" that indicated that the present era was terminating and the Messiah's coming was near. The groups considered the Yemenite Jews to be the "Gadites," descendants of the tribe of Gad (Deut. 33:20-21) and considered it a duty to assist them.[19]

After Horatio Spafford's death in 1888, his wife Anna became the spiritual leader of the community, whose members considered her to hold charismatic powers.[20] Anna abandoned universalist convictions and adopted understandings of the perfect life, sin, and death more in line with standard Holiness teachings. She took little interest in financial and commercial affairs, which were first in the hands of William Rudy, a businessman from Chicago who was one of the early members of the group, and later transferred to her sons-in-law, Frederick Vester and John Whiting.[21] Anna considered the Colony to be the biblical "Bride" awaiting reunion with God and saw its mission as setting an example of love, purity, and peace.[22] The Colony put this principle into action in extensive welfare and medical work, which reached a peak during World War I.[23]

A Swedish American evangelical group from Chicago headed by Olof Larson (1842–1919) decided to join the American group in Jerusalem. A former ship captain, Larson moved to Chicago and established an independent Swedish-speaking evangelical church with members living in a religious commune under his spiritual guidance.[24] In 1889, Larson held revival meetings in Nås in the region of Dalarna, in central Sweden, and established a local community. The Swedish Nobel prize laureate Selma Lagerlöf provided a lively description of the rise of this evangelical group of farmers and artisans and its eventual immigration to Jerusalem. The group believed that Jesus was returning soon and that true Christians would meet him upon his arrival in Jerusalem. In 1895, Anna Spafford visited Chicago and met Larson's group, who were impressed with her personality and message. Convinced that they shared the same religious beliefs, Larson and his group, about seventy persons, decided to move to Jerusalem and join the Americans. They sold their properties and proceeded to "hasten to the Holy City to await the second coming of the Lord and witness the fulfillment of Prophecy."[25] Larson's followers in Nås also decided to join the Americans. They believed that the Approach of the Last Day was imminent and they must hurry to meet their Lord in Jerusalem.[26]

The Colony, which now numbered more than 150 people, moved from the Muslim Quarter to a building on Nablus Road that was rented and later purchased from the Muslim Husseini family, and it became the center of the American Colony complex. In the 1890s, the location was not yet a densely built-up urban area, and the American Colony could develop both urban commercial enterprises and agricultural ones, including a dairy farm, a bakery, a furniture shop, a guesthouse, a tourist shop, and a photography studio. The Colony became a major economic and charitable organization in Jerusalem, leaving its mark on the city's development.[27] English was the language of choice in the Colony, which celebrated the Fourth of July, and the Swedes gradually Americanized. A number of second-generation Swedes who grew up in the Colony left for America and built their lives there. Some commented on the female leadership of the colony, which was not unusual for religious-messianic movements in America at the turn of the twentieth century but diverged from general social norms. One favorable Swedish description of the Colony and its leader is given by Lagerlöf.[28]

The Colony's theology and practices resembled those found in late nineteenth-century American premillennialist evangelicalism and Holiness teachings.[29] Daily activity in the Colony began with a morning prayer meeting, which included reading from Scripture and singing hymns used by other Holiness congregations.[30] Prayer was usually spontaneous, and Anna would sometimes receive divine revelations, defined also as the outpouring of the Spirit. The Colony declared itself to be open and welcoming to all without missionary objectives, a policy that helped facilitate good relationships with the Jewish and Muslim communities but created conflicts at times with other Protestant activists in Jerusalem. A group of local ministers expressed their resentment in a dispatch of September 28, 1897, to the American president and State Department.[31] However, Holiness groups and individuals more easily accepted the ideas and religious practices of the Colony. Evangelists who visited Jerusalem, such as William Blackstone and Dwight Moody, paid visits to the Colony, and the group also established good relations with the Keswick Holiness movement in Britain. Likewise friendships developed between the Colony and other Holiness groups in Jerusalem, such as the Christian and Missionary Alliance. This missionary organization, founded in 1888 by A. B. Simpson, had accepted premillennialist and Holiness teachings, and its leaders in Jerusalem became friendly with the Colony's leaders and sent their children to the Colony's school. Horatio Spafford's hymn "It Is Well with My Soul" appeared consistently in the Alliance's hymn collection.[32] The British general Charles "Chinese" Gordon, an ardent evangelical and premillennialist, befriended the Spaffords and lived in the Colony for a time during his visit to Jerusalem (1882-83). Among Gordon's ventures in Jerusalem was the excavation of the Garden Tomb, which he and evangelicals ever since have identified with Jesus's burial site. The place would eventually become a pilgrimage site with thousands of evangelicals visiting the place weekly. Visitors and friends like General Gordon helped turn the American Colony into a respectable local Christian group. Significantly, in 1904, an international conference of the Sunday school movement convened in Jerusalem, and the American Colony's leaders were invited to play a leading role in the convention.

The intense holiness and messianic fervor of the Colony, and its communal ideals, did not continue into the second generation. After Anna Spafford's death in 1923, her daughter Bertha took over the Colony's leadership and the austere religious atmosphere relaxed considerably.[33] For Bertha and most of the other second-generation members of the Colony, Jerusalem was not the magnified holy site where the Messiah was to arrive but an earthly city with limitations and struggles. Having abandoned the messianic faith, the second-generation members of the Colony no longer felt particularly committed to Jewish immigration and settlement in the Holy Land. They directed most of their charitable and medical work to the Arab population, often identifying with Arab needs and aspirations.[34] Without an intense religious belief system and a charismatic leader to unite them, conflicting interests led various factions of the Colony to apply to the district court concerning the division of property, and the American Colony, as a religious commune, ceased to exist in the 1930s. It became, in effect, a family business focused mainly on a hotel but also committed to community enterprises, including a children's hospital and clinic.

The American Colony in Jerusalem is best understood in the context of similar developments in religion and communal life in America. A number of communes founded in the nineteenth and twentieth centuries sought to establish new socially and morally perfect settlements, often at the geographical margins of their societies.[35] The Colony's founders and those who joined the commune in its first decades made a deliberate choice to live there and accepted the group's practices and norms of their own accord. Yet they were only partially able to transfer their values to their children, and an overt or covert rebellion against the community's regulations took place, such that norms and practices were either modified or ignored.[36]

While the commune disbanded half a century after its establishment, its influence on all spheres of life in the city, from tourism to education, was remarkable. In this it was not alone: other evangelical groups and individuals also left their mark on the city. By the turn of the twentieth century, a number of Holiness churches, including the Nazarenes and the Christian and Missionary Alliance, established congregations and educational enterprises. They were joined by the Baptists, who within a few decades built one of the largest evangelical networks in the country, attracting Arabs and Jews as well as Americans and members of other nations who settled in the country. In the 1920s and 1930s, a number of Pentecostal groups established congregations or missions in Palestine, including followers of Aimee Semple McPherson's Four Square Gospel. These groups' investment of time, energy, and resources contributed to the creation of better medical facilities, educational institutions, and employment opportunities, which affected the entire population. At times, the medical, educational, and welfare facilities offered by evangelical Christians stirred Jews, as well as Muslims and members of non-Protestant Christian groups, to establish their own alternative institutions.

Unwittingly, Jews and evangelicals offered assistance and encouragement to each other. Evangelicals such as Spafford and Blackstone saw in the growth of the Jewish population the beginnings of the realization of prophecy and a proof that the events of the end times were at hand. Jews, for their part, received medical aid, professional instruction, educational opportunities, consular protection, and a richer and safer environment.

Moreover, they saw American and European examples of disciplined and thrifty communities, which offered them inspiration and encouragement. Evangelicals in Palestine looked upon the Jews as the people responsible for building an infrastructure for a commonwealth that would serve as precursor to Christ's kingdom, so in assisting the latter they were working toward fulfilling their own prophecy. The Holy Land influenced evangelical attitudes and interactions with the Jews. Many visited or settled in the country to assist in preparing the ground for the arrival of the Lord. While at times loyalties shifted elsewhere, often the experience cemented commitments and enhanced plans for further actions. Attachment to the Holy Land and hopes for the rejuvenation of the country and the people of Israel went hand in hand. Fascination with the country and its people would continue through the years, with a new invigorated wave of evangelicals arriving after the birth of the state of Israel in 1948. In the meantime, the major venue for evangelicals to interact with the Jews was the mission.

6

Instructing Christians and Jews

Evangelical Missions to the Jews

Since the eighteenth century, missions to the Jews have occupied a central place in the agenda of evangelical Christians. Their meaning for evangelicals has gone far beyond trying to turn individual Jews into confessing Christians, though this aspect of missionary work has certainly been important. Propagating Christianity among the Jews has meant teaching that people about their true role and purpose in history. Missionaries concluded that only a handful of Jews in the current generation would be "saved" but that many others would learn about God's plans for humanity and what to expect when the Rapture took place and the events of the end times unfolded. Those righteous Jews who would read or listen to the missionary messages would recognize the events as correlating with the predictions they had read or heard and would accept Jesus as their savior. These would include first and foremost the 144,000 Jews who would become evangelists and spread the Christian message during the Great Tribulation.

Missionaries to the Jews also believed it was important to instruct Christians as to the role of the Jews in God's plans. This part of their work aimed to increase support in the Christian community for the idea of the Jews as a special people and the need to evangelize them. For most missionary groups the two aims, instructing Jews and Christians, were inseparable. Evangelical activists such as the Earl of Shaftsbury in Britain in the mid-nineteenth century and Arno Gaebelein in America at the turn of the twentieth century were advocates of the premillennialist faith, leaders in the realm of missions to the Jews, and proponents of Jewish restoration to Palestine, as well as leading spokespersons of the evangelical camp as a whole. Missions to the Jews stood high on the evangelical agenda. Run by ardent premillennialists, they managed to attract support from many Protestants who did not always fully share the missions' eschatology and biblical exegesis but were nonetheless supportive of their work. In proportion to the actual number of Jews, this missionary movement has been larger than similar efforts among other nations.

From Europe to Britain and America

The center of evangelical missionary activity directed toward the Jews has shifted throughout the years. Starting in pietist Europe in the eighteenth century, the emergence of a strong evangelical movement in Britain in the early decades of the nineteenth century gave rise to an unprecedentedly large missionary movement there. Throughout the nineteenth century, British evangelicals established numerous missions to the Jews, operating all around the Jewish world, and their efforts were followed by other English-speaking nations.[1] Evangelical missionary initiatives followed in the footsteps of pietist missions with regard to their theological perceptions, their published literature, and their more appreciative attitude toward the Jews. However, the scope of evangelicals' activity and the support it received in the English-speaking world have been much larger than the scope and the support of pietist activity in continental Europe. In a reversal of roles, pietist missionary groups in Europe from the nineteenth century onward, in places such as Scandinavia, Germany, Switzerland, and Holland, began conversing with and accepting ideas from evangelicals. The first and, for a long time, the largest mission in the English-speaking world was the London Society for Promoting Christianity amongst the Jews. The Society started as an interdenominational venture that both the established Church of England and the "Dissenters" who operated outside the established state church supported. But even when the group became fully Anglican, most of its enthusiasm and energy came from evangelicals, many of them holding to a premillennialist messianic faith.[2] The London Society acquired and brought over to London part of the Institutum Judaicum's library and translated and reproduced a number of the pietists' tracts, thus creating a direct link between the two ventures.

In its scope of activities, the Society was one of the larger and better-budgeted missionary groups of the nineteenth century. By the turn of the twentieth century, two hundred full-time paid missionaries operated in fifty-two posts around the globe, with missionary wives and volunteers aiding in the Society's efforts.[3] By that time, twenty-seven British denominations and interdenominational groups established missionary societies aiming at laboring among Jews. While often enjoying support from nonevangelical bodies, those missions were organized, directed, and run by messianically oriented evangelical Protestants. Many of them also promoted the idea of the Jewish return to Palestine as a prerequisite to the unfolding of the messianic age and combined the two agendas in their messages.

Protestant churches, which were not necessarily messianically oriented, often created special departments for missionizing the Jews or sponsored semiautonomous missionary enterprises that were evangelical in character, preached a premillennialist theology, and promoted a belief in the centrality of the Jews in God's plans for humanity. A number of groups and individuals cooperated in creating interdenominational missionary organizations, such as the Chicago Hebrew Mission. Missionaries to the Jews professionalized their vocation, published and translated tracts, organized conferences, and established schools to train missionaries to the Jews. Each mission carried unique features, but as a whole missions also created a movement. As a rule, missions held similar perceptions of the Jews and the moral and spiritual state of that people in the past, present, and the future, as well as of the obligations of the Christian Protestant community toward the Jews, and there was therefore much similarity in the messages, literature, and modes of operation.

Attempts at creating missions to the Jews in America started in the early nineteenth century but did not enjoy the same success as in Britain. Mainstream American Protestants lacked, at that time, the most important incentive to invest energy and resources in evangelizing Jews, namely an influential messianic premillennialist faith that placed Jews at the center of God's plans for the redemption of humanity. Until the Civil War, American evangelicals were mostly nonpremillennialist, but this was to change. The adoption of a premillennialist faith in the later decades of the nineteenth century by a large number of American evangelicals inspired a new enthusiasm for establishing missions to the Jews. From the 1880s onward, dozens of missions sprang up in the United States, with hundreds of missionaries busying themselves in an attempt to bring the Christian gospel to the Jewish population in America and beyond.

Like their British counterparts, American groups ventured out to evangelize a global Jewish community that, at its peak on the eve of World War II, comprised no more than sixteen million people (and would be much diminished after the war), making the Jews one of the most evangelized people on earth. From Warsaw to Capetown, and from Buenos Aires to Montreal, evangelical missions interacted with Jews via educational, medical, welfare, and literary projects. The missions served as a link between two sets of cultures: that of evangelical Protestants and that of the Jews. The missions' large and varied literature was intended to educate both communities, Protestant and Jewish, and bring them to adopt a Christian premillennial vision.

Evangelical missionaries looked upon Jews as worthy of goodwill and attention but at the same time as persons who had not fulfilled their potential and were currently spiritually and morally lacking. They demonstrated compassion for the Jews as people in need of both material assistance and the ameliorating Gospel. They were certain that their own Protestant faith, communities, and values were superior to those of the Jews. As individuals and as a people, Jews held great potential that would come to fruition when they saw the light and realized their true vocation and purpose in history. At the same time, missions to the Jews became agencies for persuading Christians of the need to relate to Jews with goodwill and to refrain from discriminating against them or treating them unkindly. Missionaries in the nineteenth and twentieth centuries also became identified with the Christian Zionist movement, viewing the evangelization of the Jews as part of a larger program: preparing the Jewish people for their historical role in helping to usher in a new era.

Alongside cooperation, there was competition over the resources and support of the Protestant community.[4] The success of missions depended on their ability to adapt themselves to the changing face of both the Jewish communities they were trying to reach and the Protestant supporters who sponsored the missions. Until the 1920s, the missions directed much of their messages and activities toward poor and needy Jewish immigrants and their children in working-class neighborhoods. The missionary enterprises utilized a variety of means to approach the Jews and interest them in the Christian message and in the missionaries' premillennialist perceptions of the advancement of history. These included preaching both in church halls and on street corners, trying to enter into discussions with curious Jews, and distributing printed materials, from leaflets to books, in homes and in the streets. They also included offering a variety of services, such as classes that helped Jews acquire new skills or study English, clinics that offered Jews free medical care, and activities for children. While many Jews benefited from the services that missions offered, and while some were curious to hear or read the missionary messages, the number of converts missions acquired was limited. This deterred neither the missionaries nor the evangelical communities that sponsored them. Missions to the Jews were important to their founders and supporters as demonstrations of commitment toward the Jewish people and as opportunities to influence their destiny.

The more successful missions changed their techniques and messages in the 1920s and 1930s (but not their theology) as they began approaching more acculturated and more economically comfortable Jewish communities. The geographical settings also changed as Jews increasingly moved from impoverished immigrant neighborhoods into middle-class neighborhoods. By that time, the evangelical community allowed Jewish converts more cultural and communal independence, and a number of missionary groups experimented with the creation of semiautonomous congregations of Jewish converts. A third stage in the development of missions started in the 1970s, when missions began trying to reach children of well-integrated middle-class Jews who had been striving to do justice to their complex identities and loyalties as Jews and as fully acculturated Americans searching for spirituality, meaning and community, as well as for their Jewish roots. At this stage, the percentage of intermarried Jews and their children had grown considerably. In all three stages, missions mostly approached Jews in transition who were searching for new sources of meaning and community in their lives. Recognizing the changing trends and deciding on which groups to concentrate their efforts and how to accommodate their spiritual and communal needs would often determine missions' success both as a movement and as separate organizations.

Starting in the late nineteenth century and still going strong at the beginning of the twenty-first century, Williamsburg Mission to the Jews, which changed its name to the American Board of Missions to the Jews and then again to the Chosen People Ministries, has been one of the largest and most influential missionary groups. Leopold Cohn, a Hungarian-born convert who received theological training in Scotland, established the mission in 1893, at first merely one among many small missions in Brooklyn, New York. Under his, and his son Joseph's, leadership, it developed into a national, and later international, organization. The Cohns were particularly well attuned to the values, sentiments, and character of the Protestant community, which supported missions such as their own. In his autobiography, *I Have Fought a Good Fight*, Joseph Cohn described the mission's main struggle as the need to successfully convince the Protestant community to recognize the Jews as a special people and to appreciate the importance of supporting the mission's efforts.

Like the London Society before it, the American Board of Missions to the Jews operated in dozens of communities in America and around the globe and produced, in its turn, a series of daughter missions, some of which have grown to prominence in the field. Established by Moishe Rosen in 1970 as an offshoot of the more veteran missionary organization, Jews for Jesus began by paying much attention to the baby boomer generation, its styles and fashions.[5] Known for its innovative and daring style, in 1974 Jews for Jesus became an independent organization, registering officially as Hineni Ministries and replacing the American Board of Missions to the Jews as the largest mission to the Jews both in America and beyond.

By the 1980s, the Chosen People Ministries, as well as other missions, began establishing and sponsoring Messianic Jewish congregations, communities of Christian Jews that have served as new means of evangelism. The rise of Messianic Judaism in the later decades of the twentieth century and the new ideology and communal experiences that came with it both challenged and transformed the character of missions. The new modes of evangelism have concentrated on the building of congregations of Christian Jews, which in their turn serve as centers of evangelism and evangelical thinking. Since the 1970s, missions to the Jews have emphasized more emphatically that becoming Christian does not eradicate Jewish cultural or ethnic identity but rather makes Jews truer to their real purpose and character.

The Jewish Reaction

Missions stirred strong and at times contradictory reactions in the Jewish community.[6] Needy Jews took advantage of the welfare services that missions offered, and many visited missionary reading rooms or attended sermons. The Jewish elite, on the other hand, resented the missions. In Jewish eyes, the missionary impulse represented a continuation of traditional Christian attitudes that had seen Judaism as obsolete after the arrival of Christianity and had refused to accept its existence outside the church. As such, missions represented hostile attitudes that were intended to undermine the Jewish position in society. Acculturated middle-class Jews were therefore often at the forefront of Jewish antimissionary activity and rhetoric.[7] Although they hardly encountered missionaries themselves, and for the most part would not have been able to read the Yiddish missionary tracts, such Jews viewed missionary work among the Jews as an insult and a threat to their own standing in society. Well-established, middle-class Jews could not understand why other

Jews would interact with missionaries and saw it as a lack of Jewish pride to use services offered by missions.[8] But their call to boycott the missions fell on deaf ears. As memoirs of Jews who grew up in the immigrant community reveal, newly arrived immigrants or working-class Jews visited the mission houses, accepted material aid, and, at times, also came to hear the missionary messages.[9]

A glimpse into conflicting Jewish attitudes is provided by an article in the *American Hebrew:*

> The missionaries have been active for some years in the neighborhood of Park avenue and 102nd street. A church there devoted to their uses is well lit up with electric lights and kept warm in winter, and with lectures and entertainment the children of the neighborhood are inveigled into attendance. Self-respecting people of the neighborhood have at different times taken the matter in their own hands and threatened to withdraw their trade from the Jewish butcher, baker, etc., who permitted their children to attend and take advantage of their outings, vacations, parties and treats. These tradesmen pleaded that no harm could come to their children, who needed the clothing and gifts they got, that the place kept them off the street, etc.[10]

This passage betrays an elitist, condescending tone toward "the Jewish butcher, baker, etc." Yet it reveals clearly the realities of Jewish cooperation with and resentment toward the missions. It explains why working-class Jews allowed their children to attend activities sponsored by missionaries and why children took advantage of such opportunities. The report suggests that their parents cared about the Jewish tradition but did not think that the missionary message could affect their children very much and felt that the services the missions offered their children outweighed the danger of their becoming Christian. Missions were aware of the Jewish apprehensions, and literature intended for Jews came to emphasize the friendly intentions of missions and calm Jewish suspicions.

Missionaries and evangelical Christians for their part cared little for liberal, secular, or Reform varieties of Judaism, which were often at the forefront of organized Jewish antimissionary activities. Missionaries and their sponsors often thought about Jews in well-defined, somewhat stereotypical categories. They were taken aback when confronted with well-acculturated Jews who had managed to reach high economic and cultural levels in the societies in which they lived. Dealing with modern culture successfully, such Jews found a comfortable alternative to the adoption of Christianity. Evangelicals could not accept that Jews could reshape their identities as they saw fit or become successful and accepted without accepting Christianity. They did not consider Judaism to be a community or tradition that could reform itself without the transforming power of the Gospel and felt that the Jews' role was not theirs to alter or choose but rather a God-given vocation. While evangelicals found the Jews to lack awareness of their role in history, they saw it as their mission to correct that.

Evangelicals, Liberals, and Missions

A case study that can illustrate many of the developments that have taken place in evangelical interactions with the Jews is that of the Department for Jewish Evangelization of the Presbyterian Church U.S.A. The history of the department provides an example of the triangular relationship that developed between conservative evangelical Christians, Jews, and liberal Protestants. In the first half of the twentieth century, the Presbyterian Church U.S.A. conducted the most extensive denominational efforts at evangelizing the Jews, and those attempts affected the emergence of Jewish Christian communities in America.

Influenced by the growing predominance of premillennialist messianic views on the Jews and their role in history, the General Assembly of the Presbyterian Church decided in 1908 to organize evangelization work among Jews on a national basis. The Presbyterian Church as a whole did not hold to a premillennialist messianic hope. In the first decades of the twentieth century, the Presbyterian Church, like American Protestantism in general, was torn between two conflicting camps and points of view that struggled for hegemony in the denomination and the power to shape its agenda and priorities. On one side stood the liberal modernists, who advocated a progressive postmillennial view of history, accepted the higher criticism of the Bible, and often favored social reform. On the other side stood the conservatives, who objected to the new academic theories of biblical exegesis, insisted on the need to be born again in order to be saved, and advocated a premillennialist understanding of the course of history.[11] Many Presbyterians were neither ardent modernists nor fundamentalists, yet the conservatives succeeded in influencing the denomination's agenda to include both pro-Zionist stands and mission- ary work aimed specifically at Jews.[12] While motivated by the biblical- eschatological faith of the conservatives, the missionary cause received support also among other elements within the denomination.

To make a case for the field of Jewish evangelism, the directors of the mission appealed to Protestant social and cultural sensitivities.[13] They claimed that Jews seeking to Americanize often abandoned their old ways and turned their back on the observance of the Jewish religion.[14] But if they did not accept Christianity in its stead, they could be lured by dangerous secular teachings, such as socialism. In articles and tracts, the mission appealed to the rank and file of the denomination to act as evangelists on a small scale and share their faith with Jewish acquain- tances. Such calls would continue to characterize evangelical missions. The mission's journal, *Our Neighbors,* saw as its aim to promote interest in Jews and Jewish evangelism among ordinary Presbyterians. The jour- nal was overtly premillennialist and was illustrated with Jewish symbols and scenes of the Holy Land. Its articles reflected the theological basis of Jewish missions, the messianic hope, and the dispensationalist under- standing of the role of Jews in history.

The Department of Jewish Evangelization set out to evangelize among the second generation of Jewish immigrants, who had been educated in the American school system and acculturated to the American scene. The mission established "community center" mission houses that often served as the beginning of Jewish Christian congregations. Jewish evangelization was a high priority for the Board of Home Missions and the second-larg- est item on its budget, the first being work among African Americans.[15]

The directors of the Department of Jewish Evangelization were non-Jews, while the field missionaries were Jews who had received training in theological seminaries or Bible institutes. Missionaries such as Aaron Kligerman in Baltimore and David Bronstein in Chicago came from the immigrant community and served as intermediaries between Presbyterian values and norms and the cultural background and expectations of the converts. This was also the case with wives of missionaries, who often worked as actual missionaries. Esther Bronstein, for example, officially was merely the spouse of the director of one of the mission's centers in Chicago, but in actuality she worked with her husband in operating Peniel, a missionary branch that the Bronsteins helped turn into a Jewish Presbyterian congregation.[16] She did not receive theological education, was not a minister, and did not conduct services or preach, but she worked with the women and youth, for whom she represented the mission and what it stood for. A firm and outgoing person, she also performed other tasks, including fund-raising.[17]

Evangelical missions, including the Presbyterian Department of Jewish Evangelization, showed concern, during the late 1930s, for the plight of Jews in Nazi Germany and its annexed territories. They were especially worried about the way "non-Aryan" Christians, Jews who had accepted the Christian faith and their children, were subject to a series of abuses. The missions tried to stir up Presbyterian public opinion in favor of those being persecuted.[18] Like a number of evangelical writers, they described the oppressive acts of the German government against Jews and the dire prospects of the Jewish population under German control. The department also made efforts to help in the immigration of a few "non-Aryan Christians" from Germany to the United States.[19] They were not alone. Other missionaries in Scandinavia, Britain, and America were engaged in similar efforts to rescue converted Jews.[20] Among other things, they could not remain indifferent to persecutions inflicted on newly converted Jews by representatives of Christian societies, since such situations undermined their missionary rhetoric about the nature of Christianity. The humanitarian efforts on behalf of converted Jews helped to strengthen the claim that the wrongs inflicted on

Jews were not done by true Christians. Evangelical missionaries were therefore among those most concerned with the fate of Jews in Nazi Germany and, later on, in Nazi-occupied Europe.[21]

Meanwhile, the department continued its program of turning missionary outposts into independent congregations.[22] Whereas the motivation was at least partially pragmatic, in actuality the Presbyterian Church sanctioned the creation of indigenous Jewish churches, among the first in the modern era. The establishment of Jewish Christian congregations was more daring than the creation of such communities by other ethnic groups. For many, such congregations seemed a bizarre hybrid of competing religious communities. Traditionally many Christians considered "Judaizing" as a dangerous deviation from Christian norms. The Presbyterians, in almost unwittingly creating such congregations, thus wrote a new chapter in the annals of Jewish-Christian relations. At that time most converted Jews joined regular churches.[23] Some converts, however, welcomed the opportunity to form communities of their own, as they felt uneasy in mainline Protestant churches, whose ways were very different from those of eastern European Jews.[24] Yet it is doubtful whether Jewish converts of that period would have found the courage to make a historically daring move and organize independent congregations without the encouragement and support of evangelical premillennialist leaders.[25]

Early congregations of evangelical Jews did not aspire to become amalgamations of synagogues and churches. They rather attempted to create a Jewish variant of evangelical communities and liturgical practices.[26] They sang Protestant hymns, but in line with evangelical premillennialist outlooks they emphasized the special mission of the nation of Israel. Congregations often avoided the use of Christian symbols, replacing them with Jewish symbols such as the Star of David. They celebrated Jewish holidays, such as Hanukkah and Passover, interpreting them in Christian terms.[27]

At the same time that conservative evangelical Presbyterians were encouraging the establishment of Jewish Christian congregations, the denomination became increasingly more liberal, and the number of conservative evangelical premillennialists within its leadership dwindled. Liberal Presbyterians stood at the forefront of dialogue with Jews.[28] Dialogue and mission did not go hand in hand. They conveyed two very different understandings of how Christians should relate to Jews.[29] Jewish participants in goodwill and dialogue groups that emerged in America, from the 1920s onward, expressed their resentment about the evangelizing of Jews and presented it as an obstacle to a respectful relationship between the two religious communities. In the aftermath of World War II, liberal theologians and activists militated against the continuation of the missionary enterprise among the Jews.[30] Protestant thinkers such as Reinhold Niebuhr, who, although not a Presbyterian himself, had much influence on theologians and intellectuals in that denomination, claimed that Jews did not need the Christian gospel, as they had a vital religious tradition of their own to sustain them.[31] The liberal demand for the abandonment of missionary work among Jews gained momentum. During the 1940s and 1950s, the budget and staff for Jewish missionary work declined steadily as the denomination as a whole became less committed to the cause.[32] The situation mirrored the atmosphere in mainline churches in general, which, during the postwar period, became marked by a division between "ecumenicals" and "evangelicals."[33] However, it went one step further: for many conservative evangelicals it was particularly important to evangelize Jews, and for many liberals it was particularly important not to evangelize them. By 1960, missions to the Jews as a denominational agenda had been phased out completely. In the 1960s and 1970s, the interfaith dialogue advanced even further, and in the 1980s the Presbyterian Church was among the more progressive churches in recognizing Judaism as a valid religion in its own right.[34]

The Department of Jewish Evangelization's policy of encouraging the independence of the missionary centers ensured the perpetuation of a number of Jewish Presbyterian communities—the oldest existing Jewish evangelical congregations. In the 2000s, conservative evangelical Presbyterians succeeded in adding a new Jewish congregation, in spite of liberal opposition. The Presbyterians, however, did not revive their missionary efforts among the Jews. While advocating appreciation of Judaism as a legitimate faith, the denomination developed a very different attitude toward Israel and its policies. Liberals did not share the evangelical commitment to biblical-messianic views of Israel, and many of them became critical of the Israeli government's dealings with the Palestinians. Following the 1967 War, and especially since the 1980s, Presbyterians have been on the forefront of liberal Christian criticism of Israel and its policies.[35] In this respect the conservatives have encountered a double defeat within liberal denominations: both in their position on missions and in their relation to Israel.

The rise and fall of Presbyterian missionary work among the Jews reflected larger developments in the mainline churches, which defined themselves more and more in liberal terms. Other American mainline churches, such as the Episcopal Church and the American Baptists, also shut down missions to the Jews in the 1950s and 1960s. Similar trends took place in other English-speaking countries as well as in Europe. Churches refrained from operating missions to the Jews, directing their energies instead, from the 1960s through the 1980s, toward reconciliation and dialogue. In Britain, which served as a leader of missionary activities during the nineteenth century and much of the twentieth, the zeal for evangelism declined sharply. The London Jews' Society, previously the largest mission to the Jews, became the project of a minority evangelical group within the Church of England. Evangelicals with a premillennialist conviction and a view of the Jews as a special people became rare in Britain. In a manner reminiscent of the Presbyterian Church U.S.A., the Church of England, as a whole, moved into the realm of dialogue and recognition, viewing Judaism as a legitimate religious community on equal footing with Christianity, and the archbishop of Canterbury removed his name from the list of sponsors of the Jews' Society. A somewhat different situation is that of the Lutheran Church of Norway, which, influenced by conservative pietist thinking, has pursued its leadership role in the realm of missions to the Jews. Norwegian Lutherans at large, influenced by liberal notions of political justice, have become, in the wake of the 1967 War, particularly critical toward

Israel and its policies. In sum, since the 1970s, evangelism of the Jews has become almost exclusively the realm of conservative evangelical Protestants. However, in the history of evangelical-Jewish relations, missions accomplished much more than the evangelization of Jews. They ultimately created cultural and literary projects and institutions that connected the Jewish community and evangelical Christianity. One of the more amazing projects was the prolific publication of vital missionary works in Yiddish.

7

Evangelical Yiddish

Christian Literature in a Jewish Language

Residents of Jewish neighborhoods in the nineteenth century and the first half of the twentieth century noticed a phenomenon that at first glance seemed like an oxymoron—Christian missionaries distributing literature in Yiddish. To many, Yiddish symbolized a unique culture that Jews had developed apart from the Christian society when they lived in Europe and in their first decades in the New World. That missionaries would use Yiddish to promote Christian beliefs and agendas seemed almost unthinkable. However, evangelical missionaries and Jewish converts to Christianity created in America and elsewhere a lively Yiddish literary subculture.

Like the evangelical missionary movement at large, the Yiddish missionary literature aimed at more than evangelizing individual Jews. Within the confines of Protestant evangelical doctrines, missionaries also expressed their literary gifts as writers and translators. Missionary writers also wished to connect with Jewish life and culture. Though missionaries produced an extensive literature over many decades, students of Jewish culture and scholars of Christian-Jewish relations have paid little attention to the missionary literature in that language.[1] This chapter fills a gap and points to the existence of a rich and varied evangelical Yiddish literature, produced by hundreds of writers over the span of a few generations.[2] Evangelical literary projects included a large number of tracts and pamphlets on Christian themes, such as the Messiah or the Trinity, a series of periodicals, the translation of the Scriptures into Yiddish, and biblical commentaries. They also included poetry, short stories, memoirs, and historical studies. In fact, evangelical Christian Yiddish literature was as rich and creative as Jewish forms of Yiddish literature.

The Rise of Evangelical Yiddish

Protestant pietist interest in Yiddish began in central Europe a few decades before evangelical Christianity began crystallizing as a movement in the English-speaking world. Pietist missions in the eighteenth century produced extensive and diverse publications in Yiddish, while in the nineteenth century such interest and creativity in the Yiddish language would become the domain of evangelicals. The nineteenth century saw the emergence of a large and vigorous movement among English-speaking evangelicals to evangelize the Jews—a movement that by the twentieth century would be centered in America. The nineteenth century also witnessed Jewish immigration from central and eastern Europe to English-speaking nations. Hundreds of thousands of Jews from German-speaking areas of Europe arrived in Britain, the United States, and other countries in the New World from the 1810s to the 1860s, to be followed by millions of mostly Yiddish-speaking immigrants from eastern Europe. Many of the newly arrived immigrants settled in poor neighborhoods in the major cities, working in the garment industry or as pushcart peddlers. Messianically oriented evangelical Protestants saw the immigrants as susceptible to their messages and disseminated their literature on street corners, in homes, and at missionary centers. Much of that literature was, particularly until World War I, in Yiddish. It was the native language of most immigrants from eastern Europe, and much of the interaction between missionaries and Jews took place in the immigrants' *mame loshn* ("mother tongue").

While many Jews made an effort to learn English, even long after settling in America (or Britain, Canada, or South Africa) a good number of them still spoke and read Yiddish. Missions recruited Yiddish-speaking missionaries and at times even taught non-Jewish missionaries to speak Yiddish. Remarkably, the first non-Jews in English-speaking countries to make a conscious effort to learn Yiddish were Christian missionaries. Speaking in Yiddish, missionaries believed, added to their credibility and thus made them more effective. It also helped them become more familiar with the Jews and their culture. A non-Jewish missionary, the

German-born Arno Gaebelein, gave advice, tongue-in-cheek, on how to speak Yiddish. Knowing German was enough, he claimed; one should "just make as many grammatical mistakes as one could."[3] In his mind, and that of many others, including Jews, Yiddish was an inferior form of proper German.

Evangelical institutions of higher learning, such as the Moody Bible Institute, established programs to train professional evangelists to the Jews, and such programs included the study of Yiddish in their curriculum. The directors of such schools thought that missionaries should be acquainted with the languages of the people they evangelized. A good knowledge of Yiddish and the ability to teach it were among the requirements of such institutions when hiring professors who would teach in their programs in Jewish evangelism. Students went with their professors on evangelizing tours into Jewish neighborhoods and were expected to gain practical training in the language. Ironically, conservative Christian schools of higher learning offered courses in Yiddish decades before secular, liberal Christian, or Jewish institutions of higher learning did so.[4] The teaching of Yiddish at the Bible colleges reflected the attitude of premillennialist evangelicals toward the Jews and their culture, which was more appreciative than that of many other Christian groups during the period.

Evangelical Journals and Tracts in Yiddish

Much of the evangelical Yiddish effort was in the literary realm. Missionaries published a large and varied selection of written material for distribution among prospective converts. Central to the missionary literature in Yiddish were periodicals, which gave expression to the missions' theological views as well as to their outlook on cultural and social issues. Missionaries also used journals as pamphlets, distributing them on street corners or handing them out in their centers. Missions often published two journals: one in English, meant to promote the mission's cause in the Protestant community, and one in Yiddish, intended for Jews. The Hope of Israel mission's English journal, *Our Hope*, for example, became one of the leading conservative journals of Protestant America and was circulated on a national basis. The Yiddish journal the mission published in the 1890s and 1900s, *Tiqwas Yisrael (Hope of Israel),* on the other hand, was distributed mainly among Jews in New York. Its name hinted at the mission's views, which stated that the Jews' ultimate hope was with Jesus.

Another noted Yiddish missionary journal during the period was *Roe Yisroel (Shepherd of Israel),* which the Williamsburg Mission to the Jews (later the American Board of Missions to the Jews) published from the 1890s to the 1960s. Like titles of other Yiddish missionary journals, *Roe Yisroel* referred to Jesus. The mission also published an English journal, *The Chosen People,* which was in circulation all through the twentieth century. Whereas *The Chosen People* was sent to subscribers and was intended to muster support for the mission among middle-class Protestants, the Yiddish journal was much shorter and was intended for distribution among prospective converts.[5] The Yiddish journal, like its English counterpart, reflected the aims and priorities of the mission. It included theological essays on topics such as Jesus, the Trinity, and the Virgin Mary, as well as articles covering more current issues such as the rise of the Zionist movement, which the mission endorsed with some reservations. The mission's leaders wished not only to propagate Christianity among the Jews but to convert them to the values of middle-class evangelical America as well.[6] Its leaders noted with pain that some Jews were attracted to, or at least tolerated, socialist and communist ideas. They sought to reeducate the Jews and make them reconsider these views. In describing an event at which Jews had sung both "HaTikva," the Zionist anthem, and the "Internationale," the communist anthem, the editor of *Roe Yisroel* remarked, "What a mishmash [hodgepodge]."

Der Vekhter (the *Watchman),* published as a supplement to the *Hebrew Christian Alliance Quarterly,* was a different kind of Yiddish missionary journal. Organized in 1915 as an association of Jewish converts to Protestant Christianity in America, the Hebrew Christian Alliance was strongly associated with premillennialist evangelical thought. Many of its members were pastors of Protestant congregations or missionaries, and the organization included on its agenda the propagation of Christianity among the Jews.[7] The Alliance people distributed their journal among members of the organization. All members read English well, and the Yiddish supplement to the quarterly was not intended for those among the Alliance members who could not read English (there were hardly any such members). The supplement was rather intended as a missionary tract to be distributed among prospective converts in the Yiddish-speaking community. It was smaller (4" x 3") and could be printed in large batches as pamphlets for missionary purposes.

Der Vekhter served another purpose as well. Unlike *Roe Yisroel* and *Tiqvas Yisroel,* where most of the articles were translations from the English versions of the journals, *Der Vekhter* presented original works in Yiddish. While the authors could read English and perhaps also write occasional articles in English, they felt more at ease writing in Yiddish. The Yiddish supplement contained some clear attempts at original literary expressions, including short stories and poetry. One might conclude that while the official purpose of the Yiddish journal was evangelism, its real aim was giving expression to missionaries with literary inclinations whose language and culture were Yiddish. The journal was published by the Hebrew Christian Alliance's "Literary Fund," and the authors writing for it had noms de plume such as Ya'ar ("Forest").[8] The Yiddish journal provides an example of the cultural world of Jewish evangelicals writing in Yiddish. They had acquired the theological beliefs of evangelical Protestantism and were living in a Protestant social milieu. But they were still connected culturally to their Jewish roots, felt more comfortable writing in Yiddish, and wrote on Jewish eastern European or Jewish American immigrant themes. Their stories or poems combined Christian evangelical theology with Jewish scenes and characters.

In addition to journals, missions produced short booklets and pamphlets in Yiddish to promote the Christian faith among Jews. These included the fifteen-page *Der Tolui* by Ya'el (also a nom de plume), which explored and promoted the Christian evangelical claim that the death of Jesus on the cross served as an atonement for the sins of humanity.[9] Another pamphlet was Aaron Kligerman's *Der Got-Mentsh—Ver iz Er?*

(The God-Man, Who Is He?).[10] As a Presbyterian missionary, Kligerman wrote mostly in English, but his Yiddish was equally good, and he wrote in that language as well. In a manner typical of missionary publications, his English tracts were intended for Christian Presbyterians whom he wished to persuade about the importance of evangelizing the Jews. His Yiddish tracts, on the other hand, were written with potential converts in mind.

Another pamphlet that deserves notice is the sixteen-page *Rosheshone (New Year's Eve).*[11] The pamphlet concentrated on a calendrical mystery: Why has the Jewish New Year been celebrated on the first day of Tishre, the seventh month, whereas the "true date," as has been shown in the Bible, is the first of Nissan, the first month? If the Jewish interpreters of the Torah—Tannaim, Amoraim, Geonim, and following generations of rabbis—erred on this crucial matter (whether intentionally or innocently), could they not have erred equally on refusing to recognize Jesus as the Messiah? The readers were encouraged to reread the Hebrew Bible in the light of Christian interpretations and see for themselves that Jesus was indeed the Messiah about whom the Hebrew Bible (or "Old Testament") spoke.

Rosheshone is a good illustration of Yiddish evangelical pamphlets intended for Jews. The author refers to the celebration of a Jewish holiday and to the Jewish sacred texts in order to make a case for Christianity. Evangelicals assumed that only those Jews who had accepted Christianity would view Christian texts as authoritative. Until then, one had to use Jewish sources to persuade the Jews to consider the Gospel. Accordingly, in Yiddish the author presents himself as a rabbi, whereas in the English translation of the pamphlet's title page he presents himself as an ex-rabbi.

American missions labored overseas and distributed tracts in Yiddish in Europe, Latin America, and Palestine.[12] The Yiddish book most widely distributed was *Dos tsveyte Kumen fun dem Meshiekh (The Second Coming of the Messiah).*[13] Like many Yiddish evangelical tracts, it was a translation from the English, in this case Blackstone's influential *Jesus Is Coming*. Blackstone's evangelical best seller was distributed by the mission he founded and led, the Chicago Hebrew Mission. Like other evangelicals, Blackstone wished that Jews, in addition to becoming believers in the messiahship of Jesus, would accept the belief in Jesus's second coming and in their special role in the imminent arrival of Jesus. In 1906, he received a large amount of money from the Milton Stewart Fund to finance missionary work and used part of the funds to finance work among the Jews. This included the translation of *Jesus Is Coming* into Yiddish and its circulation in hundreds of thousands of copies in America and Europe. The Yiddish title of the book is suggestive. The English title *Jesus Is Coming* expresses the eschatological premillennialist faith in the imminent return of Jesus to earth. The Yiddish title, *Dos tsveyte Kumen fun dem Meshiekh,* instead emphasizes that Jesus is indeed the Messiah, that the Messiah has already came to earth once before, and that soon he will come for the second time, bringing redemption to those who put their trust in him.

The translator of the book into Yiddish, Peter Gorodishz, was a missionary who worked in Russia and Poland. In his preface, he described Blackstone as "eyner fun yisroels greste fraynd" (one of the greatest friends of the Jews), who had advocated for their return to their ancient homeland. Accepting a copy of the book and reading it was thus "kosher," as it was written by a person who had expressed pro-Jewish sentiments, helped the Jewish cause, and worked against discrimination toward Jews.[14] Describing Blackstone as an advocate of Jewish causes was helpful in making his book less objectionable to Jews. Evangelical missionaries, such as Blackstone, saw themselves as friends of the Jews who evangelized them out of goodwill; they distanced themselves from the bitterness that at times had characterized Christian attitudes toward the Jews. Such a mind-set was essential for the propagation of the Gospel among the Jews, since Jews were used to seeing Christianity as an alien, hostile religion. While missionaries sometimes encountered resentment among Jews, they had no difficulty distributing their leaflets and tracts and making their voices heard in the Jewish community. Immigrant Jews encountered the missionaries and their Yiddish publications on an almost daily basis.

The Yiddish New Testament

One of the more ambitious Yiddish ventures was the translation of the New Testament into Yiddish. German Protestants had already produced Yiddish translations of the New Testament for missionary purposes. American and British evangelical missionaries, however, found such translations inadequate. In fact, evangelicals who were committed to high-quality literary productions in Yiddish considered them to be an embarrassment. Educated Jews rejected such New Testaments on literary grounds, while Jewish antagonists to missionary activity cited inaccuracies or clumsiness in the Yiddish texts as part of their efforts to delegitimize the Gospel message.[15] In actuality, such "antiquated" translations of the New Testament into Yiddish were solid literary productions, at least in the sense that their translators had worked in earnest to provide Yiddish versions of the Christian sacred text. However, for Yiddish readers of the twentieth century, eastern European Jews who grew up speaking and reading Yiddish, such manuscripts seemed alien and morbid. They were certain that such texts were actually German versions of the New Testament with minor editorial overtures for the benefit of the Yiddish readership. By the time evangelicals were preparing tracts and copies of the sacred scriptures for the Yiddish reading audience, Western Yiddish, the Jewish vernacular of the German, was in rapid decline, if not completely gone. While German Jews abandoned their Yiddish, the language thrived among eastern European Jews, who, during the period, established new, largely secular literary channels of creativity in Yiddish. These included the rise of Yiddish journals and belles lettres, political and ideological tracts, and a lively theatrical scene. Religious literature in Yiddish also thrived. With eastern European Yiddish alive and developing, the gap between it and the by now defunct Western Yiddish grew even more.

Two Jewish evangelical missionaries, Henry Einspruch and Aaron Krelenbaum, decided, each on his own, to translate the New Testament into modern literary Yiddish. Einspruch was born in 1892 in Tarnow, Galicia, a section of Poland that was then under Austro-Hungarian rule.

He was raised in a Yiddish-speaking home and studied Yiddish in the Jewish school in his hometown. In 1911 he went to Palestine as a *halutz,* a Zionist pioneer, and worked for a few weeks on a newly founded Zionist agricultural farm, where he contracted malaria and decided to leave. On his return to Poland he met a missionary, Khayem Lucky, under whose guidance he accepted the Christian faith.[16] He left Poland for America, where he could practice his new faith more openly, far from the intimidating presence of family and friends. He decided to become a missionary and took a position with the Cleveland Hebrew Mission. In 1917 he enrolled at McCormick Theological Seminary in Chicago. There Einspruch began translating the New Testament into Yiddish. His translation of the Book of Matthew was published by the American Bible Society, which sponsored the publications of many Bible translations. Upon his graduation from the seminary in 1920, Einspruch began working with the Lutheran Church, which sponsored his Salem Hebrew Mission in Baltimore, Maryland, giving him a great amount of autonomy to operate the mission as he saw fit.

Einspruch devoted much time to writing, establishing in 1928 his own missionary journal, the *Mediator.* The name was symbolic. It indicated Jesus's role as mediator between the Jews (and humanity at large) and their salvation. It might have also demonstrated the mission's purpose as a mediator between the beliefs and values of Protestant Christian America and the Jewish community. This Yiddish and English quarterly enjoyed, at its peak, a circulation of more than fifty thousand copies. While taking pride in the good Yiddish of his own journal, Einspruch was dissatisfied with the Yiddish texts the missionary movement in general provided: "Most Jewish missionaries are familiar with the derisive appellation 'missionary Yiddish.' To say that the greater part of our Yiddish tracts are a horrible mutilation of a people's language (and in this I include the Yiddish Old and New Testaments) is to put it very mildly."[17]

Einspruch's magnum opus, a Yiddish translation of the complete New Testament, was motivated by his desire to provide prospective Jewish converts with an accurate, modern edition of the Christian gospel. It also reflected Einspruch's literary aspirations as a Yiddish writer and gave him an opportunity to express his gifts. In this respect, Einspruch was not unique. The task of translating the Bible often gave missionaries with scholarly and literary inclinations an opportunity to be creative while serving missionary needs and without stepping out of line doctrinally.[18] Einspruch's desire to translate the New Testament into Yiddish might have also been inspired by a wave of translations of the Hebrew Bible into Yiddish that took place at the turn of the twentieth century.

Yiddish glosses of the Tanakh (Hebrew Bible) constitute the very beginnings of Yiddish literature, and the numerous editions of the so-called "Women's Bible," the Tsenerene, were actually also read by men who were not scholars.[19] With the rise of a more secular Yiddish-speaking culture, mostly among eastern European Jews, and the realization that many Yiddish-speaking Jews would prefer to read the Bible in Yiddish, Jewish writers had an initiative to translate the sacred text into the Jewish vernacular. A number of ambitious literary enterprises arose to translate the Jewish Bible into Yiddish. Literary luminaries such as Mendele Moykher-Sforim, Sholem Aleichem, and Y. L. Peretz translated portions of the Jewish scriptural canon. The most ambitious and complete translation into Yiddish of the Hebrew Bible was that of Solomon Bloomgarden, who chose the nom de plume Yehoyesh, and whose work came out during Einspruch's early years as a missionary.[20] Though there had been many Yiddish Bible translations, and poems based on biblical books, it was not until the poet Yehoyesh undertook his monumental rendition, which was both literary and scholarly, that a full and adequate translation of the Hebrew Bible into modern Yiddish was created. Einspruch must have been aware of the new wave of translations, and he had probably read some or all of them. Likewise, he must have been aware of and influenced by the new missionary translations of the New Testament into Hebrew. For example, Franz Delitzch's late nineteenth-century translation of the New Testament into biblical-like Hebrew, which became the most accepted one among evangelical missions and was in use throughout the twentieth century, might have served as a model for Einspruch.

Unlike Einspruch's earlier translations, this enterprise was not carried out through the American Bible Society; rather, it was his mission's independent enterprise. This demanded attending to all stages of production. Einspruch decided that to produce the book he had to acquire his own printing equipment. Some Christian presses, such as Fleming H. Revell or the American Bible Society, published books in Yiddish, as did a number of missions. But Einspruch wished the printing of his translation to be of the highest possible quality and wanted to choose the font. The cost of this project, as well as Einspruch's other literary ventures, was considerable, much more than the local Lutheran church in Baltimore was willing to spend on Yiddish literary enterprises. Einspruch approached private donors and was successful in gaining the support of a philanthropist, Harriett Lederer, for the mission and its publications. Lederer's assistance gave Einspruch's mission financial security and greater independence. When the United Lutheran Church later on lost interest in Jewish evangelism, the mission became an independent organization and assumed the name the Lederer Foundation.

The first edition of Einspruch's New Testament in Yiddish came out in 1941 as a 590-page volume. Translations involve theological and cultural choices, and in the course of his work Einspruch made some major ones.[21] It was important for him to write in good Yiddish prose, yet he tried to choose words and expressions that would promote the Christian evangelical message and would make the text more inviting to Jews. For example, he chose for his translated New Testament the title *Der Bris Khodoshe* instead of *Dos Naye Testament,* which had served as the title of the New Testament in Yiddish until the late nineteenth century. Literally, *Bris Khodoshe* does not mean "New Testament" but rather "New Covenant." The new title was probably borrowed from Franz Delitzsch's late nineteenth-century translation of the New Testament into Hebrew. Einspruch thus conveyed through the title of his translation a message that emphasized the Christian messianic interpretation of history that evangelicals promoted, namely that there would be a new covenant between God and his people.

The translation was accompanied by a number of illustrations reminiscent of those of Ephraim Moshe Lilien (1874-1925), a popular Bible illustrator. The illustrations created a familiar atmosphere meant to make the New Testament more acceptable and legitimate for Jews. The first page of the text shows an old Jewish man with a long white beard, dressed in a *yarmulke* (skullcap), and *talit* (prayer shawl), surrounded by burning candles, and reading a book. The scene suggests that the New Testament is an old Jewish book that should be read and studied like a sacred Jewish text, just as dedicated rabbinical scholars study Jewish texts deep into the night. The illustration correlates with Einspruch's translation, which begins: "Dos iz dos seyfer fun dem yikhes fun Yeyshue hameshiekh, dem zun fun Dovidn, dem zun fun Avromen," familiarizing Jesus as a descendent of David and Abraham. In his use of the crucial word *yikhes* (Hebrew *yichus*), which in Jewish culture means much more than "lineage" or "genealogy," Einspruch wisely follows earlier translators. Often used in matchmaking to point to the high value of potential brides and grooms, *yikhes* means "pedigree." It relates to honored ancestors and boosts the credentials of the *yakhsan* — the individual claiming the pedigree. Jesus, it is implied, has excellent credentials by virtue of his *yikhes.*

His missionary intentions notwithstanding, Einspruch's translation aroused the interest and appreciation of the Yiddish literary community. Meylekh Ravitsh (1893-1976), a noted Yiddish writer of the day, published a review of the work in Yiddish. At that time Ravitsh lived in Mexico City and wrote for the Yiddish daily *Der Veg.* He was not a Christian but rather a non-Zionist Jewish nationalist. He did not care for Einspruch's Christian messianic understanding of history and missionary aims, but he appreciated the translation. In his review article, Ravitsh explained to his readers why he thought it necessary for Jews to read the New Testament: "For well known reasons, the New Testament has remained for many Jews a book sealed with seven seals. And that is truly a pity, for to some seven hundred million people it is a sacred book. A cultured person should know such a work; I myself have read it and recommend it to every intelligent Jew. . . . The New Testament [is] one of the most important books in the world. How then can we Jews afford to ignore it?"

Ravitsh welcomed the new translation, which he felt was the first to do justice to the Yiddish language of that time, and remarked, "The Einspruch translation of the New Testament is unquestionably beautiful. One feels that the translator is familiar with modern Yiddish literature and that he is a master of the finest nuances of the language. In comparison with previous translations, this is truly an outstanding work."[22] Ravitsh's appreciative outlook reflected a common trend among Yiddish writers. Although they were hardly enthusiastic about missionary work among their brethren, they did not ostracize Jewish evangelical Yiddish writers, not even those who made their livelihood by missionizing fellow Jews. Contrary to a prevailing Jewish myth, the dislike of *shmad,* or Jewish conversion to Christianity, did not necessarily break converts' connections with Jews and Jewish life. It only made these connections more complicated. Einspruch's literary achievements gave him an entry into Yiddish literary circles, which had opened its doors to other converted Jewish writers as well.

Einspruch took great pride in his literary achievement, but his hope that his book would become the standard Yiddish New Testament did not materialize. A mixture of missionary and literary rivalries stood in his way. At the same time that Einspruch was working on his translation, a few thousand miles away another missionary was preparing a translation of the New Testament into Yiddish. Aaron Krelenbaum had also been born in Poland, had converted to Christianity in the early 1920s, and had moved to England, where he studied for the ministry. Like Einspruch, Krelenbaum was a premillennialist who took a messianic dispensationalist view of the course of human history and the future of Israel. He worked as a missionary with the Mildmay Mission to the Jews among the Jews in the East End of London.[23] A scholar by inclination, he learned Greek and took upon himself the task of translating the New Testament into Yiddish. Like his American fellow missionary, Krelenbaum wanted to present his readers with an accurate, respectable version of the New Testament. He, too, saw it as a personal challenge and an expression of his scholarly and literary abilities. When the two missionaries began pursuing their great literary tasks they probably did not realize that they were competing with each other. But they both possessed an almost passionate determination to translate the New Testament into Yiddish. In 1949, just a few years after the triumphant appearance of Einspruch's translation, Krelenbaum's translation appeared in England to great acclaim. Paul Levertoff, the patriarch of Jewish Christian writers, wrote on the Acknowledgments page: "I think this Yiddish translation can compare favorably with any standard translation of the New Testament, whether Hebrew, German, Russian, or any other language with which I am familiar."

In Britain, Krelenbaum's translation prevailed. However, in America too a number of missions, such as the Million Testaments Campaign, headquartered in Philadelphia, and the American Board of Missions to the Jews, decided to publish and distribute Krelenbaum's translation when it appeared in 1949 instead of Einspruch's translation.[24] The decision was not based on literary considerations. The leaders of the American Board of Missions to the Jews viewed Einspruch's missionary endeavor as competition. In their vision, their organization was to be the only mission to the Jews, and they did not wish to boost Einspruch's morale and promote his mission. Consequently, they printed Krelenbaum's translation instead.

There was an irony in the Yiddish writers' competing ambitions, as well as a tragic touch. Accurate and respectable translations of the New Testament into Yiddish came out just as Yiddish was ceasing to be the major language of the Jewish masses. Einspruch's and Krelenbaum's was the last generation that could make widespread use of their translations. Even when the two translations were published, most British and American Jews were reading English. Many historical developments worked to remove Yiddish from its common usage in Jewish life. These included the emancipation of the Jews and their integration into the societies in which they lived. The murderous Nazi policies during World War II wiped out many, if not most, of the Yiddish-speaking Jews of the time. Following the war, whether in Europe, America, or Israel, the children of

Yiddish speakers increasingly used the languages of the lands in which they were living, although many among the older generation continued to read and speak Yiddish, at least in their homes.

The End of Evangelical Yiddish

In the early 1960s, Yiddish journals, including Einspruch's *Mediator* and the American Board of Missions to the Jews' *Shepherd of Israel,* closed down, one after the other. The segment of Jews that preferred Yiddish to English had dwindled considerably and was about to disappear almost entirely. The Moody Bible Institute removed the teaching of Yiddish from its curriculum in 1965, thus bringing an era to an end. Producing literature in Yiddish or teaching Yiddish to prospective missionaries was, from the point of view of the missions, a nonproductive move.

The rise and fall of evangelical Yiddish correlated with developments in the larger Jewish culture. It had come into being at the same time that missions were trying to reach a large Yiddish-speaking Jewish population, especially in new immigrant areas, and it ended when that population dwindled and almost disappeared. Some of the dilemmas that faced Yiddish writers in America and elsewhere were shared by evangelical Yiddish writers. The culture of many of the writers was Yiddish, and writing in Yiddish allowed them to express their gifts in a language that was their own. Yet they were writing for an aging and dwindling audience. They wrote for themselves perhaps more than for others. In the 1970s, missions and the growing movement of Jewish converts to Christianity became more Jewishly assertive, emphasizing the loyalty of converts to their Jewish heritage and culture. While almost no one among the new generation of converts knew Yiddish, and many studied Hebrew, messianic Jews and missionary groups, such as Jews for Jesus, began incorporating Yiddish words and expressions into their vocabulary, thus emphasizing their attachment to their Jewish heritage.[25]

Evangelical, mostly missionary, Yiddish was never as free and creative as secular Yiddish. Operating under the auspices of evangelical organizations, and committed to a Christian premillennialist philosophy of history and a conservative view of culture, missionaries writing in Yiddish had to confine themselves to the doctrines and the worldviews of conservative Protestants. They were not allowed to discuss sexual or erotic themes and could not produce the kind of literature that many secular Yiddish writers did. They did not take part in the popular Yiddish theater that came about at the turn of the twentieth century, and they could not write plays such as those that Abraham Goldfaden and others had produced. Their theological and cultural standing drastically limited their literary scope. In this respect, they could be compared to Orthodox Jewish writers in Yiddish, who could write only on religious, social, or political themes. It was no wonder that many missionary Yiddish literary accomplishments were in the realm of translations.

Producing literature in Yiddish nonetheless meant a great deal to evangelical missionaries and Jewish converts. It was much more than a vehicle to reach Jews. Speaking and writing in Yiddish served to signify that evangelical Christians were supporters of the Jewish people and showed respect for their culture. Enemies of Jews would not speak or write in Yiddish. Since the 1960s, evangelicals have found other means to convey such a message. They have used Hebrew names, played Israeli music, expressed support for Israel, and organized tours to that country. In this realm, too, the trend among the missions has correlated with that among the general Jewish public, where the use of Hebrew and an attachment to Israel have replaced Yiddish culture.

8

Evangelical Christians and Anti-Jewish Conspiracy Theories

Not all evangelical views on Jews' culture and literary heritage were affirming; at times, they had a darker side. In 1933, for example, Arno Gaebelein, a renowned conservative evangelical theologian, published a best-selling book, *The Conflict of the Ages,* that accused the Jews of conspiring to take over the world.[1] The 1920s and 1930s witnessed a resurgence of anti-Jewish accusations and incitements, especially in European nations, such as Germany, Hungary, Romania, and France. However, the United States was also affected by the trend. Amazingly, in this case, the author considered himself to be a friend of the Jews and could point to a long record of what he considered to be demonstrations of goodwill toward the Jews and public repudiation of accusations against them.[2] Viewing the Jews as God's first nation, destined for a glorious future in the messianic kingdom, Gaebelein, a veteran missionary to the Jews, prophesied doom for the rising Nazis because of their hostility to the Jews. This, however, did not deter him from concluding, at about the same time, that *Protocols of the Elders of Zion* was an authentic document and that the global conspiracy recorded in it was unfolding in front of his eyes.[3]

Gaebelein was not the only conservative evangelical leader who accepted the authenticity of the *Protocols*. Other noted spokesmen of the movement at that time, such as William Riley, head of the World Christian Fundamentals Association, and James Gray, president of the Moody Bible Institute in Chicago, also accepted many of the accusations laid out in the *Protocols* and expressed their opinion in journals, books, sermons, and radio broadcasts.[4] Demonstrating a mixed evangelical opinion, Gray was worried that the *Protocols* would inspire anti-Jewish outbursts but nevertheless thought it likely that the document was authentic. Gray's more literal reading of the Christian Old Testament and his messianic hope ensured a great amount of goodwill on his part toward Jews and opposition to their victimization. But he believed that because the Jews did not yet accept Jesus as their savior they were capable of committing vicious acts, including the global conspiracy that the forgers of the *Protocols* accused them of conducting.[5]

The years between the two world wars saw a rise in overt anti-Jewish activity and incitement in America, with a number of popular preachers blaming the Jews for the ills of the times, including the depression of the 1930s. This atmosphere influenced, at least partially, evangelical attitudes toward the Jews. Some evangelical writers denounced overt and brutal forms of anti-Semitism and asserted that the traditional libels against Jews were false. However, a few activists adopted socially and politically exclusivist white Protestant "nativist" stands. Some, such as Gerald L. K. Smith, labored during the 1920s and 1930s on the borders of mainstream evangelicalism.[6] Others, such as Gerald Winrod, founder and head of the Defenders of the Christian Faith, received more widespread recognition in conservative evangelical circles.[7] Charles Fuller, one of the leading evangelists in America and founder of Fuller Theological Seminary, participated in the activities of Winrod's organization.[8]

The *Protocols* and the Evangelical Mind

The credit that evangelical leaders in the 1920s and 1930s gave the idea of a global Jewish conspiracy pointed to a willingness to adopt theories of global conspiracies as valid analyses of the political, economic, and cultural realities of the era. Likewise, the endorsement of such theories reflected a mood of pessimism regarding human nature and suspicion of cultural environments and political initiatives that were alien to conservative Protestantism. It further testified to long-held cultural stereotypes of Jews and their character and especially to opinions on secular, liberal, or socialist Jews, who, from the conservative evangelical perspective, had gone astray and were using their talents to cause society harm instead of good. Giving credence to the *Protocols* was also a reflection of conservative evangelical feelings of isolation and frustration.[9]

The conservatives resented the growth of a more open and pluralistic urban culture, which they associated with the Jews and which, they believed, was not grounded in Protestant Christian values and codes of behavior.[10] Among other things, they became apprehensive about the rise of the movie industry, which again many associated with the Jews and which symbolized the new non-Christian attitudes.[11] Conservative evangelicals did not share the optimism of the modernists, who held to a progressive view of the development of history. In contrast, conservative Protestants believed that humanity was going from bad to worse and that Christian civilization was crumbling under the attacks of the forces of evil, embodied in the new urban, non-Christian scene as well as the liberal modernist forces within Protestant Christianity. Unlike the liberals, who believed that humanity could overcome its limitations and backwardness on its own, the conservatives hoped for divine intervention.[12] According to this worldview, there was a constant battle between the Prince of Peace and the forces of darkness, with a growing number of people, whether from ignorance or malice, joining the forces of evil.

The messianic faith created a renewed interest in the Jews as well as some goodwill toward a people that many evangelicals came to look upon as God's chosen. In his autobiography, penned at the same time that he wrote about alleged Jewish international conspiracies, Arno Gaebelein described the relief work he had carried out among immigrant Jews of the Lower East Side of New York, explaining: "I could do just a little in paying back the debt we owe to the Jews." "How could true Christians be heartless toward Jews?" he asked.[13] Elsewhere he noted: "We should not forget that to this race—the race of Jesus—we owe our spiritual privileges."[14] However, their belief in the special role of the Jews in God's plans for humanity was not the only concept premillennialist evangelicals held regarding the Jews. "Their fraternal feelings for Jews as coheirs of the promises of God could not alter the Jews' present position as rejectors of Christ,"[15] and they were still strongly influenced by age-old views within Western Christian society on the Jews as carrying morally evil traits. The Jews, in the evangelical mind, were definitely in need of moral guidance and especially during the 1920s and 1930s were seen as major perpetrators of non-Christian ideas and movements.

Evangelical authors such as William Blackstone, Arno Gaebelein, and Alfred Thompson had developed a grudging respect for observant Jews. They claimed that traditional Jews, while they had failed to recognize the Messiah, regarded the Bible as divinely inscribed, continued to anticipate the arrival of the Messiah, and prayed for the national restoration of Israel.[16] Paradoxically, traditional and Orthodox Judaism were the only religious expressions, aside from evangelical Protestantism, for which premillennialist evangelicals found a purpose. Although they saw observant forms of Judaism as erroneous, they believed that this system of faith had a role in God's plans for humanity. Likewise, evangelicals holding to a premillennialist faith appreciated Zionists, who wished to settle Palestine and build a Jewish infrastructure in that land, as they considered these developments to be preparations for the arrival of the Messiah. This appreciation did not extend to secular, non-Zionist groups of Jews.

Indeed, the Jews whom conservative evangelical writers, such as Arno Gaebelein, William Riley, James Gray, Charles Fuller, and Charles Cook, accused of leading the world into chaos and lawlessness were those who had abandoned traditional Judaism but had chosen neither to convert to Christianity nor to become Zionists. That many Jews had left the faith of their fathers but had not accepted Christianity or become Zionists annoyed conservative Christians enormously. Instead of embracing the one true faith and finding a home for their souls as well as eternal life in becoming Christians, they chose a path that did them and others no good. Evangelicals often referred to them as "apostate" or "infidel," by which they meant nonobservant liberal or socialist Jews. Such Jews, evangelicals contended, led movements of social and political reform that undermined Christian values. "There is nothing so vile on earth as an apostate Jew," Gaebelein declared.[17]

That the Jews were God's first people also meant that they had a particular gift for destructiveness. Especially when they departed from the guidelines Judaism offered them, as inadequate as such a moral compass might be, Jews were capable of unsound personal and collective decisions. Conservative evangelicals were therefore convinced that it was within the Jews' capacity to play a major role in movements that could bring ruin down on Christian civilization, such as communism. Along these lines, Charles Cook asserted, in an article entitled "The International Jew," that "the Jewish race is morally fully capable of doing all that is charged against it. It is at present rejected of God, and in a state of disobedience and rebellion. . . . As a race Jews are gifted far beyond other peoples, and even in their ruin, with the curse of God on them, are in the front rank of achievement; but accompanying traits are pride, overbearing arrogance . . . love for material things, trickery, rudeness. . . . The unregenerated Jew usually has a very unattractive personality."[18] On Jewish involvement in revolutions, Arno Gaebelein stated more concretely: "That the Jew has been a prominent factor in the revolutionary movements of the day, wherever they may have occurred, cannot truthfully be denied . . . or that a very large majority (said to be over 80 percent) of the present Bolshevist government in Moscow are Jews."[19]

Evangelicals and the *Protocols*

Conservative evangelical Christians were not the first to embrace *Protocols of the Elders of Zion* and promote it as an authentic document. The tract had a willing audience in Europe and America before conservative evangelicals embraced it in the 1920s and especially in the 1930s, and they were by no means the only ones. Henry Ford Sr., the leading manufacturer of automobiles at the time, did more than anyone else to publicize the *Protocols* and promote the idea of a Jewish conspiracy, including on the pages of the *Dearborn Independent*, a journal he founded and financed.[20] In the early 1920s, mainstream, nonevangelical church leaders, such as George Simons and Harris Houghton, were among the first to proclaim the document genuine, giving it credence and publicizing it—so much so that they and others brought it to the attention of the political elite in Washington, and the *Protocols* became a subject of congressional investigation during the Red Scare of the early 1920s.[21] Many conservative evangelical activists stayed aloof, although some of them thought the document might be authentic. Matters changed in the late 1920s, a development reflected in the thought of Arno Gaebelein, who underwent a change of heart and became, in the 1930s, particularly bitter and suspicious.

In the early 1920s, the battle between conservative, "fundamentalist" evangelicals and "modernist" liberal Protestants reached a peak. Conservative evangelical polemics concentrated more on opposition to the theory of evolution and on insisting on the authenticity of the Christian Bible than on international conspiracies. However, in 1925, the conservative evangelical camp was severely set back by the Scopes trial in Dayton, Tennessee, with the major newspapers of the day mocking their representatives and their claims and with national public opinion turning against them. The conservative legislative campaign to prohibit the teaching of evolution suffered a defeat, and the movement in general felt humiliated.[22]

Timothy Weber has suggested that premillennialist evangelicals tended to favor conspiracy theories on a global scale.[23] By the 1930s the embattled and embittered conservative evangelical premillennialists were turning more than ever to such theories as an explanation for the decline, from their perspective, of Christian culture and values as they understood them. When adopting the *Protocols,* conservative evangelicals did not buy into a completely new conspiracy theory. They were merely modifying and adding a new detail to a wider concept of the ongoing cosmic battle that they believed was taking place between good and evil. They, like many others, believed that Jews took part in movements that promoted non-Christian regimes, including the Bolshevik Revolution in Russia.[24] Lenin, they were certain, was a Jew, as were the other leaders of the revolution. Communist or socialist political parties and regimes, they concluded, carried out the conspiracy outlined in the *Protocols.*

In 1933, the *Defender,* a publication edited by Gerald Winrod that promulgated white conservative Christian and Anglo-European nativism, provided alleged evidence for the conspiracy outlined in the *Protocols.* This time the Jews were blamed for the failure of the capitalist system, which they allegedly controlled. The Jews, Winrod claimed, ruled the world banking system and were responsible for the economic crisis of 1929 and the ensuing depression. They were also the ones in charge of the movie industry and were thus to blame for the nation's alleged decline in morality.[25] Shortly afterwards, Arno Gaebelein published *The Conflict of the Ages,* in which he outlined his understanding of the cosmic battle that was taking place between the dark forces of lawlessness and the faithful remnant of Christ's followers. Certain that the *Protocols* was not a "crude forgery," he praised Serge Nilus, the Russian who had first published it, as "a believer in the Word of God, in prophecy, and . . . a true Christian."[26] At the time the *Protocols* fit so well into the conservative evangelical philosophy of history and critique of culture that evangelical writers such as Gaebelein did not see themselves as irrational or as haters of Jews. After all they objected to anti-Jewish measures and expressed hope for the eventual conversion of that people even as they declared the Jews to be leaders of a world conspiracy to destroy Christian civilization. As far as they were concerned, they were merely stating the facts.

Opposition to the idea of the involvement of Jews in international conspiracies came from within the conservative evangelical camp itself. Jewish converts to evangelical Christianity, such as Joseph Cohn, the director of the American Board of Missions to the Jews, and Elias Newman, a Lutheran pastor and missionary in Minnesota, openly objected to what they considered unjustified defamation of the Jews. Unacceptable as their choice to convert to Christianity might have been to many Jews, in their own way these converts and missionaries were proud Jews who fought within the conservative evangelical community against anti-Jewish prejudices.[27] They shared much of the evangelical worldview, including the more literal reading of the Bible, Victorian sexual morality, and the messianic hope in its dispensationalist version. But as newcomers to Christian Protestant society they struggled on a daily basis with negative stereotypes of Jews and strongly resented the prejudices they encountered. Cohn used his mission's journal, *The Chosen People*, to fight the conservative Christian enchantment with the *Protocols*. He entered into literary vendettas with Winrod and Riley, the latter attacking Cohn as if he were the embodiment of everything evil about the Jews.[28]

Jewish activists outside the evangelical camp also responded to accusations directed against the Jews and organized to counter what they considered to be unjustified accusations, whether coming from evangelicals or others. But Jews did not necessarily differentiate between different kinds of defamers. In Minneapolis, for example, the Jewish community looked upon William Riley as an enemy, trying to discredit him as a bigot within the ranks of the Christian community.[29] Cohn and Newman could more easily make their voices heard in conservative evangelical circles than spokespersons of the Jewish community could, but they too failed to persuade Riley, Winrod, and Gaebelein to alter their positions, although they did manage, at least partially, to affect the attitudes of others in evangelical circles.

The *Protocols* Abandoned

Evangelicals' eventual abandonment of their conviction that *Protocols of the Elders of Zion* was an authentic document was not due to the protests of Jewish organizations, since evangelicals expected such denials and protests.[30] It was also not due to the effect of interfaith reconciliation, since Christian evangelical thinkers were not engaged in organized interfaith dialogue and did not see a need to conform to the emerging liberal standards of relating to other faiths. Unlike Henry Ford, they were not trying to sell cars to Jews and therefore saw no need to apologize and pretend to have changed their opinions. An important influence in changing their views was the news regarding the Jewish plight in Nazi Germany and later in other countries in Nazi-controlled Europe. At the beginning of the Nazi ascent to power evangelical Christians were divided in their assessment of the regime, some opposing it and others giving it some benefit of the doubt. By the late 1930s, it became evident to the evangelical leadership that the Nazis were not defenders of the Christian faith. Conservative evangelicals were taken aback when they discovered what they considered to be the un-Christian aspects of Nazi ideology, such as the Aryanization of Jesus, the rejection of the Old Testament, racial laws that made Jewish converts to Christianity and their children undesirable, and pagan symbols and rites.

The evangelical journal *Our Hope* was among the first to condemn the Nazi policies toward the Jews and later on to alert its readers to the devastating scope of the destruction of European Jewry.[31] Gaebelein, the journal's editor, viewed the Nazi's position vis-à-vis the Jews as a rebellion against God and predicted the downfall of the regime. The evangelist George T. B. Davis made a similar prediction, writing in 1942: "Pharaoh oppressed the Jews. He was drowned in the Red Sea. Later Haman sought to destroy the Jews. He was hung on a gallows. . . . Today, a man whose name begins with the same letter as Haman's is oppressing the Jews. . . . I know from God's word that a terrible fate awaits him."[32]

Though evangelicals did not organize politically against the Nazis' persecution of Jews, they did gradually come to realize that the Jews were not mighty conspirators but rather a vulnerable and weak people who were knocking on the doors of America and other countries and begging for asylum. By the beginning of World War II, conservative evangelical Christians began omitting the *Protocols* from their exegetical and polemical writings. Their infatuation with the document and the idea of a world Jewish conspiracy was over. This did not mean that evangelicals completely changed their minds about the Jews. Criticism of Jewish characteristics continued to appear in their writings, but the idea of an international Jewish conspiracy lost ground considerably. In 1939, for example, the aging Riley published his most well-known book, *Wanted, a World Leader!,* in which he explained world events in light of his biblical messianic faith. A relentless promoter and popularizer of the *Protocols* merely a few years earlier, he now both lashed out at and praised the Jews without referring to that document.[33]

Protocols of the Elders of Zion did not disappear completely from conservative Christian writings but rather lost favor with the more respectable and mainstream elements within that religious and cultural movement. Nativist and racist groups would persist in utilizing the tract to explain an alleged decline of Anglo-Saxon and Nordic elements in America and other societies. Since the 1940s, the *Protocols* has become a litmus test indicating where groups stand in relation not only to Jews but to the Christian mainstream as a whole. During World War II and in the postwar years, religious concord increasingly became the norm.[34] The image of Jews and Judaism improved significantly, and Judaism became one of the publicly accepted faiths in America.[35] Preachers such as Gerald L. K. Smith who persisted in attributing conspiratorial intentions to the Jews found themselves outside the mainstream and were not welcomed in polite society.[36]

Conservative evangelicalism has not remained static. As a result of reforms within Protestant fundamentalism, the mainstream has become neoevangelical: a more accommodating and open movement whose influence on American society has grown enormously, especially since the 1970s.[37] Conservative evangelical opinions on Jews have also developed throughout the years. The birth of the state of Israel in 1948, and, even more, the Israeli conquest of the older parts of Jerusalem in 1967, have turned conservative evangelicals into supporters of Jewish and especially Israeli causes. Moreover, from the 1950s to the 1980s, Israelis were fighting against Soviet-sponsored armies and guerrilla groups, often receiving Western support and evangelical sympathy. Evangelical observers noticed that the Jewish state was far from being an ally of Soviet and other communist countries. Jewish organizations were asking Christians to join their struggle to liberate Soviet Jews and to allow Jews in the Soviet Union to emigrate to Israel or to other Western nations. In the 1970s and 1980s Israel came out as an avowed enemy of the Soviet system, and world Jewry in general were recognized as victims and opponents of the Soviet state. A number of evangelical Christian groups and individuals joined the Jewish international political struggle against Soviet persecution of Jews. By that time, the conspiracy theory that the Jews stood behind communist regimes was almost completely forgotten.[38]

While leaders of other groups or movements who promoted the *Protocols* held a more consistently negative opinion of Jews, the evangelical attitude was much more complex and unstable. Though subscribing to long-held Christian stereotypical images of Jews, the evangelical leaders also regarded the Jews as a special people and anticipated a Jewish national rejuvenation. On their own terms, they were committed to goodwill toward that people. *Protocols of the Elders of Zion,* at least for a while, fit into the evangelical dispensationalist worldview because, in essence, it had been part of that worldview even before the document was forged and circulated. It took some extreme historical developments for evangelicals to abandon their belief that the *Protocols* was a genuine document. Today it appears on the websites of some white, overtly racist, Christian and neopagan groups, who see the unfolding of the conspiracy it spells out in today's political and economic situation. Within conservative evangelical circles, however, it has for the most part been forgotten. Since the 1970s, evangelicals' awareness of and sympathy for the Jewish plight during the years of the Holocaust have developed further.

9

The Evangelical Understanding of the Holocaust

Since the 1970s, the evangelical rank and file have shown growing awareness of the suffering of Jews and others during the Second World War.
Books relating to the Holocaust have become popular in evangelical
circles, often in conjunction with other themes, such as the position
of the Jews in God's plans for humanity and the moral and theological questions arising from the murder of millions of innocent people.
Biographies, memoirs, and novels have been written to inform evangelical readers about the Nazi regime in Europe from 1933 to 1945, as well
as to educate Christians on the meaning and purpose of the horrifying
events that took place during those years and how they fit into the larger
scheme of divine plans for human salvation. Such literature has further
come to set standards for the proper behavior of Christians during trying times. The writings reassure evangelicals that true Christian believers had nothing to do with the persecution and annihilation of Jews and
others and in fact went out of their way to protect such people from the
Nazis. Evangelical literature has further pointed to the horrors of the
Holocaust as a proof that all human beings need the Gospel and should
accept Jesus Christ as their savior and follow in his footsteps, thereby
assuring their status as righteous persons in this era as well as their spiritual and physical salvation for eternity.

Evangelicals Discover the Holocaust

The evangelical interest in learning about what happened to the Jews
during World War II and the wish to make sense of it morally and

spiritually corresponded in some ways to the relation of Western societies at large toward the Holocaust. From the late 1940s through the 1960s, most European and American Christians were reluctant to confront the horrors of the Nazi persecution and murder of the Jews.[1] Such interest, however, grew considerably during the 1970s and 1980s, coming to occupy an important place in Christian evangelical literature as well. During the 1970s and 1980s, evangelicals published biographies and autobiographies recounting real-life stories of both Jews and non-Jews who had suffered under the Nazi regime. Since the 1990s a new genre has taken over among evangelicals, and the representation of the Holocaust has moved to novels that reconstruct and interpret it through fictional characters and semi-imaginary events.

A major element in the evangelical understanding of the Holocaust has been the implicit claim that the evils and horrors of the Nazi regime were committed by non-Christians. True Christians, those who had undergone genuine conversions and established personal relationships with Jesus, would not, by definition, take part in such regimes and atrocities. In fact, Nazi transgressions were carried out by anti-Christians, even if nominally some or even many of them were members of churches. This outlook has not been based on a historical examination of the involvement or noninvolvement of Protestant groups with the Nazi regime in occupied Europe. The historical reality that many Protestant leaders and churches in Germany supported the regime has often been ignored by evangelical writers.[2] They have concentrated instead on the heroism of individual members of pietist or evangelical churches and have presented the actions of such outstanding persons as normative. Such literary constructions convey the message that true Christians behaved in a manner that demonstrated Christian ideals. Refusing to accept Nazi ideology or cooperate with Nazi actions, they went out of their way to protect and hide Jews, risking their own lives along the way. In evangelical narratives, good Christians and Jews have stood together against the Nazis.

Exemplary Christians and the Rescue of Jews: *The Hiding Place*

The most popular evangelical book on the Holocaust has been *The Hiding Place*. Published in the early 1970s, it was widely circulated until, at the turn of the twenty-first century, it was overshadowed by the popularity of a new genre of evangelical literature on the same topic. The narrator-protagonist of *The Hiding Place*, Corrie ten Boom, had published her memoirs nearly twenty years earlier.[3] The evangelist Billy Graham recognized the book's potential as an instructive evangelical tract and invited the Dutch heroine to the United States to lecture on her experiences. Graham also sponsored a new version of her book, coauthored by John and Elizabeth Sherrill, two professional writers, and it immediately became popular among evangelicals. Millions of copies sold in America, translations were made into a number of languages, and a film was produced.[4]

The Hiding Place tells the story of the ten Booms, a devout Dutch Reformed family who operated a watch shop in the Dutch city of Haarlem. Two unmarried sisters, Corrie and Betsie, lived with their aging father above the shop. Following the Nazi occupation of Holland, when the persecution of Jews and others began, the ten Booms gave shelter to Jews and non-Jews who were hiding from the Nazis. The family became involved in a clandestine operation to hide Jews as well as Dutch youths who were evading Nazi forced labor. The book offers a vivid account of many aspects of the rescue activity. The family had to be wary of informers and kept their rescue activity secret from those who did not take part in it. Daily life with hidden Jews is described with credibility. For example, it was difficult for the hidden persons to remain in their cramped quarters. One Jewish woman who could take it no longer gave herself up by walking out into the streets; she was recognized and arrested.

While ten Boom gives an accurate picture of Holland under Nazi occupation, indicating that only a minority were willing to save Jewish lives, her book implies that true Christian believers, brought up on biblical literalism, were in the forefront of rescue efforts. Indeed, according to Joseph Michman, the percentage of conservative Dutch Protestants who rescued Jews during World War II was more than three times the percentage in the Dutch population, making up about 25 percent of those who saved Jews.[5] Ten Boom's edited memoirs also promote the belief that the Lord guides and protects righteous rescuers. Corrie's sister-in-law, for example, insisted on speaking the truth in all circumstances. At one time, the police, who had been informed of the presence of Jews, searched the house and inquired whether a blonde, blue-eyed, "Aryan-looking" girl was Jewish. "Yes," came the answer of the sister-in-law who would not lie.[6] The poor girl was arrested but later was released, so the story goes, by the Dutch underground. Another miracle that, according to ten Boom, manifested God's guiding hand had to do with the possession of copies of the Bible. While in Ravensbrueck concentration camp, Corrie obtained a copy of the Book of Books and managed, in defiance of all regulations and inspections, to keep it, read it, and share it with others (193-94).

In actuality, the family paid dearly for disobeying the authorities. "The hiding place" was exposed. Corrie and her sister, father, brother, and nephew were arrested. Only Corrie survived. Theirs is a story of Christian martyrdom. The ten Booms kept their faith and values at all times and were a source of inspiration to the prisoners around them. Corrie portrays her father and sister as saintly figures, bringing tranquillity and hope to the prison cells and concentration camp barracks where they were interned. She herself emerges from the pages of her reminiscences as a remarkable person, highly conscientious, humorous, and humane. Readers are invited to look upon her as an exemplary Christian. Jesus, she informs the readers, was her source of strength and guidance during her time of trial, offering her solace and inspiration when she was confronted with the deaths of those dear to her (163, 189, 223).

A major message of the book is the Christian command of forgiveness and love for one's enemies. According to the narrative, the ten Booms felt sorry for the Germans, who were engaged in evil and destruction. Corrie's father voiced a premillennialist, pietist, and evangelical understanding of the Jews and their role in history when he said that the Germans were doomed because "they have touched the apple of God's eyes"

(86). Likewise, holding to a more literal reading of Scripture, the ten Boom asserted that the Jews were still God's chosen people, destined to regain their role as God's first nation. The German attempt to destroy the Jews was futile and would ultimately harm the perpetrators. After the war and the German defeat, ten Boom promoted a message of forgiveness and reconciliation. The book thus targeted Germans, too, as potential readers and converts. It carried the message that the truly converted were utterly forgiven and that Christian victims and their former persecutors were now in the same boat, that of the redeemed.

Ten Boom became a celebrity, and her story often became a venue for evangelical Christians to construct a narrative of Nazi-occupied Europe and of Christian behavior during that time. Her memoirs, however, were not the only ones that expressed the evangelical understanding of the Holocaust.

Jesus Heals Everyone: Nazi Perpetrators and Jewish Victims as Born-Again Christians

During the 1970s and 1980s born-again Christians who had witnessed the Nazi regime from different angles wrote memoirs. Although providing important historical information, the autobiographies primarily offer spiritual messages. They attempt to show the courage and righteousness of the truly converted. Taken as a whole, such books promote the idea that all people who lived under the Nazi regime, Jews and Gentiles alike, needed the ameliorating Gospel, if they had not believed in it earlier, and that once they repented and converted they were all forgiven and justified before the Lord. Evangelical narratives were perhaps the first non-German publications to look upon the Germans as victims of the war the Nazi state had initiated, even if many of them had supported that regime. Such narratives portrayed ex-Nazis as people who were for a while led astray by the powers of the devil but who redeemed themselves when they repented and accepted Jesus as their savior. Amazingly, secular memoirs and novels with similar emphases on German suffering in the last stages of the war appeared in English only in the 2000s.[7]

Autobiographical evangelical memoirs of ex-Nazis include those of Maria Anne Hirschmann, *Hansi's New Life* and *Hansi, the Girl Who Loved the Swastika.*[8] The books narrate the political and spiritual journey of a Nazi woman who became a born-again Christian. Hirschmann recounts the suffering of the Germans at the end of the war: the shock of the defeat, the fear of being raped by Soviet soldiers, and the exile to West Germany from the Sudetenland, which again became part of Czechoslovakia. Her reminiscences follow her immigration to America with her husband, who had served as a submarine officer in the German navy, their adaptation to their new homeland, and the spiritual journey that led her toward a conversion experience. "Jesus and I became friends one warm summer night under the stars. . . . I was like Paul, a chief sinner, I had rejected Christ deliberately when I became a Nazi," she wrote. "I despised His name and His life story as unacceptable to German superiority."[9]

Hirschmann states that she sought and obtained the forgiveness of God as well as of his true believers. But she complains that the Jews failed, in the years following the war, to show forgiveness. Jewish journalists "tortured" her by asking her if she knew about the concentration camps. While Germans bear guilt, she declares, Jews carry hate and prejudices (118). She asserts that she forgave her own oppressors, including the Soviets who had harassed Germans like her at the end of World War II (88). Hirschmann's memoirs end with an encounter with Corrie ten Boom. At first, she writes, she was afraid to meet this righteous Dutch savior of Jews, who, she knew, had spent time in a concentration camp. But this perfect Christian accepted her warmly. Ten Boom's attitude toward Hirschmann exemplifies the forgiveness every Christian is supposed to show toward her former enemies. Ten Boom even wrote a preface to Hirschmann's book in which she expressed that opinion. Thus Hansi's Nazi past is forgiven by both Jesus and his followers.

Hirschmann's book has been unusual, at least in English. More often it has been Christian Jews who have described, in edited evangelical autobiographies, their spiritual journeys in the midst of wartime persecution and suffering. A widely circulated book, Johanna-Ruth Dobschiner's

Selected to Live, offers a special meaning to the conversion of victims of the Nazis.[10] Like other evangelical memoirs of Holocaust survivors, it has remained in print since its first publication in the 1970s. It tells the sad story of a German Jewish family who fled from Germany to Holland. In 1940, the Nazi occupation caught up with them again. The first to be taken to a concentration camp and killed were Ruth's two brothers. Sometime later her parents too were deported to a camp. Ruth hid when her parents were arrested and lived in homes to which the Jewish council assigned her, working as a nurse in hospitals and children's homes. The deportations continued, and the inhabitants of such institutions were also rounded up and sent to death camps. Ruth was "chosen" by a clandestine Protestant Dutch network that rescued Jews and placed them in Christian homes. Her first hiding place was in the house of a Dutch Reformed minister who was later executed by the Nazis.

It was in the hiding place that Dobschiner discovered the Old and New Testaments, read them in their evangelical interpretation, and converted to Christianity. Dobschiner describes her rescuer "Domie" in terms similar to those generally reserved for Jesus. For her, he symbolized purity, love, protection for the meek, and self-sacrifice. "He died to secure my life in this world, Christ died to secure it in the next," she wrote (224). Like Domie, Jesus served as a father figure for her. When Dobschiner reached the passages in the New Testament that described his death, she mourned for him "according to the custom of my people . . . seven days" (162). In addition to being the religion of her saviors, Christianity embodied for the young woman hope for a new life, and the adoption of Jesus as a personal savior worked to overcome the loneliness of the hiding place: "With warm love He surrounded me in that bare attic. His Holy Spirit, able to be everywhere at the same time, covered me with security. I knew myself loved, even when no human being considered my needs" (197). Her survival, predetermined by God, opened her eyes to the truth of the Christian faith.

Dobschiner's autobiography was intended, among other things, to promote the evangelical faith. Its targeted audiences included Jewish readers, whom evangelicals wished to persuade about the need to adopt the Christian message. Consequently Dobschiner's narrative includes statements that are intended specifically for Jews. She describes herself before her encounter with the Christian faith as being suspicious toward Christianity. But her prejudices, she asserts, had resulted from ignorance of the true nature of that faith. Christians, she found out, were kind people. Their behavior, she decided, must result from their faith. "It must be a special religion . . . hence their kindness in taking us in" (163). "I felt protected and loved among them," she concludes (213). She claims that if Jews only knew what Christianity was really about they would embrace it wholeheartedly. When Jews encountered nominal Christians who mistreated them, they mistook Christianity for the religion of the enemy. "The trouble is that our people don't know it, they have to be told," she emphatically writes (191). Dobschiner asserts that the suffering and murder of the Jews under the Nazis was a result of Jews' not placing themselves under the protection of their savior (177-78). However, in keeping with the evangelical outlook on the Jewish people, she foresees a hope and future for the Jews in the messianic age. "God would one day send the Messiah. He would deliver Israel and call nations to see true light in God" (156).

Another widely acclaimed evangelical biography, *Pursued,* promotes a similar outlook.[11] Vera Schlamm's memories of her experiences in Nazi-occupied Europe also gave special meaning to the suffering of Jews who later found spiritual comfort in Christianity. The Schlamms were German Jews who came to Holland as refugees and were sent during the Nazi occupation to a concentration camp. But they took active steps to save their lives by obtaining passports of a neutral South American nation. Schlamm describes the life in Bergen-Belsen, the German concentration camp to which she and her family were sent. As citizens holding passports of neutral countries, they were able to receive parcels from relatives abroad and were safe from being deliberately killed. Surviving the war, the Schlamms immigrated to America, where Vera studied medicine and trained as a pediatrician. During her years in California she gradually became persuaded of the truth of the Christian message. Her conversion offered a new perspective on her experiences during

World War II, which became, in retrospect, meaningful steps in her spiritual odyssey. The book conveys the notion that Schlamm's conversion was predetermined. Jesus was waiting to embrace her and bring her under his protection, hence her survival of the horrors of the Holocaust. Although she was not yet a Christian when she underwent those travails, her survival is presented as another manifestation of the wonderful gifts God bestows on his followers. Jews for Jesus, the largest group evangelizing the Jews since the 1970s, decided to publish Schlamm's memoirs, and a member of this missionary organization coauthored the book.

Pursued is a typical convert's memoir: written with the help of professional evangelists and presenting the protagonist narrator's earlier life experiences from a perspective acquired later in life. Literary critics speak about "formulation" in the construction of such memoirs.[12] Such narratives tend, for example, to emphasize the spiritual and moral transformations that conversions bring with them. Autobiographies in general, scholars of the genre remind us, are ultimately about the present more than the past. They display not what their writers "remember" but how they understand their past as they rearrange their present identities. In this case, Jewish converts to Christianity who survived in World War II Europe tell their stories to evangelical writers from the point of view of their present selves as Christian evangelical believers. The memoirs as a whole reflect the values of evangelical Christianity from the 1970s into the twenty-first century more than those of the protagonists during the war years. Coauthors and editors have utilized the narratives to educate Christians about the horrors of Nazism and to provide models for Christian behavior during times of duress. Such life stories also convey the message that exceptional life experiences should bring Jews and others to accept the Gospel, so that the presentation of the Holocaust also serves as an evangelization tool.

A somewhat different testimony from Dobschiner's and Schlamm's is Rose Warmer's *The Journey*. Like other memoirs, *The Journey* evolved from an earlier, shorter work.[13] The evangelical community was yearning to read Holocaust survivor-converts' life stories, so Myrna Grant, a professional evangelical writer, interviewed Warmer in her evangelical

Jewish retirement community in Haifa, Israel, and came out with a best-selling biography.[14] Warmer' was born into a middle-class Jewish family in the Austro-Hungarian Empire. She studied art, music, and dance and led a bohemian life in pre-World War II Vienna and Budapest. In keeping with other converts' biographies, this book describes Warmer in her preconversion state as centered on earthly interests and pleasures and as consequently feeling spiritually and morally empty. Finally, Rose found Christ and became an evangelist. Protected by Christian friends, she could have hidden during the war, but she felt that she had a mission—to bring the message of salvation to women in the death camps (104-7). So although she could have avoided being deported, she went to a concentration camp, trusting that Jesus would protect her. She realized that she would suffer, but she also knew that she would be saved if spiritually she could stand the trial.

Since Rose was young and fit, the Nazis sent her from the concentration camp to a work squadron in Germany, where she suffered hunger and cold. But as far as she was concerned she was setting an example to the other women and bringing them a message of hope and redemption. At times she encountered anger and resentment on the part of some women, but she also found willing listeners among them. Jesus, Warmer believed, was a father, mother, brother, and sister, and she felt especially inclined to bring Jesus to those who had lost their families (118). God's guiding hand, the memoir tells us, was evident and gave her courage to continue living even when she felt completely exhausted (136). Having a Bible with her meant a great deal to Warmer, and she carefully hid the copy she had brought. When she was forced to give it up she sought ways to replace it. Once a Nazi officer gave her a copy; another time she approached the commander of the labor camp for a copy and received one (137). The fellowship of true Christian believers was also very important, and she rejoiced when she met other Christians with whom she could pray or read Scripture.

After the establishment of the state of Israel in 1948, Warmer emigrated there, settled in Haifa, and spent the rest of her life as a missionary to the Jews. The book sees a logical connection between the

Holocaust, the birth of the state of Israel, and the evangelism of Jews. Warmer saw her mission to be that of enlightening Israelis as to the true identity of their savior and the true Jewish role in history. In her book she interprets the emergence of the new state and the gathering of the Jews there as part of God's plans for humanity. She herself, she says, is living proof that God remained faithful to his people. "I was part of the promise! I had returned" (213). Warmer's journey to hell and back is presented as part of a broader spiritual journey: that of finding the Savior, submitting to his love and protection, discovering the ways in which he bestows his favors, and witnessing this to others.

A different Holocaust biography is Jan Markell's *Angels in the Camp*.[15] Like other books of its kind, it comes to educate the evangelical community about life under the Nazi regime and the horrors that befell Jews and others, as well as to give evidence about God's mercy and protection. Markell wrote down and edited Anita Dittman's testimony, which offers a window into the travails of *Mischlinge* (half-Jewish people) and their emotional and spiritual perspectives. The daughter of a Jewish mother and an "Aryan" non-Jewish father, Dittman gravitated during the Nazi period toward Christianity in order to find solace and meaning in her precarious life. Her father and mother being separated, Dittman grew up without her father, and she suggests that "perhaps my inner longing for a loving father drove me to my heavenly father so early in life" (9). Growing up in the German city of Breslau with her mother and sister, Anita joined a Lutheran congregation, whose pastor took special interest in converting Jews. Unlike "full Jews," Dittman was allowed to continue her studies in regular schools well into the war years. However, in the summer of 1944 the Nazis sent her to Barthold, a labor camp for children of mixed marriages, where the young inmates dug ditches. Finding solace in her faith, Dittman was certain that Jesus protected her and attributes her survival to his divine saving graces, as well as the goodwill of her pastor.

Like other evangelical books, *Angels in the Camp* comes to offer answers to the kind of questions readers might come up with in relating to the evils that a Christian country inflicted on vulnerable members of its own and other societies. The protagonist-narrator differentiates between "true" Christians, who remained loyal to Christian principles, and "nominal" Christians, who identified with the Nazi regime and its goals. "But those people aren't Christians; they just give real Christians a bad name," she asserts (44). The book also confronts the question of how "a loving, all powerful God would allow such horrible things to happen" and offers an answer: "Granted, millions perished, but God also allowed millions to survive" (61). The book also presents the eventual German defeat as a result of the country's brutal and unethical behavior. Like ten Boom's father, Dittman's pastor makes the claim that "the Jews are the apple of God's eye. Because Germany has harmed them, she will never be the same" (64). Like all Holocaust memoirs produced by evangelical publishing houses, the book has a clear agenda of spreading the Christian evangelical faith and emphasizing the healing powers and ever-present constructive guidance of Jesus. The book's subtitle, "A Remarkable Story of Peace in the Midst of the Holocaust," offers the message that the harsh times of the Nazi regime enabled some people to discover the truth of the Gospel and that Christian believers can find peace and reassurance even in the midst of horror.

In sum, while acquainting the evangelical community with the history of the Nazi period and the suffering it brought about, the biographies promote evangelical messages, including the role of Israel in God's plans for humanity. They portray the behavior of evangelical Christians throughout the war years as exemplary, a proof that the acceptance of Jesus as a savior guarantees correct moral behavior, courage, and an ability to survive spiritually, if not physically. The memoirs are also meant to promote the Christian imperative of forgiveness and reconciliation. The victims must forgive their repentant persecutors and accept them as fellow Christians. The destructiveness of Nazism should not work against the higher values of Christian love and unity.

Representation of the Holocaust in Evangelical Novels

In the 1990s and 2000s, the evangelical representation of the Holocaust shifted considerably. Instead of reading edited autobiographies
of Holocaust survivors who converted to Christianity, the evangelical
community learned about the events of the Nazi era through a different medium: historical novels. By the 1990s many of the heroes of the
evangelical Holocaust memoirs, including Corrie ten Boom and Rose
Warmer, had died and were no longer available for interviews or lecture
tours. More significantly, the new novels about the Holocaust were part
of a larger trend in evangelical literary tastes and means of disseminating and transmitting theological perceptions and cultural values. Novels
have come to replace theological tracts and social-political manifestos
that were previously popular among evangelicals. In the 1970s, for example, the theological-political tract *The Late Great Planet Earth* was the
evangelical best seller par excellence, selling tens of millions of copies all
around the globe. It promoted a conservative evangelical critique of culture and society, coupled with a premillennialist interpretation of history
and current world events.[16] By the 1990s, however, novels, not only for
teenagers but for adults, had become the predominant genre to promote
evangelical values in a form that readers could find exciting and attractive.[17] Authors created fictional characters, events, dialogues, scenes, and
emotions to teach readers about historical events, moral concerns, normative Christian behavior, the transforming and healing powers of the
Savior, and the challenges and travails that the future would bring.

Evangelical historical novels about the Jews often have two creators,
one responsible for researching the historical background or determining the correct theological views and the other an actual "writer"
who uses his or her literary and artistic skills to construct a compelling plot. The novels offer engaging plots, romance, heroism, suspense,
and colorful locales. Some have reached not only convinced evangelicals but nonevangelical readers as well. Through them, many readers
have become acquainted with evangelical doctrines of faith, including,
at times, the anticipation of the imminent arrival of the end times and

a premillennialist understanding of the course of world history, including the role of the Jews and Israel. A number of prominent evangelical novelists have focused on the Holocaust, the Nazis, and Jewish suffering and have confronted theological and moral questions that other series relate to only marginally.

Evangelical Christian writers have not been the first to write historical novels on the Holocaust.[18] Such books, which often included descriptions of the postwar Jewish struggles in Palestine, were popular in Hebrew and Jewish American writings long before evangelical writers began utilizing the genre. During the 1950s and 1960s, *Exodus,* Leon Uris's outstanding best seller on the Holocaust and the Jewish struggle for Palestine, enjoyed a large readership and an even greater audience when it was produced as a movie, with Paul Newman playing the fictional Israeli hero Ari Ben-Canaan.[19] Leading a ship of Holocaust survivors from Europe to Palestine in defiance of British policy, Ben-Canaan goes on to fight for the independence of the Jewish state. *Exodus* prefigured some of the evangelical dramas of the turn of the twenty-first century, which have also connected the Holocaust with the struggle for Palestine and have created scenarios in Europe and Palestine of the 1930s and 1940s. Written primarily for a Jewish audience, the book expressed a secular Jewish pro-Zionist point of view.[20] Many liberal Jews, both in America and in Israel, have since developed a more skeptical outlook on heroic Zionist narratives. Yet today evangelical novels relating to the Holocaust and the struggle over Palestine are reminiscent of *Exodus* and other popular Jewish books of an earlier period, promoting views on the situation in the Middle East from a pro-Zionist perspective. These new novels have woven together moments of Jewish, European, and Middle Eastern history with evangelical premillennialist moral codes and biblical exegeses, laced with romance and suspense.

While not as famous as Tim LaHaye and Jerry Jenkins, the authors of the Left Behind books, Bodie and Brock Thoene, have been among the most popular evangelical writers of historical novels at the turn of the twenty-first century. Their elaborate projects include a series of historical dramas on the Holocaust and another series on the Jewish struggle for a state in Palestine, with these two themes interwoven throughout both series. The Thoenes, husband and wife, have worked as a team, with Bodie doing the writing and Brock, a professional historian by training, doing the research and providing the historical setting for the books. The team has constructed fictional personalities, placing them alongside real historical figures, and has combined imaginary situations with historical ones, adding dramatic elements to make the stories more compelling. The Thoenes are committed evangelicals and premillen-nialists, and their website openly promotes an evangelical theological outlook and cultural agenda. The couple has even sponsored a mis-sionary agency, the Shiloh Light Foundation, aimed at spreading the Gospel among prisoners and other disadvantaged persons.[21] The books include study guides to promote evangelical morality and interpretation of Scripture. The guides include a list of biblical passages for those who "wish to investigate more about Jesus." The Zion Covenant series views the developments in the life of the Jewish people, and other nations as well, from a messianic evangelical point of view, using the occasion to promote the premillennialist faith in the imminent second coming of Jesus.[22] Evangelical novels on the Nazi persecution of the Jews make for exciting reading. In semifictional, suspenseful historical scenes, Hitler conspires at his headquarters with his cronies, exploring schemes to persecute the Jews and deceive the world; young, loving Jews plan their emigration, hoping to reunite in new locales; Nazi secret services plot the killing of a German diplomat in France and blame the Jews for the murder, moving forward to plan the November 1938 attack on the Jews of Germany. Intrigued and captivated, readers follow the developments with suspense as if they were watching an action film. Readers are grati-fied that ultimately justice prevails and some of the protagonists survive and reunite. They identify with attractive and positive Jewish as well as non-Jewish protagonists who stand for righteousness.[23]

Like Leon Uris, the Thoenes wished to tell "the whole story," although the novel series is often selective in the choices of events and develop-ments. Unlike *Exodus* and many other books and novels on the Holo-caust, the Zion Covenant novels pointedly omit gruesome details of the mass annihilation of the Jews. The series starts after the Nazi rise to power in 1933, follows the implementation of discriminatory measures against the Jews, and ends before the genocidal policies of the Nazis are set in motion. The authors have stopped short of actual descriptions of mass murder, but not for lack of space in a series composed of nine books. Their choice corresponds to the nature of the series and the construction of the Jewish protagonists. Amazingly and unconventionally, the Zion Covenant volumes depict the Jews, not as helpless and passive victims, but rather as active, lively persons full of ingenuity, courage, and hope. While the authors convey compassion toward Jewish suffering under Nazi persecution, they describe the Jews as alive and energized. They are people with a mission in history.

In the midst of the Jewish saga of Nazi persecution there is "an interlude" and the plot moves from European cities to Palestine during the Arab revolt of 1936-39.[24] In addition to protagonists of the larger series, with whose struggles readers of the series have become already familiar, the novel *Jerusalem Interlude* presents more characters. This volume introduces readers to life in Palestine during the Arab revolt against the British, which corresponds to the years of the Nazi takeover of Czechoslovakia and Austria before the outbreak of World War II. The series in general, and this novel in particular, draws parallels between the Nazis and Muslim Palestinians, seeing a connection between the Nazi persecution of Jews in Europe and the Arab hostilities against Jews in Palestine. It points to the German Nazis' and the Italian Fascists' backing of the Palestinian Muslims and their leader, the mufti of Jerusalem, and the money and arms they provided Palestinian fighters. The book equates militant Palestinian stands with Muslim radicalism.[25] Readers also learn about British restrictions on Jewish immigration to Palestine, which made it difficult for Jews who wished to emigrate to the Holy Land to attain their goal. Another book series dedicated to the story of the Jewish struggle for Palestine, the Zion Legacy series, has followed in the footsteps of the Zion Covenant series and continues the saga in Palestine during the Arab-Israeli War of 1947-49. The Holocaust looms in the background of the second series, with some of the protagonists being Holocaust survivors as well as veterans of the previous series.[26]

The Meaning of the Holocaust

Evangelical biographies and novels relating to the suffering of the Jews under the Nazi regime in European nations present the Holocaust as embodying a much deeper meaning than persecution and annihilation. It is a period in human history of both moral failures and spiritual triumphs. The Nazi regime and occupation were a trial that true Christians passed in an exemplary manner, having maintained their moral integrity. The Holocaust also provides a testimony that true Christians were protected even in the harshest of circumstances. They might have suffered physical harassment and even death, but such death was martyrdom, and their eternal lives had been guaranteed. Jews who survived were saved because they were predestined to play a role in history, in the rejuvenation of the land and people of Israel. Some were also called to accept their true savior, and bear witness to the Christian and Jewish communities about the saving power of Christ.

In these works, the suffering, misery, and mass murder that characterized the Jewish experience under the Nazis do not derive from brutal anti-Semitism instigated by various historical, sociological, psychological, and theological factors. They are rather the outcome of a rebellion against God: some segments of human society went astray, offering a short-lived triumph to the forces of darkness, while true Christians carried on with their values intact. The novels and biographies also convey the message that born-again Christians relate to Jews with goodwill and kindness. According to this interpretation, the Holocaust is ultimately a chapter in the Jewish and non-Jewish encounter with Christ. Nazism manifested an alienation from the knowledge of God and a shortsightedness that many of the Jewish victims shared. The remedy to the Nazi horrors is the evangelization of both Jews and Gentiles: the more people accept Christianity, the less chance there will be of such brutalities repeating themselves.

Evangelical biographies and novels convey an awareness of and sensitivity toward Jewish suffering and look upon the Jews amicably as heirs to the biblical covenant between God and Israel. The horrors they experienced during the Holocaust are seen as steps in their collective spiritual pilgrimage toward their national rebirth and eventual recognition of the true message of God. Amazingly, evangelical novels and biographies do not pity the Jews and do not treat Jews who suffered or were killed during the Holocaust as helpless, miserable victims. As a rule, they are either live heroes or martyrs: people who have fulfilled a role in God's plans for salvation. Evangelical writers have tied the birth of the state of Israel to the Holocaust, viewing both developments as a fulfillment of biblical prophecies that speak about the return of the Jews to their land. The national rebirth serves as collective compensation for the Jews for their suffering and loss. It is also a proof that God has not abandoned the Jewish people, that he has not forgotten his ancient promises to that nation, and that the Jews are still "the Chosen People."

Evangelical novels on the Holocaust at the turn of the twenty-first century differ sharply in their depiction of Jews from evangelical writings of previous generations. Jews as individuals are not mystified, vilified, or "othered." In fact, on the personal level they are very much like their Christian friends and neighbors. In the novels, the Holocaust era is a time when righteous Christians and fine Jews stand together against enemies of God and humanity, struggling for the same causes. The evangelical literature on the Holocaust has revolutionized, at least partially, evangelical literature about Jews and their history. The novels and biographies also promote the union of all true believers and the overcoming, forgiving, and healing of ethnic differences and historical grudges. This, they promise, will take place in the end times, when Jesus will return, the Jews and the rest of humanity will recognize their true savior, and the messianic age will begin its course. Both the Holocaust and the birth of the state of Israel are steps in the journey of the nation of Israel toward its ultimate union with Christ. When the Messiah comes, the Jews will accept him as their own and their national restoration will be complete. Until then, it is the duty of the evangelical community to guide the Jews and help them to restore their ancient land.

10

Evangelicals and the Birth of the Jewish State

While evangelical activists and leaders noted the plight of Jews in Europe under the Nazi and communist regimes, they also followed the growth of the Jewish community in the Land of Israel with interest and satisfaction. Their reaction on the whole could be described as supportive, yet apprehensive. They were happy to see the birth of a Jewish commonwealth in Palestine, yet they wished the new country had a different cultural and religious agenda. A number of evangelical missionaries and writers visited Palestine during the 1930s and 1940s, watching closely the developments among the Jewish community there and sending home enthusiastic reports of what they saw. The immigration of hundreds of thousands of Jews to the country; the building of new neighborhoods, towns, and villages; the cultivation of hundreds of thousands of acres of land; the establishment of cultural and educational enterprises; and the growth of a Hebrew culture there—all filled evangelicals with excitement.[1] These, they believed, were "signs of the time," indications that the current era was ending and that the arrival of the Messiah was imminent.

The evangelical response to the establishment of the state of Israel in 1948 was, on the whole, one of moral support. Evangelical journals had published sympathetic articles about the intensified Jewish struggle for a Jewish state, and American statesmen with conservative evangelical leanings had supported this agenda in the political and diplomatic struggles that preceded the birth of Israel. However, at this time no particular pro-Zionist evangelical lobby developed, and evangelicals as a group did not raise their voices in favor of American support for the Jewish state.[2] In the late 1940s, conservative evangelicalism was beginning to recover its voice in the American public arena, but this segment of American Protestantism was not yet actively organized on the national level around international causes.

Support and Apprehension

While in principle evangelicals welcomed the news of the establishment of a Jewish state in May of 1948, some also held apprehensions. Under the British rule of Palestine, Christian churches in general, and Protestant activities in particular, enjoyed the government's full protection, if not outright encouragement. A number of evangelical groups took advantage of the British favorable policies and established new communities in Palestine or enlarged existing enterprises. They and their sponsors, who were mostly in English-speaking countries, were worried that the end of the British rule would give rise to antimissionary or even anti-Christian sentiments and that Jews or Arabs might harass converts to Christianity. Gershon Nerel, who has researched the history of the Messianic Jewish community in Palestine, concluded that such worries were exaggerated, if not completely unwarranted.[3] Warranted or not, the London Jews' Society (originally the London Society for Promoting Christianity amongst the Jews) initiated, in the spring of 1948, in cooperation with other groups, and with the aid of the British government and army in Palestine, an evacuation plan: "Operation Mercy." The group sponsored the resettlement in English-speaking countries of dozens of Jewish converts. Those who left, Nerel claims, forfeited their position in the community of evangelically oriented Jewish Christians in Israel, while those who stayed behind became the leaders of the Messianic Jewish community in independent Israel.

After the birth of Israel, premillennialist evangelicals observed the young Jewish state in an attempt to interpret its significance for the advancement of God's plans in the ages. While they were not enthusiastic about the secular character of the Israeli government and society, and while they wanted more freedom of religion, some of the things they saw filled them with hope, as they meshed well with their messianic expectations.[4] The mass emigration of Jews to Israel in the late 1940s and 1950s from many parts of the world, including Asian, African, and East European countries, was one cause for encouragement. In evangelical opinion, this was a significant development, one that had been prophesied in the Bible, and a clear indication that the present era was terminating and that the events of the end of the age were beginning to occur.

However, some evangelical apprehension persisted. Israel retained the Ottoman *millet* system, according to which one's civic identity and status were defined by one's ethnic and religious background, regardless of one's personal convictions. Religious and ethnic identities were recorded at birth or upon immigration and appeared on identity cards that Israelis were required to carry at all times. The categories were very definite, and Jewish converts who immigrated to Israel at times could not register as Jews. The new state allowed missions to pursue their work and guaranteed freedom of worship. But evangelical missionaries in Israel concluded that they were not competing in an open market of religion and that the system as a whole, while not restricting their activities, did not offer them the kind of freedom of religion that America possessed. Likewise, the Israeli national ethos, which in the early years of the state was Zionist, mostly secular, and semisocialist, did not work in favor of evangelical presence and activity. Like missions in America from the 1880s to the 1920s, evangelicals had no problem reaching needy Jews, most of them new immigrants from Middle Eastern, North African, or eastern European nations. However, in spite of an extensive missionary infrastructure and aggressive efforts, from the 1940s to the 1960s, evangelicals failed to reach members of the Israeli elite. Frustrated over their disadvantage, a number of missionary leaders sought to change the relationship in Israel between church and state and create a society based on the American model.

One such visionary was Robert Lindsey, leader of the Southern Baptist community in Israel at the time. A scholar of the New Testament and a missionary, Lindsey left his mark on evangelical-Jewish relations in Israel. While translating the Gospels into modern Hebrew, Lindsey had come to believe that the Synoptic Gospels were originally written in Hebrew and that the Gospel of Luke, which in his opinion contained fewer attacks on Jews than the other two Synoptic Gospels, was the first original gospel. The Gospels of Matthew and Mark, he claimed, relied on Luke, in its original form, and on an additional source, "Q." This theory fit nicely with the evangelical missionary agenda in Israel, since it enabled evangelicals to present the New Testament as essentially lacking anti-Jewish sentiments. It also served as a cornerstone for a new school of New Testament studies, which consisted of the very unlikely match of evangelical Christians and Orthodox Jews. The Jerusalem School of New Testament Studies has been an unexpected development in Jewish-evangelical relations in the modern age. It included Lindsey and other evangelical scholars residing in Jerusalem and a number of Orthodox Jewish Israeli scholars. Among them were professors at the Hebrew University of Jerusalem, notably David Flusser, a New Testament scholar, Shmuel Safrai, a historian of Judaism during the Second Temple period, and his daughter, the historian Hannah Safrai. The Jewish scholars who joined with Lindsey in forming the school had a different agenda from that of the evangelicals. They were interested in comparing the Gospels with Jewish teaching of the period, claiming that Jesus's message was not very different from that of Jewish sages of his time. All members, for different reasons, were interested in emphasizing the Jewish origins of early Christianity. The Orthodox scholars saw Lindsey as a fellow scholar who only incidentally held the title of missionary, and they did not conceive of Lindsey as endangering Jewish souls.

If the association between evangelical missionaries and Jewish Orthodox scholars was surprising, that between the Southern Baptist missionaries and the Canaanite movement was almost in the realm of the unthinkable. The Canaanites were a small ideological-cultural group that had originated in the late 1930s, mostly around the leadership of the Hebrew poet Yonatan Ratosh. Considered radical by most Jews in Palestine of the time, they advocated building in the Land of Israel a Hebrew nation and culture, divorced from Judaism. They demanded, among other things, the separation of synagogue and state. Although the movement had at that time only a very small following and almost

no political power, it influenced Hebrew poetry and Israeli art, intro-
ducing pseudo-Canaanite motifs. Some claimed that followers of the
group had practiced what would later be known as neopagan rites,
although it is doubtful that such practices really took place.⁵ This did
not deter Lindsey from establishing close connections with Canaanite
ideologues and activists, including Yonatan Ratosh. He hired Zvi Rin,
brother of the Canaanite leader, to do translations into Hebrew of books
produced by the Baptist publishing house. Lindsey published articles in
Alef, the ideological-cultural magazine the group had produced in the
early 1950s, in which he advocated the idea of separation of church and
state. The Canaanites, for their part, viewed the Baptists favorably: "They
were the only Christian group whose language of prayer was Hebrew,"
wrote Rin. "I was also attracted to the Baptist outlook that religion was
a personal faith, and not an inherited one. . . . Similarly, I was enchanted
by their advocacy of complete separation of church and state."⁶ When
in the mid-1950s a group of secular Israelis, under the leadership of Uzi
Ornan, established a "League for the Prevention of Religious Coercion,"
Lindsey joined, but he resigned his membership after a while, following
both Christian and Jewish criticism.

Another group with which Lindsey established a relationship was
the American Council for Judaism. This American Jewish group was
founded in the 1940s to oppose the establishment of a Jewish state and
American Jewish support of this state. Members of the council advocated the idea that "nationality and religion are separate and distinct"
and rejected "the concept that the State of Israel was the national homeland of the Jewish people." Lindsey exchanged letters and views with
Elmer Berger, the executive director of this small and elitist American
Jewish group. The Baptist leader favored the establishment of the state
of Israel and stated in his letters to Berger that he saw Jewish religion
and nationality as inseparable. Where he and the American Jewish anti-
Zionist activists could find common ground was in Lindsey's rejection of
the prevailing notion among the Israeli elite that secular Zionist culture
could replace religion. For Lindsey, of course, the ideological and religious beliefs guiding Israel should have been Christian evangelical ones.

Reacting to reports from its missionaries in Israel and other countries, the Southern Baptist Convention passed a resolution on May 1955 "believing in the principle of religious freedom anywhere in the World, especially in Spain, Israel and Italy, and throughout Latin America." Israel was obviously among the countries in which the Baptists felt the nonseparation between church and state was working against them.[7] However, despite their desire for separation of synagogue and state in Israel, evangelical leaders in the country did not ignore the Israeli bureaucratic system assigned to deal with Christian groups and the benefits it offered. Evangelical representatives were in constant interaction with the Department for Christian Affairs at the Ministry of Religious Affairs, which offered Baptists and others tax returns. Like representatives of other churches, Baptists did not wish to pay the high taxes Israelis were paying on imported cars, for example. Moreover, at the same time that the Southern Baptists advocated the separation of church and state in Israel, they came to demand, on a pragmatic basis, that the state recognize them as an official religious community so they could enjoy the privileges of the Israeli *millet* system as state-sanctioned religious communities with autonomy in religious and personal matters.

In contrast to the majority of evangelicals in the country at the time, the Baptists wished to propagate Christianity among members of the country's social, political, and cultural elite. They built their centers in fashionable areas of Israeli cities, such as Rehavia in Jerusalem and Dizingof Street in Tel Aviv. Wishing to reach educated Israelis, they established Dugit, a publishing house that, among other things, published translations into Hebrew of Roland Bainton's works on Martin Luther and the Reformation. The Baptists opened a series of bookshops in Israeli cities, including one in the heart of Tel Aviv, where they promoted evangelical literature alongside scholarly Christian literature as well as books intended for tourists. Another Baptist enterprise aimed at influencing Israelis was the journal *Hayahad* ("Together" in Hebrew), published both in English and in Hebrew. Lindsey wrote extensively in *Hayahad* using an Israeli nom de plume, Reuven Lud. Other Baptist missionaries writing and publishing for *Hayahad* were Dwight Baker and Chandler Lanier. In articles as well as books, Lindsey expressed his views on Israel's role in history. Although he pointed out that he did not follow the dispensationalist interpretation of Scriptures, his understanding of the Jewish people and its role in history was messianic and very similar to that of dispensationalist premillennialists. For him, the Jews were the chosen people, and he believed God's promises for the rejuvenation of Israel in its land to be still valid. However, he expected the Jews to convert to Christianity and accept Jesus as their savior before they could be fully rehabilitated. His missionary agenda was thus, from his point of view, taking part in a historical divinely inspired plan, the rejuvenation of God's chosen nation and land. "The Jews . . . one day [will] be spoken of as having come into Christ's kingdom (Romans 11:26). . . . A certainty is that a relationship exists between Jewry and God's plan of world salvation. . . . The Jews are a remnant body in spiritual decline who nevertheless remind themselves and the world of God's beginning of redemptive history."[8]

Until the 1970s, such evangelical messages did not make inroads into the elite segments of Israeli society, since Zionist Israeli ideology and morale were at their heights. Zionism at that time was more than a political agenda. It was a social and cultural program and contained a messianic component.[9] As far as the Israeli elite were concerned, the state of Israel signified the long hoped-for realization of the Jewish people for a national rejuvenation and a negation of hundreds of years of helplessness and wandering. This reality would change in the wake of the 1973 "Yom Kippur" War, and even more after the 1982-83 Israeli war in Lebanon. Following those wars, adherence to a messianic-Zionist understanding of Jewish history diminished considerably among Israelis, especially secular Israelis. The new atmosphere would offer evangelical Christianity a better opportunity to make inroads into Israeli society, but in the early years of the state this was hardly the case.

Contrary to a common view, evangelical thinkers and leaders, including ardent premillennialists, did note and showed concern over the fate of hundreds of thousands of Palestinian Arabs who lost their homes in 1948 and became refugees in Arab lands. Although they criticized the continued Arab opposition to the creation of Israel, evangelicals also emphasized that the Land of Israel could maintain both Arab and Jewish populations. They insisted that Israel had an obligation to respect human rights and treat the Arabs fairly. One such evangelical leader was John Walvoord, president of Dallas Theological Seminary and an ardent premillennialist supporter of Israel.[10] A few conservative evangelical churches, such as the Southern Baptists, the Christian and Missionary Alliance, the Assemblies of God, and the Plymouth Brethren, have worked among Palestinians, offering relief and educational services. In striving to reconcile premillennialist teachings with the hopes and fears of Arab congregants and potential converts, they emphasized that the ingathering of the Jews in Palestine and the eventual reestablishment of the Davidic kingdom would not necessitate the banishment of Arabs from that land or the curtailing of civil rights. At least in relative terms, a certain amount of goodwill developed between Jews and Arabs who adopted evangelical Christianity. However, as Jewish and Arab evangelical communities became independent of their American sponsors and as relationships between Palestinians and Jews took a turn for the worse following the first and second intifadas, the atmosphere between Arab and Jewish "believers," as they are known in Israel, has become more strained.[11]

The Effect of the 1967 War

The 1967 War had a dramatic effect on evangelical attitudes toward Israel, much more so than the birth of the state of Israel in 1948. In fact, since the French Revolution and the Napoleonic Wars in the last years of the eighteenth century and the beginning of the nineteenth century, no other political-military event has provided so much fuel for prophetic expectations as the short war between Israel and its neighbors on June 5-11, 1967. The unexpected Israeli victory, which included taking over the historical sites of Jerusalem, strengthened the evangelical premillennialists' conviction that their understanding of Scripture was correct and that Israel was indeed created for a mission in history and was to play an important role in the events that would precede the arrival of the Messiah.[12] Evangelical attitudes toward Israel became warmer and more enthusiastic. From the 1970s onward, conservative evangelicals, especially in the United States, became ardent supporters of Israel, voicing their approval of American political and economic support for that country.[13] Many conservative Christians saw support for Israel as going hand in hand with American interests. Their pro-Israeli stand was, from their point of view, an expression of concern for the Jews and appreciation of the importance of the state of Israel in the advancement of the ages. They also believed that it was, at the same time, a fulfillment of America's historical role as well as more immediate interests.[14]

During the 1970s and 1980s, evangelical Christians also involved themselves in such Jewish causes as the facilitation of Jewish immigration from the Soviet Union, combining sympathy for Jews persecuted by the Soviet regime with a wish to see the Jews fulfill their historical role and settle the land of Israel. Evangelicals did not care much for the Soviet Union and its ideological standing and political agendas, external or internal. Even during the years of détente, conservative evangelicals, including Billy Graham, who had visited the Soviet Union, remained wary of communism and the Soviet bloc. In premillennialist evangelical writings, the Soviet Union was the "Evil Empire," the northern power destined to invade Israel during the battle of Armageddon.[15] Evangelicals were strongly affected by the cold war, its dangers, and the global struggle spearheaded by the United States against the Soviet Union and its allies. Their anticommunist stand and pro-Israeli sympathies meshed together.[16] In supporting Israel they were thus both responsible Americans and good Christians. The struggle to release Jewish (and other) prisoners of conscience and to allow them and others the right to emigrate created a bond between evangelicals and Jews. From their perspective, Israel stood on the right side of the cold war divide, and Jews, at this stage, were clearly anticommunists.[17]

The decades following the Six-Day War were marked by massive American support for Israel in terms of money, arms, and diplomatic backing. While many conservative Christians considered Israel to be important for the advancement of history, they also believed, as did many other Americans at that time, that American global interests necessitated support for Israel. A "powerful conjuncture of diverse interests and images," wrote Melanie McAlister, came to dominate the public discourse on Israel and America.[18]

Between the 1960s and the 1980s a number of American leaders considered Israel a junior ally, capable of providing pertinent intelligence services as well as a buffer against the Soviets and their allies in the Middle East. John Kennedy, a nonevangelical, began a policy of providing Israel with arms, looking upon it as an ally against Soviet advancement in the Middle East.[19] This policy was further expanded during Lyndon Johnson's administration. Johnson's evangelical Protestant upbringing might have influenced his attitude toward Israel.[20] However, Johnson was also very impressed by the Israeli victory in the June 1967 War.[21] Utilizing Western arms, Israel overcame the Soviet-sponsored armies of Egypt and Syria, thus humiliating the Soviets and adding to Western prestige. American policy makers were making decisions based on pragmatic considerations, but their attitudes toward Israel were also influenced, at times, by their biblical Christian upbringing and that of their voters. Peter Grose suggests that some Americans, especially conservatives, might have seen in Israel a country with a close experience to their own.[22] Perhaps surprisingly, this may have been the attitude of Richard Nixon. While few people have related to Nixon as a religious person, he grew up in an evangelical Quaker home. As a child he underwent a religious experience, which he recounted numerous times later. During his presidency he was particularly close to the evangelist Billy Graham, who acted as his confidant and advisor.[23] Nixon's attitudes toward Jews and Israel reflected contradictory feelings. He gave almost open expression to hostile stereotypical views on Jews that had been prevalent in Western culture for centuries, even in the presence of Henry Kissinger, his national security advisor and later secretary of state. At the same time, he promoted Jews (such as Kissinger) to unprecedentedly prominent positions in his administration and expressed admiration for Israel for its courageous stand against its enemies. During Nixon's presidency, America's relation with Israel had become closer than before, reflected in increased military and financial aid. In October 1973, when Egypt and Syria launched what turned out to be a successful surprise attack on Israel, Nixon authorized an emergency military supply to the struggling Israeli army. It was also during his presidency that premillennialist evangelicals became an organized voice in attempts to influence the American government to support Israel.

The years following the 1967 Middle East war saw a dramatic rise in evangelical influence in America. Growing in numbers and self-confidence, evangelicals have become more aggressive in their attempts to influence American political agendas. In 1976, when Jimmy Carter appeared on the national scene as a candidate for the presidency and was eventually elected president, many nonevangelical Americans discovered in surprise that evangelical Christianity was much larger and more influential than they had previously assumed. A progressive who represented a minority trend within contemporary evangelicalism, Carter was a disappointment to more conservative born-again Christians, since although he shared their basic tenets of faith he did not share their political and social views. Carter took much interest in the situation in the Middle East and strove to resolve the Arab-Israeli conflict. In 1978 he brought Egypt and Israel to sign a peace treaty. The role he played, however, was that of an enlightened American statesman who also wished to make global gains for America during the last stages of the cold war and a name for himself as a successful peacemaker. His declarations of piety notwithstanding, the premillennialist agenda of paving the way for the Davidic kingdom was not his concern. As a progressive evangelical, he was much more reserved in his attitude toward Israel than other evangelical statespersons, and he did not give preference to Israeli interests over and against Arab ones.[24]

While not officially an evangelical, Ronald Reagan, who replaced Carter as president in January 1981, was influenced in forming his Middle East policy by evangelical premillennialist views that he at times expressed openly.[25] In fact, one can look upon the Reagan administration as the beginning of long years of evangelical predominance in American policy making. American financial support for and diplomatic backing of Israel, which reached a zenith during Nixon's presidency, continued into the twenty-first century. While before 1967 Israel had relied on France for political backing, America became, in the later decades of the twentieth century, Israel's major friend and protector, at times the only one to openly back Israel in the international arena. Reagan's policy toward Israel was pursued by his successor, George Bush, who was also close to evangelicals and enjoyed their support. From the 1970s onward, a friendly attitude toward Israel has been part of the vision of most evangelicals for America's global policy. While other considerations too determined Reagan's and Bush's policies toward Israel, the evangelical conservative Christian demand that America should, when it did not conflict with her own interests, assist the Jewish state played an important part.[26]

Although Bill Clinton was raised an evangelical Christian and demonstrated great familiarity with the Bible, which he read and quoted frequently, his relationship with Israel has to be judged very differently from that of Reagan or Bush. Clinton was not a conservative evangelical statesman and, unlike Carter, did not emphasize his evangelical affiliation. He received almost no support from conservative evangelicals, who saw him as representing liberal values to which they were opposed. While in Arkansas, however, Clinton had remained a member of a Southern Baptist church. Upon his election as president in 1992, his pastor delivered a sermon that included the message that the newly elected president should look favorably upon Israel. This sermon tells us more about the effect of Christian biblical-messianic thinking on Baptists in Little Rock, Arkansas, than it does about Clinton's personal faith. Yet it is important to notice that the spiritual roots and cultural background of an American president who was friendly to Jews and showed deep concern for Israel were in the Bible Belt and were influenced by a biblical vision of the Land of Israel and its people. Clinton did his best to bring the Palestinians and Israelis to reach a peace agreement, and he remained committed to Israel's well-being even after leaving the White House. However, his outlook was that of a liberal Christian, and he tried to work with progressive Israeli statespersons to achieve his goals.

With the return of a Republican administration following the 2000 elections, large and influential parts of the constituency supporting the president held to a Christian evangelical understanding of history. Even more than previous administrations, the administration of George W. Bush, a committed evangelical Christian himself, was open to conservative evangelical values and agendas. Conservative evangelical pastors such as John Hagee found Bush accessible and sympathetic.[27] In addition to extending political and financial aid to Israel, the Christian Texan president seemed reluctant to initiate diplomatic moves that might have upset premillennialist supporters of Israel. Other considerations too played a role in determining Bush's policies concerning the Middle East. As Stephen Spector has pointed out, there were some developments over the years in what was, overall, a very friendly stance toward Israel, and Bush was not a puppet of pro-Israel lobbies. "It is true," Spector writes, "that there were limits to Bush's latitude in dealing with Israel. To compromise the Jewish state's security or to force the division of Jerusalem would certainly alienate much of his base."[28]

As important as the faiths and opinions of presidents have been, others too in the American government held conservative evangelical sentiments. The evangelical premillennialist understanding of Israel has influenced, at times more openly, the attitudes of a number of prominent American public figures.[29] One noted example was Jesse Helms from North Carolina, who served as a U.S. senator during the 1980s, 1990s, and early 2000s. A born-again Christian, Helms, as the powerful chair of the Senate's Foreign Affairs Committee, labored to limit American financial aid abroad but approved of the yearly financial support that the United States offered Israel. Helms's positive attitude toward Israel was not unique. In the 1970s to 2000s, dozens of pro-Israel evangelical organizations emerged in the United States and elsewhere. Wishing to muster political support for Israel, the leaders of such groups lectured in churches, distributed written or electronic material on Israel, organized pro-Israel conferences in Washington and other centers, and organized tours of study and support to the Holy Land. Evangelical Christian tourism to Israel has grown considerably since the 1970s, turning into a major component of the Israeli tourist industry. Evangelical ministers have cooperated with Israeli agencies in organizing tours to the Holy Land designed for born-again Christians.[30] While visiting the country, a number of such groups have also been engaged in evangelizing among Jews.

The years following the June 1967 War also saw an increase in the actual presence and activity of evangelical Christians in Israel. Visits of evangelicals to that country included field-study seminars and volunteer work in kibbutzim or archaeological digs, such as Project Kibbutz, organized by Oral Roberts University.[31] Evangelicals even established institutions of higher education in Israel. One of these has been the Holy Land Institute (currently Jerusalem University College), set up by Douglas Young, a premillennialist with a pro-Zionist orientation. This evangelical college centers on studies related to the history, archaeology, and languages of the Holy Land, as well as the Christian scriptures, and many of its students come to Jerusalem for a semester or a year. In addition, thousands of evangelical Christians have settled in Israel since the 1970s, turning the country into their permanent or temporary home. Motivated by a messianic faith, attracted to the land of the Bible, or engaged in missionary activities, evangelical Christians from all around the globe have built congregations in Israel. Many have joined or helped form communities of Jewish believers in Jesus.[32] Others have established "Gentile" congregations, such as the King of Kings in Jerusalem. Founded in the early 1980s by American and Canadian Pentecostals, the King of Kings is a vibrant congregation consisting of hundreds of charismatic Christians from all around the world and is one of the largest and most dynamic religious communities in the city.

Evangelical Organizations for the Support of Israel

Although evangelical groups who support Israel have appeared mainly in the United States, a number of pro-Israel organizations have also been established elsewhere, including in Israel.[33] One of the larger and better-known evangelical organizations for the support of Israel is the International Christian Embassy in Jerusalem (ICEJ). Its story tells us a great deal about the growing evangelical activity in Israel, as well as about the relationship that developed between the evangelical community around the globe and Israeli society and government.

In the 1970s, evangelical activists in Jerusalem founded the Almond Tree Branch, one of the first local evangelical groups that saw its aim in mustering support around the globe for Israel and its causes. Its members included some outstanding evangelicals in the country, among them Robert Lindsey and David Bivin, a Southern Baptist associate of Lindsey who also participated in the Jerusalem School of New Testament Studies and made his living in those years by running a Hebrew school in Jerusalem for interested Christians. Another noted member of the group was the founder of the Holy Land Institute, Douglas Young. Certain that Israel was to play a dominant role in God's plans for humanity, Young founded, in 1978, Bridges for Peace, also a pro-Israel organization headquartered in Jerusalem. He lent his support to the Almond Tree Branch (and later to the ICEJ), since he felt there was room for an organization more charismatic in style. An associate of Young, George Giakumakis, who directed the Holy Land Institute from 1978 until 1990, was also among the active participants in this group of Jerusalemite evangelicals, who met regularly for prayer, singing, and discussions. Other activists were Marvin and Merla Watson, from Canada, who composed "Davidic music" that was later performed at the ICEJ's gatherings. One of the more dynamic participants was Jan Willem van der Hoeven, a young Dutch minister who served from 1968 until 1975 as the warden of the Garden Tomb, where, according to the belief of a number of evangelical Protestants, Jesus had been buried. Lindsey and Young were busy with other enterprises, and Van der Hoeven emerged as the outstanding activist of the group. Van der Hoeven came with the idea of organizing large annual gatherings of Christian supporters of Israel in Sukkoth, the Jewish harvest festival commemorating the tent sanctuaries, or tabernacles, used during the Exodus. His theological rationale was twofold. First, according to the Bible (Zechariah 14:15), Gentiles were also commanded to gather in Jerusalem during the festival. Second, he pointed out that whereas Christians celebrated two of the "pilgrimage festivals" commanded in the Bible—Easter and Pentecost—there was no general Christian celebration of Sukkoth. Since the 1980s, thousands of evangelical communities have come to celebrate the seder, the Passover night Jewish festive celebration, adapting it somewhat to Christological theology. In 1979 the Almond Tree Branch launched its first yearly Tabernacles festival, a weeklong assembly of evangelical supporters of Israel, highlighted by a march through the streets of Jerusalem. Evangelicals laboring among the Jews have adopted other Jewish festivals and celebrations as well.

In 1980 the Israeli Knesset passed the "Jerusalem Law," which declared the whole of the city to be the capital of the state of Israel. In protest, almost all countries with embassies and consulates in Jerusalem moved their diplomatic staffs to Tel Aviv. This evacuation provided a dramatic point at which the Almond Tree activists announced the creation of the ICEJ, presenting it as an act of sympathy and support for Israel on the part of true Christians at a time when even friendly or neutral countries had betrayed her.[34] The ICEJ chose as its logo two olive branches hovering over a globe with Jerusalem at its center. "This symbolizes the great day when Zechariah's prophecy will be fulfilled, and all nations will come up to Jerusalem to keep the Feast of Tabernacles during Messiah's reign on earth," the ICEJ's leaders announced.[35] Israeli officials, including the recently appointed prime minister's liaison to the Christian evangelical community, the director of the Department for Christian Churches and Organizations of the Ministry of Foreign Affairs, and Jerusalem's Mayor Teddy Kollek, noted the propaganda value of the ICEJ's creation and welcomed the new organization. It made the point, they believed, that even though many countries had removed their embassies and consulates from Jerusalem because of Arab pressure the Western Christian world backed Israel. The ICEJ chose Johann Luckhoff, a South African who had served as pastor in the Afrikaner Dutch Reformed Church, as its administrative director. Van der Hoeven, who emerged as the group's ideologue, held the post of its spokesman until the late 1990s, when he abandoned this work. Van der Hoeven and Luckhoff, as well as other workers and participants in the activities of the ICEJ, point to the geographical scope of evangelical interest in Israel. While the United States serves as the hub of contemporary evangelicalism and evangelicals exercise a high degree of visibility and political influence in America, in recent decades large constituencies of evangelicals in other regions where evangelicals are on the rise, such as Latin America, have taken an interest in Jews and Israel.

The ICEJ's major aim has been to strengthen interest in Israel among evangelicals worldwide and to translate that goodwill into concrete agendas including extensive philanthropic programs in Israel. The organization has wished to represent Christianity worldwide and has made great efforts to open branches and gain supporters in as many countries as possible. In the United States, its centers of activity are mainly situated in southern states. In Europe, representatives of the ICEJ can be found in Scandinavia, Holland, Germany, Switzerland, and the United Kingdom. There are also volunteers for the ICEJ in predominantly Catholic countries—Spain, Portugal, France, and Belgium. In recent years, representatives have also worked for the ICEJ's interests in eastern Europe and the former Soviet Union. There are representatives in Australia, New Zealand, and a number of African nations; such branches enhance the organization's international image, enabling it to claim that true Christians everywhere support Israel. The ICEJ has also received support from evangelicals in Latin American countries, and thousands of Latin Americans participate in annual tours of the Holy Land that it sponsors or initiates. There has also been an attempt to attract supporters in East Asia.

The ICEJ's international work has increasingly become electronic, although it also distributes journals, brochures, and leaflets, produces DVDs and CDs of "Davidic music," and broadcasts radio programs. Representatives also recruit pilgrims for the annual Tabernacles gatherings and collect money for the organization's philanthropic enterprises in Israel. Much of the day-to-day work of the ICEJ is devoted to this international mission and to providing welfare services among new immigrants as well as needy Israelis. Aware that many Jews are suspicious of Christian charitable enterprises, the ICEJ often distributes its parcels through Israeli agencies. It has also offered financial support for the absorption of Russian and Ethiopian Jews.[36] Along with the Holyland Fellowship of Christians and Jews, the ICEJ is among the first Christian evangelical institutions that have systematically donated money to Jewish Israeli enterprises, setting new norms in the relationship between evangelical Christians and Jews. Most evangelicals involved in the fate of the Jews, by contrast, have supported missionary agencies that aim at spreading the Christian message among Jews, although such agencies too serve as pro-Israel lobbies. By the 2000s the funds evangelicals collected for welfare projects in Israel had reached tens of millions of dollars a year, making a serious impact in the community.[37] Likewise, those evangelical agencies supported, in large sums, the building and enlarging of homes and infrastructures of Jewish settlements in the West Bank.[38] The evangelical-Israeli relationship has obviously taken new directions in the decades following the 1967 War. Timothy Weber has observed that "both sides pay a price for the alliance"; among other sacrifices, some evangelicals, such as the ICEJ people, in order to build their ties with Israel, have toned down their historical commitment to evangelize the Jews.[39]

The ICEJ has made a name for itself in Israeli society. The Feast of Tabernacles serves as a colorful focal point of the year for the ICEJ, making a visible point in the capital of Israel and beyond that evangelical Christians support Israel. The activities include tours of the country for the pilgrims, a march through Jerusalem's main streets, a "biblical meal," and a series of assemblies and exhibitions in Jerusalem. Some of the gatherings have taken place in Binyanei Ha'Uma, the largest convention hall in Jerusalem with booths exhibiting publications and feature programs and enterprises promoted by the ICEJ. The ICEJ has also organized conventions outside Israel, including the United States. To promote its cause the ICEJ has hired workers with expertise in public relations and established a small office in Washington, D.C. It has also organized the "Washington for Israel Summit," pro-Israel conferences in Washington, D.C. The Israeli embassy in Washington has gladly lent it support for the conferences. Since the late 1970s, the policy of Israel's foreign ministry has been to encourage Christian evangelicals in pro-Israel activity.

Israeli officials have met with evangelists who come on visits, have greeted groups of pilgrims and have spoken at gatherings, such as those organized by the ICEJ. Sponsors of ICEJ events in Washington have included such pro-Israel evangelical organizations as the Christians' Israel Public Action Campaign (CIPAC), established in the 1980s. One supporter of CIPAC was Senator Jesse Helms of North Carolina, with whom the ICEJ's activists established a cordial relationship. One of the participants in the 1992 ICEJ conference was the Reverend Bill Criswell of the First Baptist Church in Dallas, Texas. The prestigious evangelical minister, then eighty-three years old, had long been an ardent supporter of Israel. In addition to lectures, group discussions, and prayer meetings, the conference included a "march for Israel" in Washington and the broadcasting of movies on Israel and the ICEJ's activities there. A special session was devoted to prophetic understanding of Israel's role in history.[40]

Jan Willem van der Hoeven emerged as a major speaker in the evangelical camp on Israel and its role. The evangelical leader has shared the premillennialist vision of Israel as a transitory but necessary stepping-stone on the messianic road.[41] According to that view, Israel is a positive development in the unfolding of history, and it is therefore pertinent to protect Israel against enemies that struggle to undermine it. Identifying with right-wing Israeli policies, Van der Hoeven has repudiated Arabs who militate against Israel's existence. He and his first wife, Vidad, a Lebanese Christian, have claimed that Arabs who are "true Christian believers" support the Israeli cause.[42] Van der Hoeven has expressed at times negative sentiments toward the Muslim faith, which he sees as making claims on territory that is not its own. Allah, he has claimed, is not the Abrahamic God, which Christians and Jews share, but a pagan deity that emerged in Arabia before the rise of Islam. During the Gulf Wars, he prayed to God to "crush the power of Allah," by which he meant a defeat of the Iraqi forces.[43] The attitude of premillennialist evangelicals such as Van der Hoeven toward Islam cannot be separated from their relation to

Jews and Israel.[44] This was not necessarily the case in the early decades of the evangelical-Jewish encounter, when Muslims were not yet part of the equilibrium. Early premillennialist-evangelical best sellers, such as *Jesus Is Coming,* did not bother very much with Muslims and their role in history. One can find, in the 1960s and 1970s, mention of Arabs in the writings of premillennialist leaders such as John Walvoord, Derek Prince, Billy Graham, or Hal Lindsey.[45] However, their opinions (even if not always flattering) did not necessarily relate to Islam.

Published in 1970, Hal Lindsey's *The Late Great Planet Earth* analyzed political realities and biblical prophecies through the prism of the cold war. For Lindsey, the Soviet Union and Communist China were immediate obstacles to a peaceful world order and a future challenge to the materialization of the millennial kingdom. In his understanding, Arabs fit, not very favorably, into that larger political-messianic picture. Matters changed after the fall of the Soviet Union and the transformation of China into a country open to the Western world and friendly with America. The 1990s and 2000s created new political realities, including the Gulf Wars and terrorist acts by radical fringe Muslim groups. Some evangelical activists interpreted the new developments as indications that Arab Muslim rulers and nations would play a role in the events of the end times, mostly that of the evil northern or eastern empires destined to invade the Land of Israel.[46] While some evangelical leaders have made an effort, almost in spite of themselves, to be gracious toward Islam, others, such as Franklin Graham, have not disguised their disdain.[47] Thirty-two years after the publication of *The Late Great Planet Earth,* in the wake of September 11, 2001, Hal Lindsey wrote a book dedicated to his interpretation of Arabs and Islam.[48] This time he presented Muslims as playing a negative, but central, role in world history. If previously evangelical thinkers, such as Lindsey, had tied Israel's place in God's plans for humanity to their rejection and fear of the Soviet Union, now Islam and Muslim terrorist groups came into the picture. Thus evangelical relations to the Jews have constantly been influenced by other global considerations and by additional players on the political and theological scene.

While van der Hoeven prefers Jews to Muslims, his attitude toward the Jews has been complicated. He has dedicated his life to muster support for Israel, firmly believing that the Jews are heirs of biblical Israel, God's chosen people. However, he also has harbored feelings of frustration and disappointment, for example, over the fact that many Israelis are unwilling to support right-wing political agendas. To be accepted by the world's liberals, he complained, they were willing to compromise their historical aspirations, and in so doing they were betraying their purpose in God's plans for the end of age. In a speech delivered during the ICEJ's 1989 Tabernacles celebration, he attacked moderate and left-wing Israeli politicians, declaring that giving up the territories Israel had occupied since 1967 would mark the second time the Jews had rejected God.[49]

For him, "land for peace" is not merely a political decision aimed at enhancing the well-being of Israel. Such a decision would have disastrous implications, as it would impede the divine plan for human redemption. The Jews are not just another people who can make choices according to ever-changing political needs; they have a duty and purpose in history. For the Jews to refuse to play their role would therefore constitute an unforgivable treachery toward both God and humankind. Van der Hoeven's words convey the frustration many evangelical Christians have felt regarding the Jews' refusal to accept Jesus as a savior as well as their refusal to look upon historical developments the same way that evangelicals do. In the view of these evangelicals, a second refusal on the part of the Jews to accept Jesus, or to prepare the ground for his arrival, would mean the Jews would miss their second opportunity for redemption.

Over the years the ICEJ has become one of the more controversial Christian agencies that work in the Middle East or take an interest in its fate, with the attitudes toward the group being representative of criticism toward conservative evangelical opinions at large. Middle Eastern churches, as a rule, have no contact with the organization or with similar evangelical groups and reject their messages and activities. Middle Eastern Christianity generally holds to replacement theology, the claim

that the Christian Church is the heir of biblical Israel and that Judaism has no further purpose in God's plans for humanity. Most of these
churches have Arab constituencies and are sympathetic to the Palestinian demand for national liberation. They see the ICEJ as an institution
offering one-sided support for Israel, and as members of the Middle
East Council of Churches they have signed petitions condemning its
activities. Mainline Protestants have also not been enchanted by the
ICEJ and its agenda. Such churches are committed to political justice
worldwide, supporting movements of national liberation and expressing sympathy for the Palestinians' quest for independence from Israeli
rule. In their opinion Israel should be judged, like all other countries,
on the basis of political justice. The Middle East Council of Churches
(MECC), an institution affiliated with the World Council of Churches,
represents both mainline Protestants working in the Middle East and
Middle Eastern churches. It takes a very critical view of Israel and has
officially opposed the ICEJ's Christian Zionist agenda.[50] In its May 1998
meeting in Cyprus it denounced Christian supporters of Zionism and
declared, "The consultation was referring here especially to the western
fundamentalist Christian Zionist movement and its political activities
conducted through the self-declared International Christian Embassy in
Jerusalem."[51] Evidently the very name "International Christian Embassy,"
aroused anger among members of the MECC.[52]

Although the ICEJ claims to represent all true Christians and is often
regarded as the representative of evangelical supporters of Israel, not all
evangelicals identify with its methods. Some object to its willingness to
refrain from missionizing Jews as a condition for establishing a close
relationship with the Israeli government. *Mishkan,* an English-language
magazine associated with Christian evangelizing groups, dedicated a
special issue to criticizing the nonmissionary policy of the ICEJ.[53] This
policy obviously has touched a nerve among many evangelicals who,
while supporting Israel, have remained firmly committed to evangelizing the Jews. For most pro-Israel evangelical organizations, mustering
political support for Israel has not taken precedence over spreading the
Gospel among the Jews.

Israelis and Evangelicals

How did Israelis react to the unexpected overtures of evangelical supporters? Israeli officials, one must conclude, could not always grasp
the roots and motivations of "Christian Zionists" or tell the difference
between mainline supporters and conservative evangelical ones.[54] Certainly they were unaware of the details of the Christian eschatological
hopes and had never heard of the Great Tribulation, Antichrist, or the
time of Jacob's trouble. In the early years of the state, Israeli officials
took only marginal notice of evangelical Christianity, concentrating
instead on their relationships with the Catholic Church, Orthodox and
Middle Eastern Christianity, and mainline Protestantism.[55] Israeli leaders did notice the existence of groups and individuals who supported
Israel on account of their Christian biblical faith, but they could not
make sense of their beliefs and motivations. A noted exception was Yona
Malachy, who served during the late 1960s to early 1970s at the Ministry of Religious Affairs.[56] David Ben-Gurion, Israel's first prime minister, is a case in point. He believed that Christian supporters viewed the
establishment of the state of Israel as the ultimate fulfillment of biblical
prophecies, the reestablishment of the Davidic kingdom, rather than
as a step toward the realization of the millennial kingdom headed by
Jesus. He gave expression to his views in 1961 in an address delivered in
an international Pentecostal conference, which convened in Jerusalem.
The Israeli officials who sat at the opening session were puzzled by the
coolness of the evangelical Pentecostal reaction.[57] Like Ben-Gurion, they
were not aware that messianic hopes encouraged not only support for
Israel but also aggressive missionary activity among Jews. When Oral
Roberts visited Israel in 1959, he met with Ben-Gurion.[58] The Israeli
leader demonstrated a knowledge of the nature of Roberts's activity as an
evangelist, but he might well have been unaware of Roberts's missionary
work among the Jews. Israeli leaders often chose to remain ignorant on
that subject, minimizing its importance. Trying to build good relations
with Christian groups, the Israeli government considered it essential to
assure them that the Israeli state would not interfere with their work.[59]

Orthodox Jewish activists protested against the missionaries' work in Israel, and some Jews occasionally attempted to harass missionaries, but the government refused to change its policy, and the police were given the task of protecting missionary centers.[60]

In the late 1970s, as the evangelical influence on American political life became more apparent, the Israeli government took more notice of this segment of American society and took measures to establish contact with it.[61] Among other things, Menachem Begin appointed Harry Horowitz as a special liaison with evangelical Christians. Israeli officials began receiving invitations to speak at evangelical conferences, and leading American evangelists met with Israeli leaders as part of their touring schedules in Israel. Likewise, Israeli leaders began approaching such evangelists directly, requesting support. In 1980, for example, Prime Minister Begin bestowed on Jerry Falwell, leader of the Moral Majority and founder of the conservative evangelical Liberty University, the Jabotinsky Prize as a reward for his pro-Israel stand. Israeli governments continued to nourish a cordial relationship with evangelical leaders and groups, although it seems that there is greater understanding when the more right-wing Likud Party is in power. Evangelical leaders and groups such as the ICEJ have received special privileges and prizes, such as permission to hold gatherings in the courtyard of the Knesset, the Israeli parliament, as part of its Tabernacles celebrations, or the presentation by the speaker of the Knesset of the Israeli Quality of Life Award.[62]

Ironically, many of the Israeli friends of groups such as the ICEJ are in the nationalist-religious wing of Jewish society. In July 1991 the liberal Jerusalem weekly *Kol HaIr* published an article claiming that the ICEJ was conducting welfare activities and distributing money to needy new immigrants in the offices of the Likud and Moledet (a small and now defunct right-wing nationalist party).[63] In 1988 the magazine *Nekuda*, an organ of the Jewish settlements in Judea and Samaria, published a favorable article on the ICEJ entitled "Without Inhibitions: Christians Committed to Judea and Samaria." Emphasizing that the group had no missionary intentions, it described them as pro-Israel Christians who realized that the Bible authorized the Jews to settle their land.[64]

Ironically too, one of the earliest acts of legislation by Menachem Begin's government was intended to restrict missionary activity by outlawing "the buying of converts" through economic incentives. However, Begin's coalition tried to halt the evangelization of Jews in Israel without realizing that this activity was carried out by the same elements in Christianity with whom it was trying to establish a particularly friendly relationship. The legislative initiative reflected the long-standing resentment that Orthodox and other Jews felt toward missionary activity in the country, but in the end it proved ineffective. Evangelicals were relieved when they saw the wording of the law, since it clearly did not restrict the sort of work they did. Contrary to Jewish myths, missionaries were not "buying" converts, and at any rate the Israeli government was reluctant to enforce the law.

In the mid-1990s antimissionary sentiments were again running high, and a number of Orthodox and non-Orthodox members of the Knesset came out with initiatives to outlaw missionary activity.[65] In 1996, an initial, first-round proposal passed the Knesset vote. But then the paradoxical nature of the relationship between the evangelical community and Israeli society became unprecedentedly clear. Evangelical activists operating in Israel, including Messianic Jews, called upon their evangelical supporters to raise their voices against the impeding law. "We call upon the international Christian community to join us in our opposition to this law," read one of the appeals. "As Christian believers in the God of Israel and in Jesus the Messiah and Savior of the world, we have a special respect and appreciation for the Jewish people and the nation of Israel. We seek and pray for the welfare of all of God's people in the land. We view with grave concern the erosion of Israel's democratic freedom by this proposed law."[66] Israeli embassies and consulates in America and other countries with substantial evangelical populations were virtually flooded with letters of protest against the law, and many wrote directly to the prime minister in Jerusalem.[67] Prime Minister Benjamin Netanyahu, who at first offhandedly supported the bill, changed his mind and promised evangelical activists he would oppose it. Other non-Orthodox supporters of the bill, such as Nisim Zwili, a member of the Knesset from the Labor Party, also withdrew their support of the proposed law. As a means of backing out of the law yet saving face, the government's opposition to the proposed law came in exchange for a promise by Christian groups not to evangelize. This pro forma agreement had a catch to it. The Christian groups that promised not to evangelize Jews were not engaged in such activity anyway, and those who made it their goal to missionize Jews made no promises to stop their activity.[68]

The rise and fall of the antimissionary laws reflected a number of paradoxes. Orthodox segments of the Israeli population promoted antimissionary laws, but Orthodox Israeli Jews, namely the settlers' circles, had come to rely on evangelical support, and some of them had established close ties with evangelical organizations. Similarly, the rise and fall of the proposed laws revealed, more than before, that evangelical support for Israel and the special relationship that had developed between Israel and evangelical leaders and organizations blocked any action Israel might have taken against the evangelical missionary presence. It ultimately highlighted the complexity of the relation of evangelical Christians with Jews: the evangelization of a people they see as chosen and whose country they strongly support. Likewise, it pointed to the awkward position of the Israeli leadership. Their choices of friends in the Christian world have been limited.[69] Whatever friends they had made among liberal Christians from the 1940s through the 1960, they largely lost during the 1970s and 1980s. The friendship evangelicals offered and their devotion to Israel fell on the Israeli government like manna from heaven, and they began to cultivate this friendship, even if they did not fully comprehend its theological reasoning and the scope of their newly found friends' activities.

In sum, many evangelical thinkers have been encouraged by the birth of Israel, its absorption of immigrants, and its surprising victory in the June 1967 War. They saw them as "signs of the time," indications that they had read the Scriptures correctly and that history was proceeding according to plan. Especially after the 1967 War, evangelicals went out of their way to support Israeli and Jewish causes. Establishing pro-Israel groups, or adding a strong pro-Israeli component to established missions, evangelicals became the backbone of pro-Israel lobbies in America and at times in other countries around the globe, while Arab and liberal Christian groups often considered Israeli policies and their evangelical support to be misguided.

At the same time, evangelical feelings toward the Israelis have been varied and complex. Since the 1970s, evangelicals have warmed up to Israelis and Jews in general as never before, but they have never been fully happy with Israeli values and self-perceptions. They have become more attached to Israel and have come to love the country. But they have also criticized the secular nature of Israeli culture, especially that of the political and cultural elites, and they have wished to educate the Israelis as to their true purpose in history. The reaction of Israelis to evangelicals has also been varied, although often uninformed. Israelis were glad to discover unexpected, yet devoted, Christian friends and came to welcome evangelical support, although they were at times unhappy about the missionary presence. However, the encounter between Jews and evangelicals would give birth to movements and cultural developments that neither Jews nor evangelicals could have even foreseen.

11

Evangelical Christians and the Building of the Temple

In August of 1969, a young evangelical Christian, Dennis Michael Rohan, set fire to the al-Aqsa mosque on the Temple Mount. A member of the Church of God, Rohan was motivated by a desire to bring about the messianic age and thought that clearing the ground for the building of the Temple would set the apocalyptic clock going.[1] Rohan was diagnosed as insane and sent back to Australia, and many at the time chose to believe that the burning of the mosque was an act of one unstable individual. Since the 1970s, however, a number of evangelical and Jewish groups have striven to rebuild the Temple, and some have even begun preparations for the reenactment of the Temple's ancient rituals. Their cooperation has marked a new chapter in Jewish-Christian relations, with unprecedented alliances and new visions on the part of Jews and evangelical Christians for the messianic times. Rohan's fire-setting highlighted the explosive potential of Christian and Jewish messianic hopes. Of special concern for officials, as well as those hoping for peace, in Israel and other countries has been the possibility that Jews or Christians holding such beliefs might bring about the destruction of the mosques on the Temple Mount and consequently a regional doomsday. To appreciate the passion with which many Orthodox Jews and evangelical Christians have wished to rebuild the Temple, one has to examine the role of the Temple in Jewish and Christian thought.

The Meaning of the Temple

The Temple in Jerusalem was a central institution in Israelite religion, as well as in Judaism of the Second Temple period. Kings 1 and 2 and a series of prophetic books in the Hebrew Bible reflect a struggle on the part of the Judean elite to turn the Temple in Jerusalem into the one and only spiritual center in Judea.[2] The destruction of the Temple corresponded with the collapse of Judea and the exile of Judeans to Babylon in the beginning of the sixth century BCE. When Cyrus allowed Jews to return to Judea and rehabilitate their ancestral homeland, they rebuilt a temple on Mount Moriah in Jerusalem as a matter of course. Herod the Great further enlarged the Temple, reconstructing the Temple Mount. For the Israelites and their Jewish descendants, the Temple served as the ultimate spiritual point on earth, the place where heaven and earth met. The Temple guaranteed that the Jews were reconciled with their God and therefore assured their moral and spiritual good standing. Pilgrimages to the Temple were considered essential rites, signifying piety and loyalty to the one God "in the place where He had chosen to dwell." During the Second Temple period, the Temple developed into a unifying symbol for a growingly diverse Jewish community in Palestine as well as all around the Mediterranean and Middle Eastern world. The destruction of the Temple in 70 CE created therefore a serious vacuum in Jewish communal and spiritual life, and Judaism had to start a process of adjusting itself to a life without a center.

Instead of a temple, rabbinical Judaism put its premium on sacred texts, turning Jews into "the People of the Book." Instead of a physical temple, Judaism promoted a "temple in time," making the weekly Sabbath a holy day, similar in sanctity to a holy place.[3] Jews purified themselves in honor of the Sabbath and entered the holy day in the same manner they would enter a holy space, cleaning their bodies, wearing special Sabbath clothes, and preparing festive meals. They would light candles and recite special prayers to differentiate between the sacred and the profane and would act as people do in a holy place, concentrating on spiritual activities and thoughts. Synagogues came about during the Second Temple period and developed, after the Temple's destruction, into houses of worship and learning where Jews prayed and read sacred texts. Ironically, while previously there had been competitors to the national spiritual center in Jerusalem, after the Temple's destruction it became the one and only temple to be resurrected in the fullness of time.[4] Even long generations after its destruction, Jews continued to pray to God to gather them back to Zion, rebuild Jerusalem, and recreate the Temple so as to enable them to fully atone for their sins.[5]

Though the Temple was gone, rabbis spent much time discussing issues relating to the Temple, its measures and sizes, its sacrificial system, and the alms and donations presented to it. Most rabbinical authorities throughout the Middle Ages and the Modern Era have considered the Temple Mount to be as sacred as it was when the Temple was standing. The Mishnah, the postbiblical compilation of lore and law, outlined the various degrees of sanctity of areas on the Temple Mount and the rituals of purification people needed to perform in order to enter these areas.[6] All Jews have been required to purify themselves with the ashes of a red heifer before they step on the Mount, although there are no longer red heifers to be found. Rabbis have also feared that Jews might step on restricted sacred ground, such as the Holy of Holies, which ordinary Jews, and even ordinary priests, were not allowed to enter. Most Jews have accepted the rabbinical ban, although Jews have not had much to say about the manner in which the Temple Mount was governed. During Roman times Jerusalem became a pagan city, and with the Christianization of the Roman Empire, a Christian one. Following the Arab conquest of Palestine in the seventh century CE, the new rulers of the city turned the mountain into a sacred Muslim site, building a number of mosques and chapels. While at the end of the eleventh century the Crusaders conquered Jerusalem and converted the mosques into Christian buildings, by the thirteenth century the mountain became Muslim again, and it has remained that way ever since.

In June 1967, Israel conquered East Jerusalem, including the Temple Mount. Many Israelis understood the outcome of the war in secular messianic terms as validating Israel's righteousness and the Zionist dream of creating a permanent commonwealth for the Jews. Their label "the Six-Day War" echoed the six days of creation mentioned in Genesis.[7] But most of them did not wish to rebuild the Temple.[8] Judaism had moved a long way since the destruction of the Temple in 70 CE, and Jews had come to see the building of the Temple as irrelevant or postponed to a remote theoretical future. The Israeli minister of defense at the time, Moshe Dayan, designed a policy that insisted on maintaining the *status quo antebellum* on the Temple Mount as well as in other Muslim and Christian holy sites and offered in essence autonomy to Muslims and Christians in handling their holy places.[9] In line with traditional Jewish rabbinical law, a number of prestigious rabbis, including the chief rabbis of that time, Itzhak Nissim and Issar Unterman, declared that Jews were forbidden to enter the Temple Mount.[10] In 1967, voices such as that of Shlomo Goren, chief rabbi of the Israeli army, who wished to establish a synagogue on the Temple Mount, were in the minority. When Rohan burned the al-Aqsa mosque in the summer of 1969, no Jewish group endorsed his act or declared it to be in line with its agenda or with that of the almighty. Rohan's trial records reflect a general bewilderment as to the motivation for the crime he had committed.[11] The mood in Israel changed after the Yom Kippur War of 1973, when small groups of Jews and Christians in Jerusalem organized to promote the rebuilding of the Temple. Paradoxically, external threats to Israel's territorial gains, whether through war or peace negotiations, have inspired Jewish religious nationalists to take a proactive stand, both in their settlement of occupied territories and their determination to see the Temple rebuilt.[12]

While the War of June 1967 created an unprecedented united front in Israeli public life and strengthened the government's authority, this was hardly the case after the Yom Kippur War of October 1973. The Labour leadership weakened considerably, and the reputation of Moshe Dayan diminished almost completely. Ironically, it was in the aftermath of the Yom Kippur War that the messianic excitement that followed the Six-Day War came to the surface.[13] Thousands of young people, mostly modern Orthodox, veterans of religious Zionist youth movements, and disciples of Rabbi Zvi Yehuda Kook, who became the ideological leader of the Greater Land of Israel movement, decided to settle in Judea and Samaria, formerly the West Bank of Jordan.[14] The Orthodox Zionist camp, previously a junior and peaceful part of Israeli society, became increasingly radical. The settlers of the West Bank and the Temple builders are not necessarily identical, as not all settlers have been interested in the building of the Temple and many of the Jewish Temple builders are not settlers. But the Temple builders' movement shares a great deal theologically, ideologically, and communally with the settlers' movement.[15] Since the 1980s, both movements have been part of Israel's Radical Right,[16] and some of the most volatile groups of Temple builders have come from the settlers' circles.[17]

The new groups of Temple builders reinterpreted Jewish texts, concluding that the rabbinical ban on entering the Temple Mount was erroneous and rejecting the traditional understanding that the building of the Temple should be left for the Messiah to accomplish in the fullness of time.[18] The first visible group of Temple builders, which attracted much media attention, was the Temple Mount Faithful. Led by Gershon Solomon, a disabled Israel Defense Forces veteran and a lawyer, the Temple Mount Faithful gave voice, at its inception, to a large variety of Jews interested in the building of the Temple. Among them were Orthodox and secular Jews, Labour supporters and right-wingers. This small but ideologically broad coalition could not stick together for very long, and, far from the eyes of the cameras, other groups began congregating separately, studying texts, and publishing newsletters.[19] Some of these groups were preparing for the reinstatement of the sacrificial system in a rebuilt Temple.[20]

Settlers in the West Bank were one group that turned their backs on the Temple Mount Faithful and went their own way. Some of them created an underground and planned to bomb the Temple Mount mosques, and they did not lose interest in rebuilding the Temple even after their release from prison. In the 1980s, Rabbi Joel Bin Nun, a leader of the now defunct Gush Emunim (the West Bank settlers' major organization in the 1970s), established an institute for the halachic study of the building of the Temple. In a series of publications he pointed to what he considered to be the merits of the Temple and the sacrifices there, which he believed would help reconcile God and humanity and would therefore help bring about a messianic age.[21] Other groups that formed since the 1980s, mostly in Jerusalem, have included Jerusalem First

(Reshit-Yerushalaiim), an academy for studying Jerusalem and the Temple; the Movement for the Building of the Temple (Ha Tnuaa Lekinun ha Mikdash); The Temple-Study Yeshivah (Yeshivat Torat HaByit); Unto the Mountain of the Lord (El Har Adonai); the Movement for the Liberation of the Temple Mount (Ha Tnuaa LeShihrur Har HaBayit); and the Priest's Crown Yeshivah (Yeshivat Ateret Cohanim), to name just a few.[22]

Evangelical Messianic Hopes and the Rebuilding of the Temple

The Jewish movements that have striven to build the Temple would not have acted as they did if it were not for evangelical Christians providing encouragement and assistance. Christian thinkers had traditionally seen the Temple as redundant after Jesus's sacrifice on the cross and had claimed that Jesus, the ultimate sacrifice, had atoned for humanity's sins. One did not need temple sacrifices anymore, only the mystical body of Christ. Christians often interpreted the destruction of the Temple in 70 CE as resulting from Jewish unwillingness to acknowledge Jesus's role and mission.[23] The idea that the Jews should go back to Palestine and rebuild Jerusalem and the Temple became predominant mostly among Christian messianic groups that operated outside the Christian mainstream.[24] Only with the spread of premillennialism among evangelical Protestants in the nineteenth century did Christians become interested in the prospect of the Jews building the Temple.

In dispensationalist thought, the rebuilding of the Temple became part of the events that would take place between the end of the current era and the actual coming of the Messiah to earth, with Antichrist, the Messiah's impostor, initiating it. After the Israeli conquest of East Jerusalem, premillennialist evangelicals began speculating about and anticipating the Jewish building of the Temple. After the June 1967 War, it seemed to evangelicals waiting for the imminent arrival of the Messiah that Israel held the territory on which the Temple could be rebuilt and the priestly sacrificial rituals reinstated.[25] The Temple, or rather its rebuilding, seemed to be the one event standing between this era and the next. A striking demonstration of the growing prominence of the

Temple in Christian messianic thought can be found in Hal Lindsey's *The Late Great Planet Earth,* the evangelical best seller of the time. Lindsey, like other premillennialist evangelicals, was strongly impressed by the June 1967 War and its consequences and placed Israel at the center of the eschatological drama.[26] For him, the rebuilding of the Temple and the rise of Antichrist to power were major components of the Great Tribulation, without which the coming of the Messiah could not take place. There remained, however, obstacles to this stage in the advancement of the prophetic timetable. In addition to an insufficient interest in building the Temple among the Jews, there were the Muslim mosques on the Temple Mount. While not following the example of Rohan, a number of Christian premillennialist organizations, groups, and individuals from the 1970s onward have openly promoted the building of the Temple through a variety of activities, most of them centered on helping Jews prepare for the building of the holy shrine.

Jews and Christians in Cooperation

In the late 1970s and 1980s, premillennialist evangelicals discovered groups of nationalist and Orthodox Jews who were advocating the building of the Temple and some who were even studying the Temple rituals or the manufacturing of utensils to be used for sacrificial purposes according to biblical or Talmudic measures. Christian premillennialists marveled at such groups and their activities, viewing them as "signs of the time," indications that the current era was ending and that the apocalyptic events of the end times were drawing near.[27] The Temple Institute, a museum and workshop in the Old City of Jerusalem that has housed utensils and artifacts that a group of Jewish advocates of the building of the Temple have reconstructed, has become since the 1980s a site of pilgrimage for evangelical believers in the second coming of Jesus. Evangelical tourists have been encouraged by the sight of Jews preparing implements for use in the Temple, and the visits have served to enhance the faith in the belief that the rapture of the church will take place very soon.[28] Some evangelicals have set out to assist Jewish groups in their attempts to prepare for the building and operation of the Temple. The relationship between Christian evangelicals and Jewish groups over the prospect of rebuilding the Temple began as a marriage of convenience, although the two parties have gradually warmed up to each other. Christian supporters have perceived the Jewish groups as instrumental to the realization of the messianic age, since in their vision the rebuilt Temple is a necessary stage toward that goal. Similarly, Jewish proponents of the building of the Temple have not appreciated the Christian messianic faith, but they have seen such details as being beside the point. The important thing for them has been the Christian willingness to support their work. Throughout the decades both groups have come to trust and appreciate the other party and modify their views of each other.

The first to establish contacts between Christians and Jews interested in the building of the Temple was Stanley Goldfoot. Born in South Africa, Goldfoot immigrated to Palestine in the 1930s and during the 1940s became a member of Lechi, or, as the British called it, the Stern Gang, a radical Jewish underground organization that used terrorism to force the British out of the country. He served as the group's speaker and liaison to the foreign press. A secular Jew with artistic inclinations, Goldfoot advocated a right-wing outlook on Israeli politics in an English-language satirical magazine that he published in Tel Aviv in the 1960s and 1970s. After retiring, Goldfoot relocated to Jerusalem and established the Temple Foundation, operated from his handsome Jerusalem home, and became, in the 1970s and 1980s, the Israeli contact person for evangelical Christians advocating the rebuilding of the Temple.[29] According to one source, Goldfoot established the relations that became vital from the 1990s onward between the Temple Mount Faithful and its Christian supporters.[30] In the early 1980s, Chuck Smith, a noted minister and evangelist whose Calvary Chapel in Costa Mesa, California, has been one of the largest and most dynamic charismatic churches in America, invited Goldfoot to come to California to lecture in his church.

Smith secured financial support for the exploration of the exact site of the Temple, and Lambert Dolphin, a California physicist and archaeologist, took it upon himself to explore the Mount.[31] An ardent premillennialist who believed that the building of the Temple was essential to the realization of messianic hopes, Dolphin came to Jerusalem prepared to use technological devices and methods, such as wall-penetrating radar and seismic sounding, in his search for the ruins of the previous temples. However, his attempts to search the Temple Mount for conclusive evidence regarding the Temple's exact location was frustrated by the Israeli police, who, confronted by Muslim protests, refused to allow the use of such devices on or under the Mount.[32] Most Christians and Jews aspiring to build the Temple, such as Oz Hawkins, have not waited for conclusive findings by Dolphin on its exact location. Relying on the work of an Israeli architect, Hawkins and others have embraced the theory that the former location of the Temple was between the two major mosques, al-Aqsa and the Dome of the Rock. The Temple, they concluded, could therefore be rebuilt without destroying the existing mosques, thus providing a "peaceful solution" to the problem of how to build the Temple at a site that is holy to Muslims.[33]

Christian proponents of building the Temple have not limited their efforts to discovering the exact site of the Temple. Some have searched for the lost Ark of the Covenant, adding a touch of adventure and mystery to a potentially explosive topic. The search for the "Lost Ark" has inspired a number of novels and a movie based in part on a real-life figure.[34] Some premillennialist evangelicals have also searched for the ashes of a red heifer, which are necessary, according to the Jewish law, in order to allow Jews to enter the Temple Mount, while others have supported Jewish attempts at breeding red heifers or have begun breeding such heifers on their own.[35] Christian evangelicals have taken a new interest in the Temple building and its interior plan, as well as in the priestly garments and utensils. Since the 1970s, a number of books on these subjects have enjoyed popularity in evangelical premillennialist circles.[36] The rebuilt Temple has also played an important role in evangelical novels. The Left Behind series demonstrates the importance of the building of the Temple as part of the events that precede the arrival of the Messiah,[37] and it describes one of Antichrist's "achievements" as the orchestration of the removal of the Temple Mount mosques to New Babylon.[38]

In the early 1990s, Pat Robertson, the renowned leader of the 700 Club and a onetime presidential hopeful, offered his hospitality to Solomon, leader of the Temple Mount faithful. In August 1991, the 700 Club aired an interview with Solomon. Robertson described Solomon's group as struggling to rightfully regain the Temple. "We will never have peace," Robertson declared, "until the Mount of the House of the Lord is restored."[39] Solomon, for his part, described his mission as embodying the promise for a universal redemption. "It's not just a struggle for the Temple Mount, it's a struggle for the . . . redemption of the world," he declared.[40] Such convergence between evangelical Christians and Orthodox Jews shows each side to be affected by the other. Since encountering charismatic Christians, Solomon, for example, claims to have had divine revelations not unlike those among evangelical charismatic Christians.

The close relationship between evangelicals and Jewish proponents of the Temple building has brought some Christians to modify their understanding of the role of the Temple in their vision of the end times. Initially, the building of the Jewish Temple during the Great Tribulation was stated to be merely a necessary stage on the road toward the messianic kingdom. But as Jewish activists working toward the rebuilding of the Temple learned the details of the Christian eschatological scheme, they objected to their dubious role in the service of Antichrist. Christian writers and theologians such as Randall Price have reassured them that premillennialist evangelicals expect the Temple to survive the rule of Antichrist and to function gloriously in the millennial kingdom and not only in the period that precedes it.[41] Likewise, in the Left Behind series, Antichrist is no longer Jewish.

Jewish builders of the Temple have also changed their opinion on evangelical Christians, although probably not on Christianity and its attitudes toward Judaism. These Jews have been impressed by the Christian interest and support and have noticed that some evangelical Christians are more enthusiastic about the prospect of building the Temple than most Jews, just as they support right-wing Israeli policies. The theological message of people such as Gershon Solomon has become increasingly universalist and has come to include Christians as important participants in the divine drama of salvation. Solomon has begun to put a greater premium on the Jewish idea of the Noahide Covenant. According to that idea, since the days of Noah all of humanity has been in covenant with God and has been commanded to follow elementary laws, such as "Thou shall not kill." Now such Jewish activists claim that Christians too should strive to advance the messianic times.[42] Amazingly but tellingly, in the early twenty-first century, the website of the Temple Mount Faithful is entirely in English, as are all the group's publications.[43] Their readership is composed mainly of English-speaking Christians and Jews. The group has also modified its name to signal its adherence to the idea of regaining "the complete Land of Israel." It now calls itself the Temple Mount and Eretz Yisrael Faithful.

The Building of the Temple: Christians, Jews, and Palestinian Muslims

Hopes for rebuilding the Temple have meshed with conservative evangelical Christian views on Islam. Unlike their liberal Christian counterparts, who have made, in recent years, a special effort to enter a dialogue with Muslims, many conservative evangelicals perceive Islam as a hostile faith.[44] When the Soviet Union went through a process of liberalization in the late 1980s, providing new freedoms for the churches, some evangelical premillennialists began to question their old belief that Russia was the Northern Evil Empire. During the Gulf War crisis, in the early 1990s, some, including Lambert Dolphin, suggested that perhaps Saddam Hussein's Iraq was meant to fulfill that role.[45] Similar views were voiced in the 2000s about Osama bin Laden and Al Qaeda.

The Temple Mount mosques have symbolized for some evangelicals an idolatrous domination of the sacred site on which the Temple should be rebuilt. While Christian proponents of the rebuilding of the Temple have not, as a rule, tried to pray on the Temple Mount, they have sympathized with Jews who have attempted to do so. When, in the mid-1980s, the Israeli police arrested members of the Temple Mount Faithful for trying to enter the Temple Mount and organize a prayer meeting there, evangelical supporters formed a "Committee of Concerned Evangelicals for the Freedom of Worship on the Temple Mount." They publicized their demands in leading American and Israeli newspapers and asked members of Congress to intercede on behalf of the right of Jews to pray on the Temple Mount.[46]

In assessing the dangers and tensions embodied in the struggle for the Temple Mount, one must take into consideration not only the messianic fervor of Jews and Christians but the determination of the local Muslim community and the support of Muslims worldwide. In addition to the collaboration that developed between premillennialists and Jews wishing to see the Temple rebuilt, an adversarial relation developed between Muslims and the Jewish and Christian would-be Temple builders, with the latter stirring strong negative reactions among the former.[47] The unhidden agenda of some Jewish and Christian groups who wish to change the status quo on the Temple Mount has helped make the Haram al-Sharif a symbol of national liberation for Palestinian Muslims. The Mount and its mosques were sacred to Muslims, especially in Palestine, even before the new fascination that Jews and Christians have developed toward it. In Jerusalem, for example, Muslims announced their completion of a hajj to Mecca by painting pictures of the Temple Mount mosques on the entrances to their homes. Sovereignty over the Mount played a prominent part in the peace talks that took place between Palestinians and Israelis in the late 1990s and caused a breakdown of the negotiations. The visit of Ariel Sharon to the Temple Mount in September 2000 was understood as a symbolic act of intrusion that stirred Palestinians to start the Second Intifada. As far as they are concerned, the Temple Mount is a Muslim site and they have no wish to share it.[48]

Muslim fears have some foundation. Rohan's attempt to burn the Al-Aqsa mosque has been largely forgotten, as most media and public attention has turned to new Christian and Jewish radical groups. In the mid-1980s, the Israeli security services uncovered what soon became known as the Jewish Underground (Ha Mahteret ha Yehudit). The group consisted of religious nationalist settlers, disciples of Rabbi Zvi Yehuda Kook, who were stocking illegal weapons and explosives. The group's main agenda was to prepare a settlers' army for the event of an Israeli withdrawal from the West Bank or the Golan Heights. Members of the group were involved in acts of sabotage, and a number of them were planning to blow up the Temple Mount mosques. The discovery of the group, whose members included leaders in the settlers' community, sent shock waves through the Israeli public, and members of the group were put on trial and sent to prison. And despite right-wingers' disapproval of the government's policy of "land for peace," no Jewish underground group of such size has organized in Israel since. The discovery of the Jewish Underground stoked fears that a small but determined group of political extremists would succeed in blowing up the mosques. Unlike Michael Rohan, members of the group had army training, including, for some, training in handling explosives. Protecting the Temple Mount mosques became a priority for Israeli security services.[49]

A number of other incidents have also demonstrated, since the 1980s, the dangers that Christian or Jewish groups might bring to the region by trying to destroy the Temple Mount mosques. In 1984, the Israeli police arrested another group that had planned to bomb the mosques on the Temple Mount, storing explosives and ammunition for that purpose. The group came to be known as the Lifta Gang, a name it received from its residence in a semiabandoned Arab village on the western outskirts of Jerusalem. Israeli newspapers described a curious commune that held to a mixture of Jewish and Christian messianic faiths. According to one source, the group was associated with and received assistance from premillennialist Christians in America.[50] The Lifta Gang was just as dangerous as the Jewish settlers who had planned at about the same time to blow up the mosques. Its weapon stockpile included American-made LAW (light antitank weapon) shoulder-held missiles as well as a large amount of TNT. In the case of the Lifta Gang, individuals' messianic hopes came together with little regard for accepted social or legal restraints, because of either psychopathologies or criminal or quasi-revolutionary tendencies. One could not help wondering what would have happened if the group had not been stopped before carrying out its plans. The Lifta Group's potential for destruction notwithstanding, its existence was completely overshadowed by the discovery of the Jewish settlers' underground groups that had similar plans. As far as the public was concerned, it was a marginal group politically, socially, and religiously and was soon forgotten.

Even symbolic attempts to claim the Temple Mount as a Jewish or Jewish and Christian site have had explosive consequences. The Temple Mount Faithful have made it their habit to try to enter the Temple Mount on Jewish festivals in order to conduct prayers. On Sukkoth, the Feast of the Tabernacles, in October 1990, the Temple Mount Faithful planned to enter the Temple Mount and this time prepared to lay an alleged cornerstone for the future Temple. The police did not allow them to enter the Mount and they left the place. But Muslims on the Mount felt threatened and threw rocks at Jewish worshippers at the Wailing Wall, down below the western wall of the Temple Mount. The atmosphere became volatile as Muslim demonstrators chased the small police unit off the mountain, and Israeli antiriot police stormed the area a short while later. Dozens of demonstrators and police officers were killed or wounded.[51]

The possibility that Christian and Jewish messianic hopes would bring about a miniapocalypse gained momentum in the late 1990s. As the year 2000 approached, journalists, scholars, and government officials became preoccupied with the dangers that this symbolic year might bring, and the approaching turn of the millennium stirred the messianic imagination. Many looked upon Y2K, a predicted global computer breakdown, as a potential catalyst of the apocalypse. Of special concern for those taking interest in the developments in the Middle East was the fate of the Temple Mount mosques. Should the mosques be bombed or seriously damaged, all hell might break loose. This time the Israeli public and media targeted evangelical protagonists of the Second Coming as potential troublemakers and forgot, for a moment, that Jews could come up with similar schemes.[52] For a while Israelis as well as Americans showed unprecedented interest in the details of the evangelical messianic scheme. Terms such as "the Rapture" and "the Great Tribulation," previously unknown outside evangelical circles, became in 1999 almost household words. In April 1999, Israeli security rounded up members of a messianic group called Concerned Christians that had come to Jerusalem to take part in the events of the end times and, according to official Israeli reports, to commit mass suicide, or perhaps to damage the mosques, on the Temple Mount. Members of the group were consequently deported. Toward the latter months of 1999, Israeli fears that premillennialist evangelicals might try to blow up the mosques bordered on hysteria. Israeli security forces arrested and deported dozens of evangelical Christians, most of them harmless persons, who had made Jerusalem their home in hopes of witnessing the Second Coming of Jesus.[53] Likewise, the Israeli government refused entrance to the country to "suspicious" Christians. Israelis believed that messianically oriented Christians might bring about a catastrophic event at the Temple Mount, and their fears in this respect concentrated on Christians instead of Jews.

From the 1990s onward, the peace negotiations between the Israelis and the Palestinians, including the Oslo peace agreement and the pullout from Gaza, have caused alarm among Jewish settlers as well as among some premillennialist Christians.[54] For most Christians and Jews expecting the messianic age, hopes for the rebuilding of the Temple have remained as strong as before.[55] However, one cannot tell what would happen if Israel gave up its official control of the Temple Mount. Some fear that such a prospect might stir a handful of Jews and Christians to take drastic steps in an effort to "secure" the Jewish (and indirectly Christian) control of the mountain.

The possibility that some evangelical Christians and Jews would try to destroy the old Muslim mosques in order to prepare the ground for the messianic age has stirred concern among observers of the developments in Jerusalem. Granted, most Christian and Jews committed to the idea of building the Temple are law-abiding and would not support terrorist acts. Fears that nationalist Jews or evangelical premillennialists would become involved in a plot to bomb the mosques relate to the extreme margins of the movements, but such concerns are only too real. And Christians and Jews are not the only ones making claims to the mountain. Muslims have turned the Haram al-Sharif into a symbol of their title to Palestine and are passionately committed to defending it.

What happens if Israeli or Palestinian security forces fail to detect plots to blow up the mosques in time? Will a local doomsday then begin in Jerusalem?

Beyond such concerns, observers are amazed by the relationship that has developed between Jews and Christians over the prospect of the building of the Temple. It has brought about scenes that are almost unimaginable, including Christians marveling at and receiving reassurance for their messianic faith from Jews studying the priestly codex in preparation for the reinstatement of the sacrificial system. Although each of the groups has a somewhat different vision for the messianic times, they all share the same agenda for the near future. Accordingly, they have formed historically unprecedented friendships and alliances, difficult to imagine at other times and places. Such interactions and alliances have even brought the Jews and Christians involved in them to modify their opinions and theological perceptions. The cooperation of Christian and Jewish advocates in plans to rebuild the Temple strikingly diverges from the familiar historical dynamics of Jewish-Christian interactions.

12

Evangelical Jews

The Rise of Messianic Judaism

In the 1970s and 1980s, both Jews and Christians were surprised to
see the rise of a large and vigorous movement of Christian evangelical
Jews. Considering the two faiths to be completely separated from each
other, many observers considered such an amalgam bizarre, like a cup
of "half coffee and half tea." Attempting to overcome the historical differences between the two religious traditions, these Jewish converts to
Christianity often defined themselves as Messianic Jews instead of using
the Hellenistic term *Christian*. The new name highlighted the messianic element in Christianity and pointed to the movement's ideology of
emphasizing the Jewish roots of the Christian faith. Since the early centuries of the Common Era, the understanding of most Christians and
Jews had been that Christianity separated itself from Judaism, claiming
to have inherited its place. Some Jewish converts to Christianity in the
modern era had envisioned an amalgam of the two faiths, and the late
modern era witnessed a number of attempts to create congregations of
Hebrew Christians. However, this time the movement was larger and
more assertive in its Jewish-Christian ideology. And while at first both
Jews and Christians saw such groups as a symptom of "crazy times,"
many, especially evangelical Christians, have come to accept the new
movement and even support it.

Since the 1970s, this movement of Jewish believers in Jesus has grown
considerably. Its development sheds much light on the changing relationship between evangelical Christians and Jews.

Historical Background

The roots of the new movement can be traced to pietist and evangelical attempts, in the modern era, to promote the idea that Jews who had embraced the Christian faith could maintain elements of their Jewish identity. Pietist and evangelical missions to the Jews created an ideology that, at first mostly in theory, made being Jewish and Christian at the same time possible. Evangelical missions promoted Jewish symbols, such as the Star of David and the menorah, and claimed that accepting the Christian faith did not contradict retaining a Jewish identity but rather completed it. This innovative position involved abandoning the traditional Christian claims that the church had inherited God's promises to Israel. Motivated by a premillennialist view that considered the Jews to be the chosen people and heir to the covenant between God and Israel, evangelicals began a journey of altering their attitudes toward Jewish customs and symbols.

Premillennialism would become a central element of the theology of Jewish evangelical groups, serving as a source of commitment for bringing Jews to accept Jesus as their savior, as well as offering an ideology that justified maintaining Jewish identity, customs, and symbols. Following in the evangelicals' footsteps, first Hebrew Christians and later Messianic Jews embraced the definition of Christians as people who had undergone experiences of conversion, or being born again, and had accepted Jesus as their personal savior. Likewise, Messianic Jews adopted evangelical ways of reading the Bible and evangelical codes of personal morality on matters of family and sexuality.

There were a number of attempts in the eighteenth and nineteenth centuries to create Hebrew Christian "brotherhoods," or "houses," designed to serve as centers for Jews who had converted to pietist or evangelical Christianity. Such experiments were mostly short-lived.[1] Jews who converted to Christianity did not see a need to remain in such centers and for the most part moved on, searching for their place in Protestant society. Jewish converts established associations in Britain in 1860 and in America in 1915, but most members of these Hebrew Christian organizations were active missionaries or ministers in various Protestant churches, and their willingness to create separate Jewish Christian congregations was limited.[2] In the late nineteenth century Joseph Rabinowitz, a Zionist activist who converted to Christianity, established a congregation of Christian Jews in Kishinev, Russia. The dispensationalist-oriented Mildmay Mission to the Jews sponsored this experiment.[3] Evangelical leaders were impressed by Rabinowitz's work, and in 1893 Dwight Moody, the prominent American evangelist, invited Rabinowitz to America to evangelize at the World Columbian Exposition.

In the early 1890s, the Hope of Israel mission established a congregation of Jewish converts to Christianity in the Lower East Side of New York. The mission's directors, Arno Gaebelein and Ernest Stroeter, advocated the then unusual idea that Jews who had accepted Christianity had the right to remain observant and to follow Jewish customs and rites.[4] Like other attempts at building Jewish congregations in the nineteenth century, this unique experiment was short-lived. The converts themselves wished to leave the Lower East Side and move to Protestant middle-class neighborhoods. As a whole, at that time, the evangelical community did not see a particular merit in encouraging the establishment of Jewish-Christian communities. For Christians, "Judaizing" had traditionally been considered heresy, and many still expressed suspicion at the idea of separate Jewish congregations. Converts were reluctant to congregate with other fellow Jews, since they did not feel that the Protestant environment approved of separate communities of Jewish Christians.[5]

Attitudes changed slowly, with some missionaries, in the early decades of the twentieth century, initiating the establishment of Jewish Christian congregations. The directors of the Department of Jewish Evangelization of the Presbyterian Church U.S.A. considered it more economical to create independent Jewish congregations that would serve as centers of evangelization. They also believed that many converts would feel more at home in communities of their own, where being ethnically Jewish and acting Jewish was normative, but at the same time they envisioned a socially and culturally Jewish version of Presbyterian churches. Some of those congregations made timid attempts at creating a unique Jewish

Christian liturgy, but for the most part they followed the Protestant Presbyterian hymnology. The novelty of the Messianic Jewish movement in the 1970s and its Jewish Christian ideology was that a set of notions and aspirations that had previously been expressed only sporadically, partially, and hesitantly found a stronger and more assertive voice.

Messianic Judaism, the Early Years

Messianic Judaism represented a new generation that possessed unprecedented freedoms of choice and experimentation, including the amalgamation of traditions that previous generations had considered alien and hostile to each other. Before the 1970s, the evangelical missionary claim that Jews could be true to their Jewishness while adopting the Christian faith did not hold much water with potential Jewish converts. In Jewish and Christian minds alike, Jews were Jews, and Christians were Christians. But for the generation that came of age in the 1960s and 1970s, things were often different. They felt that they could make their own choices and did not have to abide by old taboos, which they believed they could transcend. The new movement attempted to turn conversion to Christianity into an exciting option, offering a new, young version of Christianity that rejected traditional views of Judaism as an alien faith. Messianic Jews were well aware of older attitudes and reacted by developing a sense of historical mission—a sense that they were crossing historical boundaries. They believed that they were working to heal wounds and bring together the truth and beauty of both Christianity and Judaism: faith in Yeshua with the belief in the special role of Israel in history.

In the early 1970s, the term *Messianic Judaism* came into public use, designating groups or individuals who viewed themselves as fully Christian and fully Jewish and were confident about their right to express both identities. The term, however, was not entirely new, having been used in internal debates in the community of Jewish converts to evangelical Christianity as early as the beginning of the twentieth century. At that time, it referred to a minority of converts who wanted to retain elements of the Jewish tradition and law.[6] When the term was revived in Israel in the 1940s and 1950s, its meaning changed and it came to designate all Jews who had accepted Christianity in its evangelical form. The word *Meshichyim* (messianic) linked the movement to the Jewish tradition and overcame the sense of alienness that the word *Notzrim* (Christian) would have provoked.[7] Adopted in America in the early 1970s, the term *Messianic Judaism* began to be used in other parts of the globe. At the turn of the twenty-first century many Jewish Christians have begun using the term *Jewish believers in Jesus* to designate all Jews who have adopted Christianity but still maintain a Jewish identity. In the first phase of the movement, during the early and mid-1970s, Jewish converts to Christianity established on their own initiative congregations that were largely independent of the control of missionary societies or Christian denominations. However, most congregations of Messianic Jews that have appeared since the late 1970s were established with the assistance of missionary societies, who had come to appreciate the success of such communities in promoting conversions of Jews to Christianity. Yet the independence of the early congregations shaped much of the image and self-perception of the movement.[8]

Messianic Judaism was greatly influenced by the atmosphere that developed in America in the late 1960s and early 1970s. A number of evangelists attuned to cultural trends established missions or ministries intended for members of the counterculture. Some ventures, such as Chuck Smith's Calvary Chapel, have left an enduring mark on the mainstream of evangelical charismatic Christianity in America and elsewhere. By the early 1970s, the evangelical community was ready for new groups to appear on the scene and promote new styles of worship and communal engagement, provided that they followed evangelical theology and morality. Jewish converts too had changed, and their sense of what it meant to be Jewish had been transformed. Among other things, the Six-Day War in June 1967 had strongly affected Jewish self-perceptions. The war raised the converts' status within the larger evangelical milieu and boosted their pride in their Jewish heritage and their desire to maintain Jewish identity. Jewish evangelical writers such as Louis Goldberg published articles and books in which they interpreted the war, conveying a sense of devotion and attachment to Israel and Jewish heritage.[9] The same years also saw dramatic changes in the way Americans related to ethnic cultural heritages. Like African Americans and Native Americans, Jews were taking a renewed interest in their "roots" and were emphasizing their unique cultural attributes. Whereas previously the trend for Jews was to eradicate tribal features, the trend in those years reversed.[10] For Jews, as for others, the resurgence of ethnicity was not merely nostalgia; rather, it involved incorporating their perceptions of their collective past and heritage into their current identities. In such an atmosphere, the prospect of Jews joining Anglo-Saxon, "Gentile" Christian congregations and disappearing into that milieu seemed less attractive. At this time, the encounters of Jewish converts with the evangelical community reinforced notions of ethnic pride, since evangelicals were taking a renewed interest in the Jews and their culture.

Early Congregations

Although it advocated an independent movement of Jewish converts, Messianic Judaism remained an offspring of the evangelical community, striving for recognition within the larger evangelical culture. The ideology, rhetoric, and symbols that evangelicals had promoted for generations provided the background for the rise of the new movement, and within a few years most evangelical activists came to accept the movement as a legitimate part of evangelical Christianity.

From the perspective of the members of the new evangelical Jewish groups, their movement had broken away from older forms of Jewish expressions within evangelical Christianity. But in effect there was a direct link between the older forms of Jewish involvement with evangelicals and the new Messianic Jewish expressions. Beth Messiah in Cincinnati is a case in point. Its founder and first leader, Martin Chernoff, began as a missionary on behalf of the American Association for Jewish Evangelism, a conservative evangelical missionary group with an overt premillennialist theology. A convert to Christianity, Martin Chernoff settled in Cincinnati with his family in the late 1950s after working as a missionary in Atlanta. In the late 1960s and early 1970s, many Jewish students at the University of Cincinnati responded to Chernoff's evangelism and came to believe in Jesus as the Messiah. This dynamic group of educated young people produced, in later years, a number of the leaders of the Messianic Jewish movement in America. The Cincinnati congregation chose to become independent from missionary control, acquiring a more assertively Jewish character and, in contrast to the American Association for Jewish Evangelism and other major missions to the Jews during the period, became charismatic. It incorporated enthusiastic modes of prayer that included music and dancing and the raising and clapping of hands during services. Like other congregations of its kind, the new community struggled from the 1970s onward to find a path that would give expression to its Christian beliefs, its charismatic style, and its Jewish roots. The move toward the incorporation of Jewish elements was gradual, as would be the case in other Messianic Jewish congregations, and was not without internal debates and struggles. The congregation eventually chose to conduct its weekly prayer meetings on Friday nights, asked its male members and guests to wear yarmulkes during the services, and asked women to perform the ceremony of lighting Shabbat candles. It also installed an ark in the prayer hall.

The community also manifested its affiliation with the charismatic movement. In the 1990s, for example, the congregation adopted a practice known as the Toronto Blessing or "being slain in the Spirit," a devotional event in which, inspired by the Holy Spirit, members fall to the floor. Members of the community have kept in touch with other charismatic congregations around the world. On traveling, for example, to Israel, they visit and pray at charismatic Messianic congregations rather than at noncharismatic ones. Messianic congregations serve as centers of evangelism. Members invite friends to attend services, and curious observers and seekers also come by. Almost all sermons are evangelistic in nature, promoting the Christian evangelical creed and striving to inspire the visitors in the audience to convert. Such messages emphasize the necessity of accepting Jesus as a savior, the need of Jews, like all other people, to be born again in Christ, and the view that Jews become better Jews when they accept Jesus. Messianic leaders consider their achievements in evangelism to surpass those of missions to the Jews when the manpower and resources spent are compared, and they regard their enterprises to be beneficial for the propagation of the Gospel among the Jews.[11]

Christian and Jewish Reactions

The evangelical community, whose theology and message helped bring about the rise of Messianic Jewish congregations, at first reacted with suspicion to the new movement. In the eyes of a number of missionaries, for example, Messianic Judaism, at least potentially, represented misguided forms of Jewish Christian expressions that could compromise the status and achievements of the historical evangelical interaction with the Jews. They were concerned about a new movement of congregations outside the auspices of established missions or denominational bodies. The missions were dependent on the support and trust of the larger evangelical community, and some missionaries and older Hebrew Christians feared that the new movement of Messianic Jews was going beyond the accepted theology and customs that the evangelical community was willing to tolerate.[12]

However, many Messianic Jews would have concurred with the ideas voiced by some of their critics. They did not try to join the synagogue but rather attempted to become a new subdivision within evangelical Christianity with its own characteristics and set of congregations. They certainly did not wish to go beyond the accepted theological and moral norms of the evangelical world. Although the Fellowship of Christian Testimonies to the Jews, as an association of missionaries, was suspicious toward the Messianic Jewish movement, its members invited Larry Rice, the general secretary of the Messianic Jewish Alliance, to present a defense of Messianic Judaism. This sign of openness in the midst of suspicion proved significant. The missionary movement began coming to terms with Messianic Judaism and its methods, adjusting itself to the new changes. Attempting to advance the cause of evangelism among Jews, missions tried to make the most out of the Messianic program. By the 1980s, groups such as the American Board of Missions to the Jews began sponsoring Messianic congregations.

The change in the missions' attitude had to do with the realization that the evangelical community at large was actually open to the new movement's style and methods. There was a certain amount of uncertainty in evangelical circles during the early and mid-1970s concerning Messianic congregations. It was a new development, and many in the evangelical community were uninformed as to its exact nature and purpose. Major evangelical publications such as *Christianity Today, Missiology*, and *Moody Monthly* published articles to inform their readers and let spokesmen of Messianic Judaism present their case.[13] As such accommodations indicate, there was no rejection or censorship of the movement. The evangelical community was willing to listen and to be persuaded. One article by *Christianity Today* focusing on a Jewish family of converts was entitled "More Jewish Than Ever—We've Found the Messiah."[14] Louis Goldberg, director of the Department of Jewish Studies at the Moody Bible Institute, published a more theological essay in the same magazine entitled "The Messianic Jew."[15] Goldberg claimed that Messianic Jews were part of the church—the body of the true believers—but that they were not merely Christians who happened to be of Jewish origin. As Jews, they had a special role in serving as witnesses to their brethren. So the call to the evangelical community to accept Messianic Jews as a legitimate group included the idea that they should serve effectively as evangelists to other Jews. Nonconverted Jews, regular Christians, and Jewish believers in Jesus each had different roles in history, the Moody professor asserted.

Goldberg's openness to Messianic Judaism made the program he directed at the Moody Bible Institute attractive to the new generation of converts. A number of Messianic Jews became interested in the kind of education the program offered. Similarly, the new, dynamic missionary organization Jews for Jesus built a working relationship with the department, and students in the program did fieldwork in Jews for Jesus. Since the 1980s, graduates of the program have pursued careers not only as missionaries but also as leaders and pastors of Messianic congregations and institutions. In the 1990s, Michael Rydelnik became director of the program, while Goldberg, who retired, joined the ranks of Jews for Jesus. Neither the professors nor the Messianic Jews who studied at the Moody Bible Institute were "traditionalists" who wore yarmulkes or kept the Jewish dietary laws.

Another open defender of Messianic Judaism was James Hutchens, who wrote a doctoral dissertation at the evangelical institution Fuller Theological Seminary, "A Case for Messianic Judaism." Hutchens, who converted to Judaism while holding to his belief in the messiahship of Jesus, advocated Messianic Judaism as a means for Jews to accept the Christian faith while retaining the cultural components of their Jewish heritage. Beyond "the core faith," the cultural trappings were variable, he contended, and were matters of choice.[16] Other evangelical institutions of higher learning, such as Trinity Evangelical Divinity School, Moody Bible Institute, and Dallas Theological Seminary, also opened their doors to Messianic Jews. Being admitted to such schools signaled acceptance by the core evangelical community. The *Moody Monthly*, the bulletin of the Moody Bible Institute, published, in 1972, an article entitled "A Breakthrough for Messianic Judaism?," presenting the movement positively and noting its potential for converting large numbers of Jews. "The ministry of sharing Jesus with Jewish people is a much more rewarding enterprise than it was a decade or so ago," the journal noted.[17] The growing positive response of members of the evangelical camp toward Messianic Judaism is best illustrated by a book published in the early 1980s by an evangelical scholar, David Rausch. Rausch traveled throughout the fledgling congregations of the late 1970s and early 1980s and wrote about what he encountered with much sympathy.[18] He set out to defend Messianic Judaism in the pages of the more liberal *Christian Century*. "The fact that Judaism and Christianity are not incompatible has, it seems, been a well-guarded secret," he approvingly quoted a Messianic leader.[19]

Liberal Protestants looked at times less favorably upon the new movement. The years in which Messianic Judaism made its debut were the heyday of Jewish-Christian dialogue. A number of Protestant denominations as well as interdenominational bodies had come out with declarations absolving the Jews from the deicide charge and asserting the legitimacy and validity of the existence of Judaism alongside Christianity.[20] Most significantly, liberal Christian groups closed down their missions to the Jews. From the liberal point of view, there was no need for Jews to turn to Christianity, certainly not to conservative evangelicalism, a form of Christianity many liberals cared little for anyhow.[21] The liberals were interested in speaking with "real" Jews and learning from a "sister religion," not from Messianic Judaism, which they did not consider to be a valid form of the religion they were now looking at in a new light. Many liberal Christians now joined the Jews in viewing the evangelizing of Jews as a sign of disrespect toward Judaism. Moreover, dialogue between Christians and Jews was based on what was then a common perception: that Christianity and Judaism were entirely separate from each other and in need of reconciliation. Messianic Judaism posed an alternative path of reconciliation based on blurring the differences between the two faiths. Most Jews and Christians at the time did not view this option as viable, and some, including those committed to dialogue, resented it.

Evangelicals were not bothered by liberal Christian or Jewish objections. Missionary societies, such as the Chosen People Ministries, Jews for Jesus, Ariel Ministries, and denominational missionary bodies such as the Assemblies of God, the Christian and Missionary Alliance, the Southern Baptist Convention, and rather out of line and controversially, the Presbyterian Church U.S.A., decided to establish and support congregations of Messianic Jews.[22] The American Board of Missions to the Jews, which at first was very skeptical, became a major sponsor of Messianic congregations. This became the major means through which the veteran mission now attempted to propagate Christianity among the Jews.[23]

While the American Board embraced the idea of Messianic congregations and turned them into its means of evangelism, it influenced their character, and as a result they have become more reminiscent of the Hebrew Christian congregations of the 1930s through the 1960s. As a rule, prayers have not followed traditional Jewish customs, arks have not been placed in assembly halls, and services have not included chanting from the Torah. For the most part members have not worn yarmulkes or *talitot* (prayer shawls). In describing the first congregation in northern Chicago, its first pastor, John Bell, spoke about "planting the Jewish oriented Church." Another missionary of the American Board wrote: "If we can share the Gospel with a Jewish accent, we can have a local congregation with a Jewish flavor that is reaching out to Jews and Gentiles."[24] Missionary organizations, however, appropriated the Messianic Jewish terminology. Perhaps not surprisingly, the American Board of Missions to the Jews decided in the 1980s to change its name to the Chosen People Ministries. The name demonstrated a wish not to be identified with "missions" and instead to emphasize a premillennialist understanding of the Jewish people and its role in history. In a manner typical to ethnic evangelical communities, a number of Messianic congregations share buildings with other congregations, signifying affinity in faith and agenda. As remarkable as the rise of Messianic Judaism has been, it has not been the only group to amalgamate ethnic practices with evangelical faith and values. It was not a coincidence that when the evangelical group the Promise Keepers launched a major rally in Washington, D.C., in 1997, two groups of born-again Christians who participated in the rally were particularly visible. Messianic Jews came to the gathering wearing *talitot*, prayer shawls, and holding *shofarot*, ram's horns, and Native Americans came dressed in their traditional attire and decorated with American Indian symbols. Both groups signified the inclusiveness of the rally, which gave space to all sorts of conservative evangelicals at the same time that it demonstrated a common set of values. It also signified the acceptance of evangelical Native American and Jewish as well as other ethnic groups by the larger community of born-agains.[25]

The new movement challenged traditional Jewish understanding of the legitimate boundaries of Judaism as a religion and as a community. Many Jews also shared, from the 1960s onward, prevailing liberal images of evangelicals as opponents of cultural openness and progressive values.[26] However, the Jewish community's reaction to the new and innovative movement of converted Jews was not always unified or consistent. Significantly, Jewish activists and writers often viewed missionaries and converts within the larger framework of "cults" or "bizarre" new religious groups who were out there to captivate innocent souls.[27] Scholars have pointed to common themes that appear in anticult literature, including the claims that the new groups are deceptive and that they intentionally lie about their true activities. This theme has appeared in the Jewish literature on Messianic Jews.[28] Many Jews have not taken seriously the Messianic Jewish assertion that one can embrace Christianity and remain Jewish and have considered the groups to be either fraudulent or "crazy." Giving expression to what was a common Jewish perception, Rabbi Ronald Gittelsohn wrote in an article in *Midstream:* "Jews for Jesus is only one of several aberrant religious or pseudoreligious cults flourishing today on the American scene."[29] Gittelsohn's relating to Messianic Judaism as "Jews for Jesus" is not unique. To this day, many Jews and non-Jews confuse the two movements and are often unaware that Jews for Jesus is a specific organization that in fact has had a complicated relationship with the Messianic Jewish movement as a whole. Gittelsohn also saw a need to offer a psychological explanation for the attraction of young Jews to these groups: "What a blessed and wonderful relief to throw all this heart-breaking, backbreaking, brain breaking worry onto a gentle Messiah who will solve everything? Jesus or Krishna, or Sun Myung Moon—represents to them the kind, loving daddy they knew, or for whom they desperately yearned as children, the daddy who would answer all their doubts, assuage all their hurts."[30] Jewish anticult literature often directed its criticism as much against mainstream Jews as against Christian groups. Jewish writers accused Jewish parents of failing to raise their children in committed Jewish homes, criticized the Jewish community for its inadequacy in making Judaism attractive to the younger generation, and criticized Jewish education for failing to transfer Jewish knowledge and spirituality to the next generation. Many of the writers also criticized Jewish congregations for a lack of spirituality, warmth, and a sense of community.

The visibility and relative success of the new Jewish Christian groups stirred Jewish activists to establish new venues of education and emphasize the spiritual dimensions of Jewish life. This approach is reminiscent

of the Jewish reaction to Christian missionaries in the nineteenth century and the first half of the twentieth century, when Jewish activists saw
a need to offer welfare services to counter missionary activities. Jewish
outreach, both Orthodox and liberal, developed mostly in the last third
of the twentieth century. Among other goals it has aimed at offering
spiritual and communal Jewish alternatives to the non-Jewish religious
groups that Jews began joining by the tens of thousands. Here too, Jewish outreach activists have not differentiated between Messianic Jewish
groups and other new religious movements. Much of the outreach motivation has come from the realization that Judaism is now competing in
an increasingly open market of religions and that if Jews wish to maintain their constituency they must enter the competition.[31]

Jewish activists have also founded specific organizations aimed at
combating missionaries, Messianic Judaism, and new religious movements in general. These include Jews for Jews, its name unmistakably
inspired by that of Jews for Jesus. Disbanding after a few years, it was
replaced by a new organization, Jews for Judaism.[32] The group has sponsored lectures on university campuses, published antimissionary literature, and organized demonstrations at Messianic Jewish gatherings. In
Israel, the ultra-Orthodox organization Yad L'Achim (A Hand for the
Brethren) has made a name for itself in combating missionaries and
congregations of Jewish believers in Jesus.[33] The antimissionary groups,
however, have been, as a rule, small in size, budgets, imagination, and
scope of activities. Their often short-lived histories have indicated their
standing in the list of priorities of the Jewish community. American Jews
have given large sums of money to such causes as the arts, higher education, and social projects, but they have not shown the same generos-
ity toward combating missionaries or Messianic Judaism and have not
considered the fight against them to be an important cause. Unlike the
Anti-Defamation League, such organizations have not become household names in the Jewish community, and many Jews have not even
known they existed.

On rare occasions Jews have turned to violence against Messianic
Jews. Such behavior has been mostly the initiative of individuals or small

groups. In February 1980, two young men entered a Messianic Jewish congregation, Ahvat Zion (Love of Zion), in Encino, Los Angeles, and removed a Torah scroll from the Ark of the Covenant. The men claimed that the use of the scroll by a Christian congregation desecrated the Jewish scriptures. However, for members of the congregation, as well as the police and the general public, it was an intrusion and a theft. According to newspaper reports, the Messianic Jewish congregation in Philadelphia, Beth Yeshua, encountered opposition when it tried to build its center in a Jewish neighborhood. An unidentified Orthodox group called for an after-service social gathering on Friday night not far from the Messianic group's prayer house as a protest against the activities of the new congregation. The appeal to come to the protest echoed common Jewish perceptions of Messianic Jews: "Jewish residents of Overbrook Park: there is a cult in your midst. Like the Moonies and the Krishnas. . . . They are the Messianic Jewish Movement."[34]

By the 1980s, Jewish educators and activists thought that they should prepare Jewish youth for a possible encounter with the new rhetoric of Christian evangelism and Messianic Judaism. From the 1970s onward, a number of Jewish activists published "know what to answer" books and pamphlets in response to, among others, Jewish Christian groups and their faith. These tracts did not speak in one voice but represented various viewpoints. *What to Say When the Missionary Comes to Your Door,* by Lawrence M. Silverman, a Reform rabbi, was one such brochure.[35] Expressing a progressive Jewish viewpoint, it included sentences such as "The messianic age will come to pass in this world!" and "We do not believe that personal salvation and eternal life should be overriding concerns in one's life." Many traditional and most Orthodox Jews would probably not have agreed with Silverman. The Department of Youth Activities of the Conservative movement circulated a different guidebook, *The Missionary at the Door—Our Uniqueness,* a collection of essays such as "Why Aren't We Christians?" The guide illustrates some of the problems mainline Jews have been facing in trying to counter Messianic Jewish groups, who demonstrate pride in their ethnic identity and make extensive use of Jewish symbols and language. The discussion guide thus insists that Judaism is a religion and not merely an ethnic group and that being a "Jewish-Christian makes no more sense than [being] a capitalist-communist."[36]

The writers of "know what to answer" publications were perhaps right to assume that many young Jews did not have ready answers to Messianic Jewish assertions. It is doubtful, however, that such tracts could have made a significant difference when such Jews encountered individuals or communities propagating a Jewish-friendly version of the Christian faith. In contrast to both Jewish and Christian perceptions, many of the Jews who become attracted to Christianity do not join their new faith merely for theoretical, theological reasons. The Messianic Jewish environment offers them a sense of community and spiritual and moral content. Promoting a conservative worldview, their new evangelical faith has also made demands and imposed clear boundaries and guidelines in the realm of personal morality. From their point of view, the newly converted have found in their new religious communities more nurturing environments than in liberal Jewish congregations or in secular, unaffiliated Jewish or non-Jewish life.

Jewish reactions have not remained static. Many Jews have continued to look upon Messianic Judaism suspiciously as a bizarre development. However, in recent decades some have reconsidered their position. Messianic Judaism has not faded away; in fact, it has grown in numbers and confidence and has turned into a permanent feature of the religious and cultural scene in Jewish population centers around the globe. Some liberal Jews have begun looking at communities of converts in a new way. Articles in *Moment* and the *Jerusalem Report*, appearing in the 1990s and 2000s, treated Messianic Jews respectfully and presented their case in a surprisingly impartial tone—a long shot from the articles of the 1970s and 1980s, which related to that movement in a condescending manner or attributed to it conspiratorial motives. The writers of the newer articles described the converts in realistic terms as normal people whose faith offered them meaning and a sense of purpose. In 2000, Dan Cohn Sherbok, a Reform rabbi in Wales, wrote a book on Messianic Judaism in which he called upon Jews to accept the movement. Stirring surprisingly little controversy, the book was praised for its openness and pluralistic attitude.

An Evangelical Jewish Subculture

While struggling to be accepted as genuinely Jewish and Christian, Messianic Jews, from the 1970s onward, have built their own subculture, complete with conferences and organizations, youth movements and summer camps, prayer books and hymnals, and numerous websites, books, and periodicals, including theological, apologetic, and evangelistic treatises. One series of Messianic conferences, the Messiah Conferences, has been held since the 1980s at the Mennonite evangelical Messiah College in Pennsylvania, a place that was chosen, among other considerations, for its name. Sponsored by a number of Messianic organizations, the gatherings demonstrate the movement's varied activities and groups, which have included bands of singers and dancers, youth ministries, and missionary organizations such as Ariel Ministries and Jews for Jesus. Messianic hymns resemble contemporary evangelical ones, and the music is unmistakably the rock-influenced New Christian Music, yet many of the hymns have been written and composed by Messianic Jews, offering an opportunity for songwriters and musicians within the community to express literary and musical talents.[37] Hymns often relate to Israel's role in history, convey a Messianic hope, and refer to Jesus as Yeshua. Messianic hymnals often include Israeli songs.[38]

Messianic Judaism has developed since the 1970s into a large movement. By the early 2010s, there were about three hundred Messianic Jewish congregations in America, with a noticeable presence in evangelical life going beyond those numbers. There are about one hundred communities in Israel and dozens more in Europe, Latin America, and the former Soviet bloc. Whereas previously membership was almost insignificant in comparison to the larger Jewish population, the size of the current movement is larger than that of Reconstructionist Judaism or Humanistic Judaism. While creating their own set of congregations and their own culture, Messianic communities follow mainstream conservative evangelical social and cultural norms. For example, all Messianic rabbis or ministers are men, although women, often unofficially, fulfill leadership roles. Remarkably, for many Messianic Jews, adherence to central Christian evangelical tenets of faith and morality is what has allowed them to adopt and promote Jewish rites and customs.

While creating a subculture of its own, Messianic Judaism is not a fully unified or uniform community. There are many subdivisions and groups within the larger definition. A major division between charismatics and noncharismatics reflects the same division within the larger evangelical community, where, since the 1970s, the charismatics have been on the rise. Their advocacy of a direct personal encounter with the divine and their more joyful and expressive services have appealed to many Jewish converts. At times, charismatic Messianic Jews have formed organizations separate from noncharismatic fellow evangelical Jewish believers. However, despite differences, the mutual campaign to be recognized by the evangelical community as genuine Christians and by Jews as authentic Jews, and the basic sense of identity as Messianic Jews, have often overshadowed the divisions.

Another difference between Messianic congregations is over observance of Jewish tradition and rites. On the one end of the spectrum are those who have adopted the name of Messianic Jews but have been very hesitant to observe Jewish rites and customs and have adopted a liturgy close to that of non-Jewish "Anglo-Saxon" congregations. On the other end of the spectrum are those who advocate extensive incorporation of Jewish rites, such as the wearing of yarmulkes during prayer and at times even on a daily basis (although the number of such people is very small). Some have introduced into Messianic services such rites as the wearing of *talitot* by leaders of the communities, and some reading from a Torah scroll as part of the service, as well as chanting of prayers according to traditional Jewish melodies and the holding of the major weekly services on Friday nights or Saturday mornings. None, however, have claimed that there is a requirement to observe such rites in order to be justified in the eyes of God.

Many Messianic congregations have found a middle position along this spectrum. One feature that has helped create larger uniformity has been liturgical compilations. John Fischer, a pastor of a Messianic congregation in Florida and director of Menorah Ministries, has edited a Messianic Jewish *siddur* (prayer book) that has become popular in the Messianic movement.[39] The *siddur* picks and chooses elements of the traditional Jewish prayer book, making up for passages it leaves out with prayers that give expression to faith in Jesus and his role as the Redeemer. Almost all congregations celebrate Jewish holidays, the most popular of which is Passover, in which the liturgy from a Messianic Haggadah is read.[40] The manner in which Messianic congregations choose to celebrate the Passover points to the dialectical approach of the movement, which promotes attributes of the Jewish heritage while remaining within the theological boundaries and public approval of evangelical correctness.

One of the more popular versions of the Haggadah, Eric Lipson's *Passover Haggadah: A Messianic Celebration*, is distributed by Jews for Jesus, attesting to the Messianic Jewish spirit the mission has decided to adopt. Written entirely in English and assuming no prior knowledge of Jewish customs, it maintains features of the traditional celebration, such as "the Four Questions," the four cups of wine, and an additional fifth cup for Elijah the Prophet, although many Messianic Jews prefer to drink grape juice instead of wine. Lipson's version cuts out passages of the traditional Haggadah, most notably those of the *midrash*, rabbinical elaboration on the Exodus story. Instead, the text offers numerous quotations from the New Testament, such as from John 20:19 on Jesus's appearance before his disciples after his resurrection from the dead.[41] The Haggadah also includes prayers relating to Jesus and his role as a savior, including "Blessed art Thou, O Lord our God, king of the Universe, who had sent Thy son, Thine only son, Y'shua the Messiah, to be the light of the world and our Paschal Lamb, that through him we might live."[42]

J. Ron Tavalin has also produced a Haggadah, *Kol Hesed Messianic Haggadah*. "The Messianic Believer's Haggadah," Tavalin explains in the

preface, "differs from the traditional Haggadah in that we who maintain the Messiahship of Yeshua (Jesus) see an even greater blessing and
redemption than that one contained in the book of Exodus. Even as the
Israelites were redeemed from Slavery to Pharaoh, so all peoples, Jew
and non-Jew, through the New Covenant of the Messiah, are redeemed
from bondage to sin and death." While Tavalin's Haggadah incorporates
Hebrew, it is intended for uninitiated participants, both Jewish and non-
Jewish, and it offers both a glossary of terms and ample explanations
throughout the text. *Kol Hesed* also eliminates the *midrash* passages,
instead bringing in Jesus and his role as the Redeemer. The first blessing
reads: "Blessed are you, O Lord our God, King of the Universe, who has
sanctified us through faith in Yeshua Ha Mashiakh and commanded us
to remove the leaven."

Celebrating Passover night became, by the 2000s, fashionable in the
evangelical camp, a reality that has worked in favor of Messianic communities. Now evangelical churches, by the thousands, are conducting
seder demonstrations, often under the leadership of Messianic Jewish
guests. This has become a common means for groups, such as Jews for
Jesus, to approach the evangelical community, advertise their agenda,
influence evangelical culture, and apply for funds. "See the link between
the ancient festival of redemption and Christ as the Lamb of God," reads
a brochure by Jews for Jesus, which calls upon churches to "invite Jews
for Jesus to visit your congregation."[43] Evangelicals have shown growing interest in Jewish matters, historical and contemporary. Evangelical
scholarship in the last generation has paid attention to the Jewish roots
of Christianity, a reality that works to enhance interest in Jewish holidays that go back to Jesus's era and that are mentioned in the Hebrew
Bible and the New Testament.[44]

Messianic Jewish congregations differ as to the percentage of Jews
versus non-Jews they have as members. According to a survey conducted by Michael Schiffman in the early 1990s, most Messianic congregations had percentages of Jewish membership between 25 and 50
percent.[45] The percentage of intermarried couples within the congregations surpasses the average for the Jewish population affiliated with

non-Messianic synagogues.[46] In Israel, at the turn of the millennium, 30 percent of Messianic Jews were intermarried, a much higher percentage than in the general Jewish population in the country.[47] Thus Messianic congregations are centers of evangelism for non-Jews as well. Although the communities are theologically evangelical, the non-Jewish members resemble, at least partially, non-Jews joining conventional synagogues. In both cases, non-Jews show interest in elements of the Jewish tradition and become members in houses of worship that define themselves as Jewish, incorporating Jewish customs, folklore, and humor into the celebration of the Jewish Sabbath and holidays.[48]

No comprehensive survey on the socioeconomic makeup of Messianic congregations has so far been conducted, so assessing this aspect of Messianic life can be based on impressions only. Yet it seems that with noted exceptions most members are in the lower or middle-middle classes, are college educated, and hold stable jobs.[49] Compared to the larger Jewish population, these congregations lack prestigious professionals, intellectuals, academics, and people of standing in the media and the arts. This is gradually changing with a growing presence of scholars, a reality that affects the theological discourse in the movement. Early Messianic communities consisted mostly of converts of the baby boom generation who came of age in the 1960s and 1970s, but they have been joined by younger converts, and in a growing number of congregations a second generation of Messianic Jews who have grown up in the movement are making an impact.

An important feature of Messianic Jewish culture has been its special vocabulary. It has been strongly influenced by the evangelical rhetoric of conversion, yet it has used terms that reflect the movement's unique sensitivities. The terms *mission* and *missionary* have been abandoned.[50] Rather than "evangelizing," Messianic Jews speak about "sharing," and "witnessing," and rather than "converting" they speak of "coming to the faith," or "coming to know Yeshua." They speak about "believers" to designate born-agains and differentiate between "Gentile believers" and "Jewish believers," the first being non-Jewish evangelical Christians and the second, Jews who have accepted the Christian evangelical faith.[51] The vocabulary helps shape a communal spirit among the converted. Converts learn this language along their spiritual and communal journey toward conversion, and their adoption of it signifies their acceptance of Messianic theological perceptions and communal norms.[52]

In principle, members of Messianic congregations do not smoke or gamble, and they refrain from drinking hard liquor and often other kinds of alcoholic beverages. Similarly, they promote a conservative sexual morality, not unlike that of evangelical Christians or Orthodox Jews.[53] Most Messianic Jews, like conservative evangelicals in general, subscribe to conservative social and political views, seeing themselves as patriotic Americans or Israelis. Messianic Jews support Israel out of an understanding similar to that of premillennialist evangelicals. Their relation to Israel serves to reaffirm their Jewish identity at the same time that it carries the theological perceptions and political agenda of the evangelical camp. Like evangelicals in general, Messianic congregations organize tours to Israel, establishing personal attachments to that country.[54]

The new Messianic Jewish messages and vocabulary have transformed the position of the evangelical faith in Israel. In previous decades missions concentrated their efforts on the poor, immigrant neighborhoods in Israeli cities, making very few permanent converts. But since the 1970s Messianic Jewish communities have reached the heart of Israeli culture and society. Young men and women who grew up in Israel, were immersed in its culture, and served in its army joined the movement by the thousands. Israeli society has changed dramatically since the early days of the state. It has moved away from the pioneer spirit of the prestate era and the early years of independence to become a Western-oriented consumer society. Following the Yom Kippur War of October 1973, the older Israeli elite, who were mostly European born, secular, and labor oriented, lost much of their self-confidence. Faith in Zionism as an all-encompassing ideology, providing hope, meaning, and a sense of purpose, weakened considerably. With the fading away of a central secular national faith and the moral and spiritual vacuum it left, there was plenty of room for alternative faiths to make their way in the Israeli spiritual and communal market.[55]

In the years following the Yom Kippur War, thousands of young Israelis joined new religious movements that had not been represented in the country just a few years earlier, including EST, the Church of Scientology, the Hare Krishnas, and the Unification Church. Thousands became "returnees to tradition" and joined Orthodox forms of Judaism. Many others accepted the Christian faith, mostly in its evangelical Messianic Jewish form. The community of Messianic Jews in Israel grew considerably from the 1970s on. From no more than a few hundred people in the mid-1960s, it grew to over fifteen thousand by the 2010s. Some of the growth came from immigration, as hundreds of Jewish converts to evangelical Christianity from America settled in Israel, and thousands arrived from the former Soviet Union and Ethiopia. Jews (and their non-Jewish spouses) who had converted to Christianity in the former Soviet Union or in Ethiopia often joined Messianic congregations in Israel. Such a choice helped them reconcile their loyalty to their Christian faith with the culture of their new country and served to ease the tensions of building their lives in Israel. By the 2010s, the demography of the Messianic congregations was a far cry from the realities of the earlier years of the state. It became evident that this Israeli evangelical movement had been making converts in almost all segments of society. Much of the stigma surrounding conversion to Christianity had faded away, at least in the non-Orthodox community, as Israeli culture became more inclusive and tolerant and as new religious movements became part of the Israeli scene.[56] For many secular Israelis, Messianic Jews had become just a friendly new religious movement, not a threat to Israeli society. A public opinion poll solicited by Messianic Jewish activists in the late 1980s discovered that most Israelis were willing to accept Messianic Jews.[57] Since the 1990s, Messianic Jews have marched under their own banner in the yearly Jerusalem marches, something that could not have taken place earlier. This is not to say that Messianic Jews did not encounter opposition and even occasional harassment, almost always from ultra-Orthodox circles, but the larger Israeli society opened to that option much more than before.

Ironically, autobiographical accounts have signaled that the converts find Israeli secular culture and values unsatisfactory.[58] In this, again ironically, they share similar outlooks with the many returnees to tradition who have become Orthodox Jews and, like them, reject open and permissive aspects of Israeli culture. This accounts, among other things, for the bitter animosity of the Orthodox propagators of the faith toward Messianic congregations, since they have felt that they compete for the same pool of potential converts. For similar reasons, Messianic Jews have held a less than favorable attitude toward Orthodox Jews.

Even though Messianic Jews reject some Israeli ways and values, their relationship with Israeli society has improved in the past few decades, and they have come to feel much more at home in it. Their religion's relative appeal and greater success may come from its growing legitimacy and its posing as an alternative to some of the other options within Israeli culture.[59] It has provided a sense of community within a society that, as a whole, has lost much of its sense of unity, cohesion, and purpose. As in America, the terminology adopted by the Messianic Jews in Israel has helped in the process of creating a community as well as a sense of finding a home for the soul. Those joining Messianic congregations have called themselves *maaminim* (believers) and have spoken about "lehagea laEmuna" (becoming a believer) and not about their "conversions." They remain "Yehudim" (Jews) and not "Notzrim" (Christians), even after their conversion.

The Messianic Jewish community in Israel is far from being uniform. In addition to manifesting the divisions that exist in America, congregations operate in a number of languages, including Hebrew, English, Russian, and Amharic. Messianic congregations often depend on missionary support; many of them are located on the property of churches, and foreign missionaries take part in the life of many communities. Menahem Benhayim summarizes the atmosphere: "Most Israeli congregations and fellowships reflect the Evangelical Christian streams from Calvinist to Charismatic, which have influenced their leaders and members. We sometimes hear gentile Christian visitors from abroad making much significant comments during visits to Israel, 'Oh, we feel so much at home here; the service and atmosphere was just like ours!'"[60] He concludes by expressing a wish for more independent and authentic Israeli content to Messianic Jewish life in the country. Since the turn of the twenty-first century, both in America and in Israel, Messianic Jews, especially intellectuals and scholars, have been increasingly calling for more independence from Christian groups and agencies.

In recent years, Messianic Judaism has made its mark not only in Israel but also in the former Soviet Union. The opening of the countries of the former Soviet Union gave American evangelicals unexpected new territories where they could encounter Jews and propagate the Gospel among them. In this realm, too, missions to the Jews were like many other evangelical missions to the former Soviet bloc once the communist regimes there crumbled.[61] Many evangelical groups had been active in the former Soviet Union since the early 1990s, and Soviet Jewry proved to be a promising and fertile group for evangelism. The use of Messianic vocabulary and the Jewish Christian option proved attractive to many Soviet Jews. After seven decades of communist rule, which destroyed Jewish educational, cultural, and religious infrastructure, most Jews there were ignorant of Jewish knowledge and practices, and a high percentage of them had intermarried. They had no preconceived notions of what Judaism was supposed to look like and no concept of the theological and liturgical content of traditional forms of Judaism. For some, Messianic Judaism was the only Judaism they had ever encountered, and the Messianic option allowed them to connect with their Jewish identity and roots while maintaining or embracing Christianity.

Like Israel, the countries of the former Soviet Union became something of a promised land: a place that called for a special mission and effort, that conveyed a sense of enthusiasm and triumph. Missions and Messianic Jewish organizations sent dozens of evangelists, organized tours, and established seminars to train local activists. They helped build a handful of Messianic congregations. Jewish observers have remarked that the Messianic congregations are often larger, younger, and more active and enthusiastic than conventional Jewish synagogues in the former Soviet Union.[62]

A Theological Coming of Age?

Having built a diverse and growing subculture within the larger evangelical camp, Messianic Jewish thinkers have produced a series of theological and apologetic tracts that have come to define and defend the movement's unique path. Among the Messianic Jewish theologians at the turn
of the twenty-first century are Stuart Dauermann, John Fischer, Arnold
Fruchtenbaum, Richard Harvey, Daniel Juster, Mark Kinzer, Gershon
Nerel, Rich Robinson, Tsvi Sadan, and David Stern, to name but a few.
Their work expresses a spectrum of opinions. However, one claim that
several of them have made concerns the antiquity of the movement.
According to that notion, Jews who have embraced Christianity are following in the path of the original Christians, making Messianic Judaism
a continuation of the earliest and one of the most authentic forms of
Christianity. David Stern, a leader and thinker in the Messianic Jewish
movement in Israel, has translated and edited a Messianic Jewish New
Testament. In it, he has changed St. Paul's traditionally titled Epistle to
the Hebrews into a Letter to Messianic Jews.[63]

A major trend has been a gradual move to a more independent form
of Jewish Christian thought. This development has manifested itself
in the work of Arnold Fruchtenbaum, a relatively moderate Messianic thinker. In the 1970s, Fruchtenbaum defined himself as a Hebrew
Christian and was skeptical about the more assertive forms of Messianic
Judaism.[64] In *Hebrew Christianity: Its Theology, History and Philosophy*,
Fruchtenbaum defended Hebrew Christians and presented them as solid
Christian believers in good evangelical standing. At this time, the more
assertively Jewish Messianic Jews would not have shared his views on
where Jewish converts should look for community, as he declared that
"the Hebrew Christian should be a member of the local church along
with Gentile believers."[65] Fruchtenbaum modified his views a number
of years later, and Ariel Ministries, which he founded and led, has been
instrumental in the establishment of a number of Messianic Jewish congregations. In 1985, Fruchtenbaum defended the right of Jewish believers
in Jesus to establish congregations and observe Jewish rites if they so

wished, as long as they looked upon it as an option and did not consider it a requirement toward salvation.[66]

The Messianic Jewish Manifesto has been one of the better-known Messianic theological tracts of the late twentieth century. In it David Stern presents the merits and goals of the movement as many evangelical Jews have understood them: "By providing a Jewish environment for Messianic faith, Messianic Judaism is useful in evangelizing Jews" and "It is useful in focusing the Church's attention on the Jewish people."[67] The last argument relates to the role of Messianic Jews within the evangelical camp. They have served, since their inception, as a lobby within the larger evangelical camp for giving high priority to the evangelization of the Jews as well as support for Israel and defense of Jewish rights around the globe. Stern's declaration that Messianic Jews are not half Christian and half Jewish but rather 100 percent Christians and 100 percent Jewish has become a cornerstone of mainstream Messianic Jewish self-understanding at the turn of the twenty-first century.

An important feature of Messianic Judaism in this respect has been the predominance of the premillennialist faith in the second coming of Jesus. At the turn of the twenty-first century, David Brickner, the current director of Jews for Jesus, published *Future Hope: A Jewish Christian Look at the End of the World*. The book advocates the premillennialist messianic faith and its view of the Jews and at the same time is intended to serve as a tool for evangelism among the Jews. "The millennium," Brickner promises, "contains some special provisions for Israel."[68] Dispensationalism offers a special meaning to Messianic Jews, as it convinces them that the Jewish people have a special role and mission in history, are heirs to biblical Israel, and serve as a central nation in the messianic times. This aspect of the evangelical faith can give Messianic Jews a sense of pride and self-esteem within the larger evangelical community. It also adds more vigor to their attempts to evangelize their ethnic brothers and sisters. Likewise, overcoming the schism between Judaism and Christianity has added to their sense of historical mission. "The Messianic Jewish community will be the vehicle for healing the worst schism in the history of the world, the split between the Christians and the Jews," declares David Stern optimistically.[69]

The relative success of the movement of Messianic Jews and its acceptance in conservative evangelical circles have paradoxically encouraged growing theological independence among evangelical Jewish thinkers. At the turn of the twenty-first century, a number of thinkers on both sides of the Atlantic have come up with new interpretations and suggestions about how to understand and practice this unique amalgamation of Judaism and evangelical Christianity. Gershon Nerel, an Israeli Messianic intellectual, has advocated for a greater reliance on the sacred scriptures. A historian by profession, Nerel has engaged in extensive research on the history of Jewish believers in Jesus in twentieth-century Palestine and views the early activists, before the rise of the current movement, as worthy sources of inspiration. An ardent premillennialist, Nerel views Israel as fulfilling an important role in God's plan for humanity and criticizes Christians who would like to undermine its achievements.[70] Especially since the intifada, Palestinian and Jewish believers in Jesus have often differed over their visions for the Land of Israel, or Palestine, and Nerel has pointed to Palestinian Christian unfavorable media coverage and interpretation of Israel and its actions.[71] Like Nerel, Tsvi Sadan grew up in Israel and served in its armed forces. He too became a believer in Jesus as a young man searching for meaning and, like Nerel, completed a doctoral degree at the Hebrew University, researching the attitudes of Jewish thinkers toward Jesus.[72] An editor of *Kivun*, a Messianic Jewish Israeli journal, Sadan has developed an independent understanding of the Jewish faith in Jesus, believing that Messianic theology can free itself from conventional evangelical theology. While he sees faith in Jesus as essential and the Christian sacred scriptures as authoritative, he has come to consider many other features of Protestant dogma and theology as open for discussion.[73]

While not all as daring as Sadan, a group of American Messianic Jewish thinkers have organized to develop innovative Jewish Christian thought. Wishing to cut the umbilical cord with missionary patrons and sponsors, at least on the intellectual level, they have advocated an independent approach on the part of Messianic Jews.[74] Mark Kinzer and Stuart Dauermann are founders and leaders of Hashivenu ("Bring us Back," in Hebrew), a group of Messianic Jewish intellectuals who promote a more independent Jewish Christian culture and thought. A number of such thinkers have asserted, in the last few years, that Jewish Christians should, at least in certain instances, look for inspiration in Jewish, postbiblical sources, over and against postscriptural Christian texts that may not be very relevant anymore. Jewish Mishnaic sages may at times be more appropriate sources than sixteenth-century Protestant reformers, for example.[75] While having few members, Hashivenu has made a name for itself in evangelical Jewish circles.[76] Using traditional rabbinical Jewish language, the group has expressed its agenda: "We seek an authentic expression of Jewish life maintaining substantial continuity with Jewish traditions. . . . It is our conviction that *Hashem* brings Messianic Jews to a richer knowledge of himself through a modern day rediscovery of the paths of our ancestors—*Avodah* (liturgical worship), *Torah* (study of the sacred texts), and *Gemilut Chasadim* (deeds of loving-kindness)." Significantly, while most Messianic Jewish congregations and leaders have not identified with the new group, and some have expressed criticism, the movement and its leaders have not been rejected or treated like pariahs.[77] The Hashivenu group has established the Messianic Jewish Theological Institute, which provides an online graduate school for Messianic Jewish leaders and activists, publishes the journal *Kesher,* and organizes conferences.

While looking to strengthen the intellectual basis of Messianic Judaism, Hashivenu also promotes connections with nonevangelical groups of Jewish believers in Jesus. The first such conference took place in Helsinki in June 2010 and included, besides Messianic Jews, representatives of Jewish converts to Christianity in its Catholic and Greek Orthodox versions who wish to maintain their Jewish roots.[78] Such groups are smaller in size than the evangelical Messianic Jewish movement and, as a rule, do not advocate the same assertive Jewish ethnic and religious symbols and rites as the evangelically oriented Messianic Jews have done.[79] Hashivenu and its circle point to the growing diversity within the larger Messianic Jewish movement, where different communities and individuals have placed greater emphasis on varied components of the Jewish Christian amalgam. At the same time, one can look upon Hashivenu as an avant-garde of the movement at large, which in the last decades has generally been promoting and reclaiming Jewish rites, texts, customs, symbols, and language.

In sum, Messianic Judaism has been the outcome of the energetic evangelical engagement with the Jews and the effect of the biblical-Messianic dispensationalist theology on evangelical Jewish converts. The spirit of the age has also brought about development from small, moderate, and hesitant forms of Hebrew Christianity to the more dynamic and assertive movement of Messianic Judaism. The movement has reflected larger trends, such as the transition from a melting-pot paradigm to a new interest in and emphasis on roots and ethnic pride, and the ease of a new generation in crossing boundaries and picking, choosing, and bringing together rites, customs, and ideas from different traditions. Messianic Judaism has challenged long-standing definitions of Judaism and Christianity as well as the conventional wisdom on the relationship between the two religious traditions. It has proposed a different solution to the age-old difficulties between the faiths. While the initial reaction of many Christians and Jews was shock or mockery, the Messianic Jewish movement has carved a niche for itself within the evangelical community and has been largely accepted as a legitimate subdivision within that larger culture. This should be attributed not only to evangelicals' increasing willingness to give more room to ethnic expressions but to their growing appreciation of Jews and the Jewish tradition in their midst. In spite of the Messianic Jewish commitment to Jewish identity and its incorporation of Jewish symbols and customs, the acceptance of the new movement by the Jewish community has been slower and more limited. However, while Jews have traditionally viewed conversions to Christianity as desertion from the Jewish ranks, their opposition to Messianic Jews has weakened throughout the years, and many Jews have come to treat the movement with some respect.

Ironically, while advocating conservative views on political, social, and cultural issues, this evangelical Jewish movement is postmodern in that the individuals and communities drawn to it possess multiple identities and loyalties and struggle to negotiate among them. Such hybridization has become prevalent in contemporary evangelical communities and has worked in favor of evangelical growth and energy.[80] It has also been evident in Jewish choices, which, since the 1960s, have often tended toward innovation and amalgamation of different traditions and practices. For example, there is now a large movement of Jewish practitioners of Buddhism, most of whom have not seen a contradiction between their Jewish identity and their Buddhist practices. Other hybrids have amalgamated Hasidic Judaism or hippie culture. Still, the rise of Messianic Judaism is more extraordinary than the rise of Jewish Buddhism. Judaism and Buddhism had not made conflicting claims over the same religious legacy and have not developed a long history of bitterness and accusation. The evangelical Jewish movement has signaled a new openness on the part of conservative evangelical Christianity and the development of alternative means of easing the historical tensions between the communities and reaching rapprochement between them.

CONCLUSION

In the history of relationships between religious communities the interactions between evangelicals and Jews have been extraordinary. In no
other instance have members of one community of faith considered
another group to hold a special role in the divine course of human
redemption and to be their God's first nation. Likewise, there are not
many situations in which a religious tradition views a country in another
part of the globe as the locale of great events leading from one era to
the next. This belief is particularly remarkable in light of evangelicals'
insistence on the exclusivity of the Christian faith as the only true fulfillment of God's commands and as the only means to assure justification and salvation and their view of America as a special nation with a
role in history. Such elements in the evangelical relation to the Jews are
revolutionary and unique, while others are more traditionally Christian.
Together, they have determined the nature of the unusual, seemingly
contradictory, evangelical understanding of the Jews. While in previous generations long-held Christian attitudes often prevailed, in the last
generation one can detect erosion in stereotypical attitudes and a greater
friendliness toward Jews as a people.

Most evangelicals have moved away from traditional Christian supersessionist claims and, while maintaining their claim to the exclusivity
of the Christian faith, have come to view the Jews as people who have
not been cast away by God and who are about to resume their role as
a chosen nation. Amazingly, evangelicals have only indirectly been
influenced by the liberal atmosphere of interfaith reconciliation. Their
revolutionary departure from older Christian norms crystallized long

before mainstream Christian groups gave up on supersessionist paradigms. While earlier groups promoted similar understandings of Jews and their role in God's plan for humanity, only with the rise of evangelicalism in the late modern era have a large and influential group of Christians come to regard the Jews as a people with a mission in history, separate from that of the church. This theological breakthrough notwithstanding, the relationship between evangelicals and Jews has proved to be complicated, often marked by older suspicions, stereotypes, and frustrations that the evangelical understanding of the role of the Jews could not entirely do away with. Evangelical-Jewish interactions were therefore marked by seeming paradoxes and anomalies.

Evangelical thinkers and activists have consistently expressed hopes for the redemption of the Jews and their eventual rehabilitation as a nation. They have showed concern over the well-being of the Jews and have at times tried to protect communities of Jews from persecution. Thousands of evangelicals have devoted long years of their lives to evangelizing Jews, considering their work to be a sign of goodwill and dedication. Likewise, evangelical groups and individuals have lent their support throughout the last century to Jewish public causes, such as facilitating Jews' emigration from countries in which they had been persecuted. Evangelicals have also provided material help to needy Jews and have offered young Jews education and medical care. Many evangelicals have become loyal friends of the state of Israel. At the same time, evangelical Christians have viewed the Jews as a people who failed to recognize the true Messiah and thus halted the materialization of the kingdom of God on earth, as well as deprived themselves of eternal life and more sound moral guidelines. The belief in the role of the Jews in the imminent arrival of Jesus has often served as a mitigating element in the evangelical evaluation of the Jews and the basis for a new involvement with the Jews as individuals and communities. But it has not been able to fully erase old European images of Jews, and such stereotypes have persisted for many years alongside more favorable attitudes.

The evangelical interaction with Jews has developed throughout the years. In the last generation evangelical relations to the Jews have undergone apparent changes and have become more generous and friendlier than ever before, although residues of mixed opinions have remained. The unprecedented relationship that has developed between Jews and evangelicals has brought about scenes that are almost unbelievable. These include evangelical Christians marveling at and receiving reassurances for their faith and understanding of history from secular Jews struggling to establish a Jewish state in Palestine and from observant Jews studying the priestly codes in preparation for the reinstatement of the sacrificial system in a rebuilt Temple. Something of a symbiosis has developed between conservative evangelical Christians and Jews, as one group has helped to sustain the faiths and agendas of the other. This has especially been evident in the encouragements that evangelicals and Zionist Jews have offered each other, especially Israeli and evangelical leaders following the 1967 War. It has become prevalent between particular groups of evangelicals and Jews over the vision of "greater Israel." Although each of the groups has held a somewhat different view of the messianic times, they have often shared similar hopes and agendas for the near future.

In their interactions with Jews, evangelicals did not follow liberal Christians who, from the 1960s through the 1980s, worked systematically to improve relations between the faiths and to construct theologies that legitimized the existence of Judaism alongside Christianity. Evangelical attitudes toward Judaism and Jews have also improved, but along a different trajectory: in particular, interfaith dialogue has played only a marginal and almost negligible role.[1] Evangelicals would not modify their basic outlook that all humans should be born again in Christ and that evangelism was both legitimate and charitable. But evangelicals too were influenced, albeit indirectly, by the new interfaith spirit. While less careful at times than liberal Christian leaders, evangelicals too have adopted more culturally correct approaches. Evangelical tracts and textbooks, like their liberal counterparts, attest to the removal of controversial or insulting statements.[2]

Unlike liberal Christian groups, evangelicals have been unwilling to grant Judaism an equal standing to that of Christianity. But they have come up with agendas that have been friendlier toward Jews than older Christian attitudes. In actuality, developments in liberal and evangelical attitudes toward the Jews, although different in character, have together brought about a revolution in the way Christian America has come to relate to the Jews. Despite sharp differences, evangelical attitudes accord in some ways with liberal ones.[3] Evangelicals have refused to look upon Judaism as an "elder brother" or "sister religion," but they have recognized positive, often instrumental, elements in Judaism and Jews that other branches of the Christian religious tradition have not always shared. Evangelicals have found means of easing the tensions and improving relations with Jews, though different from those of the liberals. The changes brought about by both groups have created an unprecedented improvement in the relations of Western Christianities in general and American Christianity in particular toward the Jews. However, in contrast to the liberal paradigm of reconciliation through mutual recognition between two theoretically equal traditions, evangelicals have suggested blurring the line. They have allowed for and later even encouraged the creation of congregations of evangelical Jews. Groups and churches within the larger movement have adopted in the last generation Jewish symbols, terms, and customs, including the celebration of Jewish holidays.

While liberal Christians have treated their understanding of Judaism and their relation to Israel as two separate issues, evangelicals (with the exception of the smaller progressive wing of the movement) have made no such differentiation. For evangelicals, Israel has been the focal point of their interest in the Jews and their hopes for the future and, in their own eyes, the ultimate proof of their dedication to that people. They scorn liberals for their critical attitude toward Israel and have come to support that country's policies, at times more than many of Israel's own citizens, as well as American Jews.

A Continued Fascination

The evangelical-Jewish relationship is an ongoing affair. Some have seen the evangelicals and Jews as strange bedfellows, thus offering a political utilitarian explanation to the enchantment. There has certainly been an element resembling a marriage of convenience in the evangelical-Jewish interaction. However, as this book has demonstrated, marriages of convenience can also become affectionate throughout the years. And the evangelical-Jewish connection has gone far beyond the realm of politics.

The relationship between evangelicals and Jews has not been one-sided. The mutual rewards the two groups have provided each other perhaps explain their continued and persistent fascination with each other. The evangelical discourse on the Jews, in all its complexity, has shown that Jews are central to evangelical Christians' definition of their own faith and community and their articulation of their own role within larger historical developments. Evangelicals have spent time, energy, hope, and resources trying to influence the life of the Jews, and their engagement with that people has been both extensive and creative. However, theirs has not been an unrequited love. On their own terms they have been very successful. From early on, evangelicals have managed to reach Jews in different walks of life, establish contact with leaders, create alliances, and at times engage in mutual projects. Moreover, evangelicals have managed to disseminate their ideas among Jews, stir interest in their faith among some, attract a few converts, and even establish congregations of converts as well as intellectual cultural venues of evangelical Jews.

No less important have been the assurances evangelicals have derived from what they have considered to be fulfillment of prophecies. In the developments in the history of the Jews—Zionism, the Jewish settlement of Palestine, the birth of the state of Israel and the June 1967 War—they have found validation of their philosophy of history and their reading of Scripture.

Each side has considered the other a useful ally and has considered the other's faith, at least partially, a blessed source of support for its own cause. This attitude has included, at times, both liberal and observant Jews. For the most part, Jewish understanding of the evangelical faith has been even more limited than evangelical knowledge of rabbinical Judaism. Jews have not been informed of the nature and details of the religious beliefs that motivate the interest and goodwill of Christians toward them, but for many of them this is beside the point. Others, at times, have been wary of or have resented evangelical pressure, although not always consistently. Whether Jews have accepted, encouraged, hesitated over, or rejected evangelical overtures, their perceptions of evangelical beliefs and culture have been perhaps even less nuanced than evangelical knowledge on Jewish culture and faith.[4] Jews as a rule have been unaware of the scope of evangelical involvement with them and their culture and the full impact of such encouragement. Although many have been aware of the missionary presence, they have not necessarily been aware of its sources and intentions. Many others have come to notice the political implications of evangelicals' willingness to support their causes. Few have noticed the borderland hybrid literature and community cultures that evangelicals have sponsored.

Following the 1967 War, evangelical involvement with the Jews reached a zenith. The opinions of members of both communities regarding one another have improved considerably, with evangelical Christians making efforts to be more attuned to Jewish sensitivities in their writings and speeches and with some Jewish leaders openly encouraging evangelical support. Actual day-to-day encounters on a nonmissionary basis between Jews and evangelicals have increased, and a growing movement of evangelical Jews has often acted as a go-between for the two communities. Public opinion polls confirm such impressions. A survey that sociologists conducted in the early 1960s discovered that in America conservative Protestants were more likely to hold prejudices against Jews than mainline Protestants or Roman Catholics.[5] However, a similar survey conducted in the late 1980s discovered a remarkable improvement in evangelical opinions on Jews.[6] This has been partially the result of the changing image of the Jews in American culture and the growing importance of Israel to evangelicals. But it has also been due to a dramatic growth in evangelical encounters with real Jews. While previously evangelicals encountered Jews only in books or sermons, since the 1970s millions of evangelicals have met and conversed with actual Jews, taken tours to Israel, and met with Israeli officials, and some have spent time as volunteers in kibbutzim or as students in educational programs in the country. Changing demographics have also played a part. Many American Jews have moved to "Bible Belt" areas, and evangelicals and Jews have increasingly encountered each other as neighbors, colleagues, or customers. A growing awareness of Jewish suffering under the Nazis in Europe during World War II and under the Soviet regime after the war has also influenced evangelical opinions and attitudes.

Such developments have met with some opposition and controversy. Antagonists of Israel or of conservative evangelical Christianity have scorned evangelical Messianic expectations as illegitimate and cultlike.[7] Some Jewish leaders have criticized the flourishing of the friendship, as have Christian leaders outside the ranks of conservative evangelical Christianity.[8] However, the friendship between evangelicals and Jews, or at least between certain groups of evangelicals and Jews, has become, if anything, warmer. In that respect, it has both progressed and regressed, becoming more amicable and at the same time more sectarian. Many of the mutual ventures have involved hardline evangelicals and Jews, with more liberal-minded members of both traditions critiquing what they have come to see as an alliance of radicals.

This does not mean that Jewish-evangelical relations are now based solely on love and appreciation. One must remember that evangelical devotion toward the Jews does not result from unconditional love; rather, it springs from a certain mode of interpretation of biblical passages and certain expectations in the political realm. The positive elements in evangelical attitudes toward the Jewish people, as well as activity on the Jews' behalf, have derived primarily from evangelicals' unique perception of the Jews' role in God's plans for humanity. Those attitudes are also products of political views that are conservative and patriotic in nature, supportive of America and its allies, and convergent with a biblical Christian view of America, the Jews, and the Holy Land. In the last decades, the perception that Israel is America's ally has reinforced evangelical Christian support of Jewish and Israeli causes, as well as worked toward gradual eradication of older stereotypes and antagonisms.

Will the relationship between evangelicals and Jews continue to be as close and extensive in the coming years? This depends on a number of considerations. For many decades evangelical-Jewish relations have been influenced by changing political and cultural atmospheres, as well as by actual contacts between evangelicals and Jews and the friendships and alliances they have formed. Such developments are difficult to predict. Few could have foreseen, merely half a century ago, groups of Orthodox Jews and evangelical Christians cooperating over the prospect of building the Temple or the growth of a large and innovative movement of evangelical Jews. However, it is doubtful whether this unique relationship could continue along similar lines without the continued prominence in evangelical circles of a biblical, messianic faith that views the Jews as historical Israel and places them at the center of the drama of the end times. A second condition is the continued existence of at least a moderately vibrant Jewish nation and a Jewish state in some part of the historical Kingdom of David. At the turn of the twenty-first century, it seems that at least in the near future evangelical Christians will remain strongly invested in the life and destiny of the Jewish people and that a committed evangelical-Jewish relationship will remain a high priority of both communities.

NOTES

INTRODUCTION

1. On the reaction to the conversation, see David Vest, "They Don't Know How I Really Feel: Billy Graham, Tangled Up in Tape," *Counter Punch*, March 5, 2002, www.counterpunch.org/vestgraham.html.

2. Billy Graham, *Just As I Am: The Autobiography of Billy Graham* (New York: Harper Collins, 1997), esp. 353–55.

3. "Billy Graham and the Jews," n.d., www.beliefnet.com/story/102/story_10204_1.html.

4. On William E. Riley and his attitude toward Jews, see Yaakov Ariel, *Evangelizing the Chosen People: Missions to the Jews in America, 1880–2000* (Chapel Hill: University of North Carolina Press, 2000), 111–12, 118–19, 188–89; William V. Trollinger, *God's Empire: William Bell Riley and Midwestern Fundamentalism* (Madison: University of Wisconsin Press, 1990).

5. "A Statement by Evangelist Billy Graham on Intolerance and Prejudice following Release of Nixon White House Tapes," March 16, 2002, http:///jmm.aaa.net.au/articles/175.htm.

6. Ariel, *Evangelizing the Chosen People.*

7. On the large variety of evangelical expressions at the turn of the twenty-first century, see Randall Balmer, *Mine Eyes Have Seen the Glory* (New York: Oxford University Press, 1987).

8. Kevin Roose, *The Unlikely Disciple: A Sinner's Semester at America's Holiest University* (New York: Hachette Book Group, 2009).

9. See Mark Noll, *American Evangelical Christianity: An Introduction* (Oxford: Blackwell, 2000), 56–66.

10. Byron Johnson and Nancy Isserman, eds., *Uneasy Allies: Evangelical and Jewish Relations* (Lanham, MD: Lexington Books, 2007), esp. 19–48, 103–54; Mark Silk, "The Protestant Problem(s) of American Jewry," *Studies in Contemporary Jewry* 24 (2010): 126–40.

11. Jackie Feldman, "Constructing a Shared Bible Land: Jewish Israeli Guiding Performances for Protestant Pilgrims," *American Ethnologist* 34 (2007): 349–72.

12. See, e.g., Motti Inbari, *Jewish Fundamentalism and the Temple Mount* (Albany: State of New York University Press, 2009), 89–94.

13. Tsvi Sadan, *A Flesh of Our Flesh: Jesus of Nazareth in Zionist Thought* (Jerusalem: Carmel, 2008), 88.

14. See Yona Malachy, *American Fundamentalism and Israel* (Jerusalem: Hebrew University Press, 1978), 103–9.

15. See Margaret Brearley, *The Anglican Church, Jews and British Multicultural-ism,* Posen Papers in Contemporary Antisemitism (Jerusalem: Vidal Sassoon International Center for the Study of Antisemitism, 2007), http://sicsa.huji.ac.il/ppbrearley.pdf.

16. Paul Merkley, *Christian Attitudes towards the State of Israel* (Montreal: McGill-Queen's University Press, 2001).

17. Regina Sharif, *Non-Jewish Zionism: Its Roots in Western History* (London: Zed, 1983); Stephen Sizer, *Christian Zionism: Road Map to Armaggedon* (Leicester: Intervarsity Press, 2004); Irvine H. Anderson, *Biblical Interpretation and Middle East Policy: The Promised Land, America and Israel, 1917–2002* (Gainesville: University Press of Florida, 2005).

18. On the history, theology, and political agendas of progressive evangelicals, view Brantley W. Gasaway, "An Alternative Soul of Politics: the Rise of Contemporary Progressive Evangelicalism" (PhD diss., University of North Carolina, 2008).

19. See the website of the organization Jews on First, who describe themselves as "defending the First Amendment against the Christian Right"; www.jewsonfirst.org.

20. Sergio Minerbi, *The Vatican and Zionism* (New York: Oxford University Press, 1990); Uri Bialer, *Cross on the Star of David* (Bloomington: Indiana University Press, 2005). An exception has been Malachy's *American Fundamentalism and Israel.*

21. An exception is Nahum Sokolow, *History of Zionism, 1600–1918* (London: Long-mans, Green, 1919).

22. Albert E. Thompson, *A Century of Jewish Missions* (Old Tappan, NJ: Fleming H. Revell, 1905); Robert I. Winer, *The Calling: The Hebrew Christian Alliance* (Phila-delphia: Hebrew Christian Alliance, 1990).

23. See, e.g., Timothy P. Weber, *On The Road to Armageddon* (Grand Rapids, MI: Baker Academic Press, 2004); Victoria Clark, *Allies for Armageddon: The Rise of Christian Zionism* (New Haven: Yale University Press, 2007).

24. David S. Katz, *Philo-Semitism and the Readmission of the Jews to England, 1603–1655* (Oxford: Oxford University Press, 1982); Eitan Bar-Yosef, *The Holy Land in English Culture, 1799–1917: Palestine and the Question of Orientalism* (Oxford: Oxford University Press, 2005).

25. David Rausch, *Zionism within Early American Fundamentalism, 1878–1918: A Convergence of Two Traditions* (New York: Edwin Mellen Press, 1978); Merkley, *Christian Attitudes;* Shalom Goldman, *Zeal for Zion: Christians, Jews, and the Idea of the Promised Land* (Chapel Hill: University of North Carolina Press, 2009).

26. Clark, *Allies for Armaggedon;* Stephen Spector, *Evangelicals and Israel: The Story of American Christian Zionism* (New York: Oxford University Press, 2009); Motti Inbari, *Jewish Fundamentalism.*

27. Weber, *On the Road;* Sizer, *Christian Zionism.*

28. Shoshanah Feher, *Passing over Easter: Constructing the Boundaries of Messianic Judaism* (Walnut Creek, CA: AltaMira, 1998); Carol Harris-Shapiro, *Messianic Judaism* (Boston: Beacon Press, 1999); Gershon Nerel, "Messianic Jews in Eretz Israel, 1917-1967" (PhD diss., Hebrew University, 1996); *Yiddish Culture in Britain: A Guide* (Frankfurt: Peter Lang, 1990); Jorge Quiñónez, "Paul Philip Levertoff: Pioneering Hebrew-Christian Scholar and Leader," *Mishkun* 37 (2002):21-34.

29. See Billy Graham, *World Aflame* (Garden City, NY: Doubleday, 1965), and Hal Lindsey, *The Late Great Planet Earth* (Grand Rapids, MI: Zondervan, 1970), both best sellers, one in the 1960s and the other in the 1970s.

30. Lynn Neal, *Romancing God: Evangelical Women and Inspirational Fiction* (Chapel Hill: University of North Carolina Press, 2007).

1. THE ROOTS AND EARLY BEGINNINGS OF THE
EVANGELICAL-JEWISH RELATIONSHIP

1. Luther removed the Jewish Apocrypha on the basis that they were noncanonical, with the exception of the book of Judith, which he included in his collection but not as a canonical reading. The book would disappear from Protestant Bibles later on.

2. See Ronald H. Bainton's classical study *Here I Stand! A Life of Martin Luther* (New York: Signet, 1950).

3. Jeremy Cohen, *Living Letters of the Law: Ideas of the Jew in Medieval Christianity* (Berkeley: University of California Press, 1999); Kenneth Stow, *Jewish Dogs: An Image and Its Interpreters* (Stanford: Stanford University Press, 2006).

4. Luther's complicated and changing attitudes toward the Jews have received much scholarly attention. For an updated comprehensive study of the subject, see Thomas Kaufmann, "Luther and the Jews," in *Jews, Judaism, and the Reformation in Sixteenth-Century Germany,* ed. Dean Phillip Bell and Stephen G. Burnett (Leiden: Brill, 2006), 69–104; see also Peter von der Osten-Sacken, *Martin Luther and die Juden* (Stuttgart: Kohlhammer, 2002).

5. Joy Kammerling, "Andreas Osiander's Sermons on the Jews," in Bell and Burnett, *Jews, Judaism.*

6. See G. Sujin Pak, *The Judaizing Calvin: Sixteenth-Century Debates over the Messianic Psalms* (New York: Oxford University Press, 2010).

7. See John Calvin's major theological tract, *Institutes of the Christian Religion,* ed. John T. McNeill, 2 vols. (London: S.C.M. Press, 1961); William J. Bouwsma, *John Calvin: A Sixteenth-Century Portrait* (New York: Oxford University Press, 1988).

8. Calvin, *Institutes* 2.30.

9. Salo Wittmayer Baron, "John Calvin and the Jews," in *Harry Austryn Wolfson Jubilee Volume,* ed. Saul Lieberman (Jerusalem: American Academy for Jewish Research, 1965), 2:141–63.

10. See Calvin's commentary to Matt. 27:25.

11. See Myriam Yardeni, *Huguenots and Jews* (Jerusalem: Zalman Shazar Center, 1998), 83–112; J. Van Den Berg, "Eschatological Expectations Concerning the

Conversion of the Jews in the Netherlands during the Seventeenth Century," in *Puritans, the Millennium and the Future of Israel: Puritan Eschatology, 1600–1660*, ed. Peter Toon (Cambridge: James Clarke, 1970), 137–39; Frank E. Manuel, *The Broken Staff: Judaism through Christian Eyes* (Cambridge, MA: Harvard University Press, 1992), 92–98.

12. Gershom Sholem, *Shabbatai Zvi: The Mystical Messiah* (New York: Schocken Books, 1970).

13. Frank Felsenstein, *Anti-Semitic Stereotypes: A Paradigm of Otherness in English Popular Culture* (Baltimore: Johns-Hopkins University Press, 1995).

14. See Christopher Hill, *The English Bible and the Seventeenth-Century Revolution* (Harmondsworth: Penguin, 1994).

15. Barbara W. Tuchman, *Bible and Sword: England and Palestine from the Bronze Age to Balfur* (London: Macmillan, 1983), 80–101; David S. Katz, *Philo-Semitism and the Readmission of the Jews to England, 1603–1655* (Oxford: Clarendon Press, 1982); Hill, *English Bible;* Eitan Bar-Yosef, *The Holy Land in English Culture, 1799–1917* (Oxford: Clarendon Press, 2005); Christopher Hill, "Till the Conversion of the Jews," in *Collected Essays 2: Religion and Politics in Seventeenth Century* (Brighton: Harvester, 1986); Robert M. Healers, "The Jews in Seventeenth Century Protestant Thought," *Church History* 46, no. 1 (1979): 63–79; Avihu Zakai, "The Poetics of History and the Destiny of Israel: The Role of the Jews in English Apocalyptic Thought during the Sixteenth and Seventeenth Centuries," *Journal of Jewish Thought and Philosophy* 5 (1996): 313–50; Mel Scult, *Millennial Expectations and Jewish Liberties: A Study of the Efforts to Convert the Jews in Britain up to the Mid-Nineteenth Century* (Leiden: Brill, 1978); Mayir Verete, *From Palmerston to Balfour* (London: Frank Cass, 1992); Franz Kobler, *The Vision Was There: A History of the British Movement for the Restoration of the Jews to Palestine* (London: Lincolns-Prager, 1956); Peter Toon, "The Latter Day Glory," in *Puritans, the Millennium,* 23–41; Carl F. Ehle, "Prolegomena to Christian Zionism in America: The Views of Increase Mather and William E. Blackstone Concerning the Doctrine of the Restoration of Israel" (PhD diss., New York University, 1977), 47–61.

16. Toon, "Latter Day Glory," 26–32.

17. Ibid., 32–34.

18. Iain H. Murray, *The Puritan Hope* (London: Banner of Truth Trust, 1971); Avihu Zakai, *Exile and Kingdom: History and Apocalypse in the Puritan Migration to America* (Cambridge: Cambridge University Press, 1992).

19. John Winthrop, "A Model of Christian Charity," quoted in Perry Miller and Thomas H. Johnson, *The Puritans* (New York: American Book Company, 1938), 198–99; H. Richard Niebuhr, *The Kingdom of God in America* (New York: Harper, 1937); Ernest L. Tuveson, *Redeemer Nation: The Idea of America's Millennial Role* (Chicago: University of Chicago Press, 1968).

20. Ehle, "Prolegomena to Christian Zionism," 61–192. See Le Roy E. Froom, *The Prophetic Faith of Our Fathers*, 4 vols. (Washington, DC: Review and Herald,

1946–54), 3:19–143; Sidney H. Rooy, *The Theology of Missions in the Puritan Tradition* (Delft: W. D. Meinema, 1965),

21. Ehle, "Prolegomena to Christian Zionism," 67–69.

22. Ibid., 69–73.

23. Peter Toon, "The Question of Jewish Immigration," in *Puritans, the Millennium*, 115–25; Scult, *Millennial Expectations*, 17–34; Tuchman, *Bible and Sword*, 121–46; Katz, *Philo-Semitism*.

24. Philip F. Gura, *Jonathan Edwards: America's Evangelical* (New York: Hill and Wang, 2005).

25. On Edwards's treatment of the Jews, see Rooy, *Theology of Missions*, 297–306; Ehle, "Prolegomena to Christian Zionism," 192–96.

26. Walter Beltz, "Gemeinsame kulturelle Codes in koexisteierenden Religionsgemeinschaften, dargestellt und untersucht an Beispielen der Messiasdiskurse in den Reisetagebüchern des Institutum Judaicum et Muhammedicum J. H. Callenbergs," in *Sprache und Geist: Peter Nagel zum 65 Geburstag* (Halle: Druckerei der Martin-Luther-Univ. Halle-Wittenberg, 2003), 11–20.

27. The institute was officially called the Institutum Judaicum et Muhammedicum, but its activity among the Muslims was secondary and it quickly became known as the Institutum Judaicum.

28. Institutum Judaicum, *Catalogus* (Halle: Institutum Judaicum, 1739).

29. Christoph Bochinger, "Die Dialoge zwischen reisenden Studiosi und Juden in religionswissenschaftlicher Perspektive," *Jewish History Quarterly* 4 (2006): 509–20.

30. Johann Heinrich Callenberg and Wilhelm Christian Justus Chrysander, *Schriften zur jiddischen Sprache*, facs. ed. (1733; repr., Marburg: N. G. Elwert, 1966).

31. Institutum Judaicum, *Catalogus* (Halle: Institutum Judaicum, 1733), in the archive of the Frankische Stiftung, Ad 263 (6) i8° ("Lehrer der christlichen Erkänntnis").

32. Arno C. Gaebelein, *The Prophet Daniel* (New York: Our Hope, 1905).

33. Institutum Judaicum, *Catalogus* (Halle: Institutum Judaicum, 1748), 5.

34. Giuseppe Veltri, "Die Diarii des Callenberg-Instituts: Eine Quelle zur jüdischen Kulturgeschichte in der ersten Hälfte des 18. Jahrhunderts," *Jewish History Quarterly* 4 (2006): 652–61.

35. Peter Vogt, ed., *Zwischen Bekehrungseifer und Philosemitismus: Texte zur Stellung der Pietismus zum Judentum* (Leipzig: Evangelische Verlagsanstalt, 2007).

36. Timothy P. Weber, *Living in the Shadow of the Second Coming* (Chicago: University of Chicago Press, 1988).

37. Among the exceptions are Baruch Mevorach, "Messianic Hopes within the Discourse on the Emancipation of Jews and Early Reform" (PhD diss., Hebrew University, 1966); Alan T. Levinson, *Between Philosemitism and Antisemitism: Defenses of Jews and Judaism in Germany, 1871–1932* (Lincoln: University of Nebraska Press, 2004).

38. See, e.g., Clarke Garrett, *Respectable Folly* (Baltimore: Johns Hopkins University Press, 1975); W. H. Oliver, *Prophets and Millennialists* (Auckland, New Zealand:

Auckland University Press, 1978); Yaakov Ariel, "The French Revolution and the Resurgence of Christian Eschatology," In *The French Revolution and Its Impact: A Collection of Essays,* ed. Richard I. Cohen (Jerusalem: Zalman Shazar Center, 1991), 319-33.

39. Ernest Sandeen, *The Roots of Fundamentalism: British and American Millenarianism, 1800–1930* (Grand Rapids, MI: Baker Book House, 1978); Weber, *Living in the Shadow.*

40. Leon Festinger, Henry W. Riecken, and Stanley Schachter, *When Prophecy Fails* (1956; repr., London: Pinter and Martin, 2008); Ronald L. Numbers and Jonathan M. Butler, eds., *The Disappointed: Millerism and Millenarianism in the Nineteenth Century* (Knoxville: University of Tennessee Press, 1993).

41. Sandeen, *Roots of Fundamentalism*; Weber, *Living in the Shadow.*

42. See, e.g., David Rausch, *Zionism within Early American Fundamentalism, 1878–1918: A Convergence of Two Traditions* (New York: Edwin Mellen Press, 1978).

43. George M. Marsden, *Fundamentalism and American Culture: The Shaping of Twentieth-Century Evangelicalism, 1870–1925* (New York: Oxford University Press, 1980).

44. "Niagara Creed," in Sandeen, *Roots of Fundamentalism,* 273-77.

45. Joel Carpenter, *Revive Us Again: The Reawakening of American Fundamentalism* (New York: Oxford University Press, 1997).

46. Christian Smith, *American Evangelicalism: Embattled and Thriving* (Chicago: University of Chicago Press, 1998); James K. Wellman Jr., *Evangelical versus Liberal: The Clash of Christian Cultures in the Pacific Northwest* (New York: Oxford University Press, 2008).

47. See Caitlin Carenen, *The Fervent Embrace: Liberal Protestants, Evangelicals, and Israel* (New York: New York University Press, 2012).

48. See Arthur Hertzberg, *The French Enlightenment and the Jews* (New York: Columbia University Press, 1968); John Toland, *Nazarenus: Or, Jewish, Gentile and Mahometan Christianity* (London, 1716).

49. See Conrad Hoffmann, *Our Jewish Neighbors,* pamphlet, Home Missions Council of North America, n.d., in Archives of the Presbyterian Church USA, Philadelphia.

50. See Christian Wiese, *Challenging Colonial Discourse: Jewish Studies and Protestant Theology in Wilhelmine Germany* (Leiden: Brill, 2005).

51. See George L. Berlin, *Defending the Faith: Nineteenth-Century American Jewish Writings on Christianity and Jesus* (Albany: State University of New York Press, 1989).

2. THE EVANGELICAL MESSIANIC FAITH AND THE JEWS

1. See Norman Cohn, *In Pursuit of the Millennium* (New York: Oxford University Press, 1970).

2. Bart Ehrman, *Jesus: Apocalyptic Prophet of the New Millennium* (New York: Oxford University Press, 2001).

3. Augustine, *The City of God* (New York: Image, 1958), especially ch. 20.

4. Cohn, *In Pursuit of the Millennium.*

5. Christopher Hill, *The World Turned Upside Down: Radical Ideas during the English Revolution* (London: Penguin, 1991).

6. Gershom Sholem, *Shabbatai Zvi: The Mystical Messiah* (New York: Schocken Books, 1970).

7. Ernest Sandeen, *The Roots of Fundamentalism: British and American Millenarianism, 1800–1930* (Grand Rapids, MI: Baker Book House, 1978).

8. See, e.g., Barbara W. Tuchman, *Bible and Sword: England and Palestine from the Bronze Age to Balfur* (London: Macmillan, 1983); Donald M. Lewis, *The Origins of Christian Zionism: Lord Shaftesbury and the Evangelical Support for a Jewish Homeland* (New York: Cambridge University Press, 2010).

9. Charles H. Spurgeon, "Restoration and Conversion of the Jews," sermon 582, June 16, 1864, www.spurgeongems.org/chsbm10.pdf, and "Joy Born at Bethlehem," sermon 1026, December 24, 1871, www.spurgeon.org/sermons/1026.htm.

10. George John Stevenson, *Sketch of the Life and Ministry of the Rev. C. H. Spurgeon: From Original Documents* (New York: Sheldon, Blakeman, 1857), 74.

11. Spurgeon, "Joy Born at Bethlehem."

12. Dennis Swanson, "Charles H. Spurgeon and Eschatology: Did He Have a Discernible Millennial Position?," 1996, www.spurgeon.org/eschat.htm. This highly learned essay shows convincingly that Spurgeon was an ardent premillennialist but hardly a dispensationalist, although contemporary dispensationalists have adopted Spurgeon as their own.

13. Charles H. Spurgeon, "The Church of Christ," sermon 28, June 3, 1855, www.spurgeon.org/sermons/0028.htm.

14. David Bebbington, *Evangelicalism in Modern Britain: A History from the 1730s to the 1980s* (New York: Routledge, 1989), 81–86.

15. See "The Epistle of Barnabas," in *Early Christian Writings*, ed. B. Radice (Harmondsworth: Penguin Books, 1981).

16. On Ribera and the emergence of futurism, see Le Roy E. Froom, *The Prophetic Faith of Our Fathers*, 4 vols. (Washington, DC: Review and Herald, 1946–54), 2:484–93.

17. See, e.g., Arnold D. Ehlert, *A Bibliographic History of Dispensationalism* (Grand Rapids, MI: Baker Book House, 1965); Erich Geldbach, *Christlich Versammlung und Heilsgeschichte bei John Nelson Darby* (Wuppertal: Brophaus, 1971).

18. Timothy P. Weber, *Living in the Shadow of the Second Coming* (Chicago: University of Chicago Press, 1988).

19. On Darby's life and career, see Clarence B. Bass, *Background to Dispensationalism* (Grand Rapids, MI: Eerdmans, 1960).

20. John N. Darby to Prof. Friedrich A. G. Tholuck, letter 226 [1850s], in *Letters of John Nelson Darby*, 3 vols. (Sunbury, PA: Believers Bookshelf, 1971), 3:298.

21. Ibid.

22. Edmund Gosse, *Father and Son,* ed. Michael Newton (1907; repr., New York: Oxford University Press, 2004).

23. John Nelson Darby, "The Rapture of the Saints," in *The Collected Writings of John Nelson Darby*, 34 vols., ed. William Kelly (Sudbury, PA: Believers Bookshelf, 1972), 11:118–67. For more recent expositions of the dispensationalist belief in the rapture, see John F. Walvoord, *The Rapture Question* (Findlay, OH: Dunham, 1957); Hal Lindsey, *The Rapture* (New York: Bantam Books, 1983); and Tim LaHaye and Jerry R. Jenkins's novel *Left Behind* (Wheaton: Tyndale House, IL, 1995).

24. See William E. Blackstone, *Jesus Is Coming*, 2nd ed. (Chicago: Fleming H. Revell, 1886), 65. The idea that the true believers would be saved from the turmoil of the Great Tribulation had already appeared in Jewish messianic literature of the Second Temple period, as well as in such Jewish literature of later periods. See David Flusser, "The Reflection of Jewish Messianic Beliefs in Early Christianity" [in Hebrew], in *Messianism and Eschatology*, ed. Zvi Baras (Jerusalem: Zalman Shazar Centers, 1983), 132–33. Opponents of the Rapture theory are well aware that the idea behind it is that the true believers will escape the Great Tribulation, and they build their arguments accordingly. See, e.g., George E. Ladd, *The Blessed Hope* (Grand Rapids, MI: Eerdmans, 1960), 11.

25. Walvoord, *Rapture Question*.

26. The scriptural reference to the rapture of the saints is 1 Thess. 4:16–17: "For the Lord himself shall descend from heaven with a shout, with the voice of the archangel, and with the trump of God: and the dead in Christ shall rise first: Then we which are alive shall be caught up together with them in the clouds, to meet the Lord in the air: And so shall we ever be with the Lord." In the mid-1970s, David MacPherson repeated this claim with much vigor. He claimed to have uncovered what he considered to be "the incredible cover up," namely, Darby's use of a vision of the secret rapture of the saints that a young Scottish woman named Margaret MacDonald had had in 1830, without giving her any credit for it. Dave MacPherson, *The Incredible Cover Up: The True Story on the Pre-Tribulation Rapture* (Plainsfield, NJ: Omega Publications, 1975); Dave MacPherson, *The Great Rapture Hoax* (Fletcher, NC: New Puritan Library, 1983).

27. Darby, "Rapture of Saints."

28. See, e.g., John N. Darby, "The Covenants," in *Collected Writings*, 3:44–56; James H. Brookes, *Israel and the Church* (Chicago: Fleming H. Revell, n.d.), 42–50; Cyrus I. Scofield, *Scofield Reference Bible* (New York: Oxford University Press, 1909), 20. For a more recent exposition of the subject, see Hal Lindsey, *The Promise* (Eugene, OR: Harvest House Publishers, 1982).

29. For a chart that illustrates the differentiation between God's plans for Israel and his plans for the church, see Clarence Larkin, *Dispensational Truth or God's Plan and Purpose in the Ages* (Glenside, PA: Published by the author, 1920), 19½ [sic].

30. C. H. Mackintosh, *The Lord's Coming* (Chicago: Moody Press, n.d.), 113.

31. James H. Brookes, *Maranatha: Or the Lord Cometh* (St. Louis: Edward Bredell, 1874), 425–26; William E. Blackstone, *The Millennium* (Chicago: Fleming H. Revell, 1904), 59; Scofield, *Scofield Reference Bible*, 914–15; Arno C. Gaebelein, *The Prophet Daniel* (New York: Publication Office, "Our Hope," 1936), 135.

32. George M. Marsden, *Fundamentalism and American Culture: The Shaping of Twentieth-Century Evangelicalism, 1870–1925* (New York: Oxford University Press, 1980).

33. James Barr, *Fundamentalism* (Philadelphia: Westminster Press, 1978), 40–54; James Barr, *The Scope and Authority of the Bible* (Philadelphia: Westminster Press, 1980), 77–78.

34. Cyrus I. Scofield defined *dispensation* as "a period of time during which man is tested in respect of obedience to some specific revelation of the will of God." *Scofield Reference Bible*, 5.

35. For a recording of the division of history in the writings of a few premillennialists, see Ehlert, *Bibliographic History of Dispensationalism*; Charles C. Ryrie, *Dispensationalism Today* (Grand Rapids, MI: Baker Book House, 1965), 84.

36. Based, according to dispensationalist belief, on Jer. 30, Dan. 12, Matt. 24, 2 Thess. 2, and Rev. 7. For a chart that illustrates the order of the eschatological events according to the dispensationalist belief, see J. Barton Payne, *The Prophecy Map of World History* (New York: Harper and Row, 1974).

37. Scofield, *Scofield Reference Bible*, 918. Scofield divided the seven years that separate, according to the dispensationalist belief, the rapture of the saints and the arrival of Jesus into two periods. Only the second one, in his view, would be tumultuous.

38. Blackstone, *Jesus Is Coming*, 65.

39. Henry Ironside, *Who Will Be Saved in the Coming Period of Judgment* (New York: Loizeaux Brothers, n.d.), 12–14; Arno C. Gaebelein, *Hath God Cast Away His People?* (New York: Gospel Publishing House, 1905), 28–29, 69.

40. See, e.g., Hal Lindsey, *The Late Great Planet Earth* (Grand Rapids, MI: Zondervan, 1970), 98–113. The dispensationalist image of the Antichrist was based on Rev. 3, Matt. 24, and 2 Thess. 2.

41. Thomas S. McCall and Zola Levitt, *The Coming Russian Invasion of Israel* (Chicago: Moody Press, 1974). For an exploration of the attitude of premillennialists to Russia since 1917, see Dwight Wilson, *Armageddon Now! The Premillennarian Response to Russia and Israel since 1917* (Grand Rapids, MI: Baker Book House, 1977).

42. Blackstone, *Jesus Is Coming*, 226–27.

43. See Bass, *Background to Dispensationalism*, 29; Weber, *Living in the Shadow*, 23; Yona Malachy, *American Fundamentalism and Israel* (Jerusalem: Hebrew University Press, 1978), 133.

44. See Merrill Simon, *Jerry Falwell and the Jews* (Middle Village, NY: Jonathan David, 1984).

45. See Joan Didion, "Mr. Bush and the Divine," *New York Review of Books*, 2003, November 6, 2003, 82.

46. LaHaye and Jenkins, *Left Behind*, 6–14.

47. On the Jews in the *Left Behind* series, see Yaakov Ariel, "How Are the Jews and Israel Portrayed in the *Left Behind* Series," in *Rapture, Revelation and the End*

Times, ed. Bruce Forbes and Jeanne Kilde (New York: Palgrave Macmillan, 2004), 131–66.

48. Ibid., 246–50; Tim LaHaye and Jerry B. Jenkins, *Assassins: Assignment Jerusalem, Target: Antichrist* (Wheaton, IL: Tyndale House 1999), 9–13.

49. See, e.g., LaHaye and Jenkins, *Left Behind*, 415; Tim LaHaye and Jerry B. Jenkins, *Nicolae: The Rise of Antichrist* (Wheaton, IL: Tyndale House, 1997), 369; Tim LaHaye and Jerry B. Jenkins, *Tribulation Force: The Continuing Drama of Those Left Behind* (Wheaton, IL: Tyndale House, 1996), 208.

50. LaHaye and Jenkins, *Tribulation Force*, 277.

51. LaHaye and Jenkins, *Left Behind*, 70.

52. Thomas Ice and Randall Price, *Ready to Rebuild* (Eugene, OR: Harvest House, 1992).

53. See Melani McAlister, "An Empire of Their Own," *Nation*, September 22, 2003.

54. See, e.g., "Left Behind: Bad Fiction; Bad Faith," www.godweb.org/leftbehind.htm.

55. Amy Johnson Frykholm, *Rapture Culture: "Left Behind" in Evangelical America* (New York: Oxford University Press, 2004), 21.

56. Gertrude Himmelfarb, *The Jewish Odyssey of George Eliot* (New York: Encounter Books, 2009).

57. Jonathan Hess, *Middlebrow Literature and the Making of German-Jewish Identity* (Stanford: Stanford University Press, 2010).

58. Abraham Mapu, *Ahavat Tsion* (1853; repr., Tel Aviv: Dvir, 1950).

59. Yemima Avidar-Tchernowitz, *Shmona be-Erkvot Ehad* (Tel Aviv: Tverski, 1960).

60. Larry Collins and Dominique LaPierre, *O Jerusalem* (New York: Simon and Schuster, 1972).

61. LaHaye and Jenkins, *Left Behind*, 80.

62. Marilou H. Flinkman et al., *The Chalice of Israel: Four Novellas Bound by Love, Enchantment, and Tradition* (Uhrichsville, OH: Barbour, 2001).

63. "Cup of Courage," in Flinkman et al., *Chalice of Israel*.

64. See, e.g., LaHaye and Jenkins, *Nicolae*, 225–50.

65. See Yaakov Ariel, "Jewish Suffering and Christian Salvation: The Evangelical-Fundamentalist Holocaust Memoirs," *Holocaust and Genocide Studies* 6 (1991): 63–78.

66. Marc H. Tanenbaum, Marvin R. Wilson, and A. James Rudin, *Evangelicals and Jews in Conversation* (Grand Rapids, MI: Baker Book House, 1978).

67. Tim LaHaye and Jerry B. Jenkins, *Soul Harvest: The World Takes Sides* (Wheaton, IL: Tyndale House, 1998), 245.

3. EVANGELICAL THEOLOGIANS, INSTITUTIONS, AND PUBLICATIONS AND THE JEWS

1. A. G. Mojtabai, *Blessed Assurance: At Home with the Bomb in Amarillo, Texas* (Boston: Houghton Mifflin, 1986).

2. James H. Brookes, *Maranatha: Or the Lord Cometh* (St. Louis: Edward Bredell, 1874), 389–445.

3. James H. Brookes, *"I Am Coming": A Setting Forth of the Second Coming of Our Lord Jesus as Personal-Private-Premillennial* (London: Pickering and Inglis, n.d.);

James H. Brookes, *Till He Comes* (Chicago: Fleming H. Revell, 1895), is almost identical to "I Am Coming."

4. Brookes, *Till He Comes,* 81.

5. See, e.g., James H. Brookes, "Israel and the Church," *Truth* 7 (1881): 117–20, 165–69.

6. James H. Brookes, "The Purpose of God Concerning Israel as Revealed in the Prophecy by Daniel," *Truth* 9 (1883): 514.

7. James H. Brookes, "Salvation Is of the Jews," *Truth* 19 (1893): 331.

8. James H. Brookes, "How to Reach the Jews," *Truth* 19 (1893): 135–36.

9. James H. Brookes, "Jewish Promise," *Truth* 11 (1885): 211–14; Brookes, "How to Reach the Jews," 134–36; James H. Brookes, "To the Jew First," *Truth* 19 (1893): 325–27.

10. Brookes, "Jewish Promise," 211–14; James H. Brookes, "Work among the Jews," *Truth* 20 (1894): 15–16.

11. Brookes, "Purpose of God," 502.

12. Brookes, "How to Reach the Jews," 135.

13. Ernest Sandeen, *The Roots of Fundamentalism: British and American Millenarianism, 1800-1930* (Grand Rapids, MI: Baker Book House, 1978), 132–61.

14. On the Niagara conferences, see also C. Norman Kraus, *Dispensationalism in America: Its Rise and Development* (Richmond, VA: John Knox, 1958), chs. 4 and 6.

15. Great Commission Prayer League, *The Fundamentals of the Faith as Expressed in the Articles of Belief of the Niagara Bible Conference,* pamphlet (Chicago: Great Commission Prayer League, n.d.).

16. James F. Findlay Jr., *Dwight L. Moody: American Evangelist, 1837–1899* (Chicago: University of Chicago Press, 1969).

17. For a classic literary depiction of a revival meeting, see Mark Twain, *The Adventures of Huckleberry Finn* (New York: Harper and Row, 1960), 111–16.

18. Even passages in Moody's messages that can be interpreted as premillennialist do not necessarily carry a distinct dispensationalist attribute. See Findlay, *Dwight L. Moody,* 410; Stanley M. Gundry, *Love Them In: The Proclamation Theology of D. L. Moody* (Chicago: Moody Press, 1976), 177–78; Sandeen, *Roots of Fundamentalism,* 180. A similar claim was made regarding the eschatological thought of Charles H. Spurgeon. See Dennis M. Swanson, "Charles H. Spurgeon and Eschatology: Did He Have a Discernable Millennial Position?" www.spurgeon.org/eschat.htm.

19. Note Dwight L. Moody's "The Second Coming of Christ," in *The Second Coming of Christ,* by Harriet Beecher Stowe et al. (Chicago: Bible Institute Colportage Association, 1896), 16–32.

20. Dwight L. Moody, *The New Sermons* (New York: H. S. Goodspeed, 1880), 535; Findlay, *Dwight L. Moody,* 253.

21. See, e.g., Dwight L. Moody, *Twelve Select Sermons* (Chicago: Fleming H. Revell, 1881), 118; Dwight L. Moody, *Glad Tidings* (New York: E. B. Treat, 1876), 105.

22. Dwight L. Moody, *"To the Work, to the Work!" Exhortations to Christians* (Chicago: Fleming H. Revell, 1880), 117.

23. Moody, *Twelve Select Sermons,* 113; Dwight L. Moody, *Great Joy* (New York: E. B. Treat, 1887), 454–55; Moody, *Great Joy,* 456; M. Laird Simons, *Holding the Fort: Comprising Sermons and Addresses at the Great Revival Meetings Conducted by Moody and Sankey* (Philadelphia: John C. Winston, 1880), 221.

24. Moody, *Twelve Select Sermons,* 65.

25. See, e.g., Dwight L. Moody, *Daily Meditations* (Grand Rapids, MI: Baker Book House, 1964), 201.

26. Dwight L. Moody, *Overcoming Life and Other Sermons* (New York: Fleming H. Revell, 1896), 10.

27. Moody, *"To the Work,"* 118.

28. Moody, *Daily Meditations,* 48, 128.

29. See, e.g., the denunciation of Moody by Rabbi Sabato Morais of Philadelphia in *Jewish Messenger,* January 21, 1871, quoted in Naomi W. Cohen, *Encounter with Emancipation: The German Jews in the United States, 1830–1914* (Philadelphia: Jewish Publication Society, 1984), 256.

30. Cohen, *Encounter with Emancipation,* 256.

31. See Moody's words in "Mr. Moody's Toughest Job: Trying to Persuade a Jew to Embrace Christianity," *New York Sun,* March 12, 1876, front page.

32. H. B. Hartzler, *Moody in Chicago: Or, the World's Fair Gospel Campaign* (New York: Fleming H. Revell, 1894), 96–101, 120–25; Richard K. Curtis, *They Called Him Mister Moody* (Garden City, NY: Doubleday, 1962), 280–81. On Adolf Stoecker and his role in propagating anti-Semitism in Germany, see Franklin H. Littell, *The German Phoenix* (New York: Doubleday, 1960), 33–34.

33. Hartzler, *Moody in Chicago,* 101.

34. See, e.g., a letter signed by "J. R." to the editor of *American Israelite,* December 10, 1875.

35. Moody, *Daily Meditations,* 72; Moody, "Second Coming of Christ," 31; Dwight L. Moody, "The Second Coming of Christ," *Northfield Echoes* 3 (1896): 281.

36. Dwight L. Moody, *To All People* (New York: E. B. Treat, 1877), 354.

37. Dwight L. Moody, *The Home Work of D. L. Moody* (New York: Fleming H. Revell, 1896), 67, 354.

38. Ibid., 355.

39. Robert E. Speer, *D. L. Moody* (East Northfield, MA: Northfield Schools, 1931).

40. Moody, *Great Joy,* 212–13.

41. George C. Needham, "The Future Advent of Jesus," *Northfield Echoes* 1 (1894): 498, 499, 496–97.

42. On Abraham Ben Oliel, see Albert Thompson, *A Century of Jewish Missions* (Old Tappan, NJ: Fleming H. Revell, 1905), 178–79.

43. Florence E. Ben Oliel, "Palestine and the Jews," *Northfield Echoes* 1 (1894): 143–44.

44. Ibid., 147, 142–43.

45. Nathaniel West, "History of the Premillennial Doctrine," in *Second Coming of Christ, Premillennial Essays of the Prophetic Conference Held in the Church of*

the Holy Trinity, New York City, ed. Nathaniel West (Chicago: Fleming H. Revell, 1879), 313–404.

46. W. R. Nicholson, "The Gathering of Israel," in West, *Second Coming of Christ,* 222.

47. Ibid., 228–31.

48. Ibid., 232.

49. Ibid., 233, 234, 235. Nicholson tried to outline his scheme by bringing in an abundance of quotations from Scripture.

50. Nathaniel West, "Prophecy and Israel," in *Prophetic Studies of the International Prophetic Conference, Chicago, Ill., November 1886,* ed. George C. Needham (Chicago: Fleming H. Revell, 1886), 122.

51. Ibid., 124–35.

52. William E. Erdman, "The Fullness of the Gentiles," in Needham, *Prophetic Studies,* 56–57.

53. William G. Moorehead, "The Final Issue of the Age," in *Addresses in the Second Coming of the Lord Delivered at the Prophetic Conference, Allegheny, Pa., December 3-6, 1895,* ed. Joseph Kyle and William S. Miller (Pittsburgh: W. W. Waters, n.d.), 10.

54. George M. Marsden, *Fundamentalism and American Culture: The Shaping of Twentieth-Century Evangelicalism, 1870–1925* (New York: Oxford University Press, 1980); Timothy P. Weber, *Living in the Shadow of the Second Coming* (Chicago: University of Chicago Press, 1988).

55. William G. Moorehead, "The Conversion of Israel and the Conversion of the World," in *Addresses of the International Prophetic Conference: Held December 10-15, 1901, in the Clarendon Street Baptist Church, Boston, Mass.* (Boston: Watchword and Truth, 1901),38.

56. Ibid., 40.

57. Ibid., 43.

58. William B. Riley, "The Significant Signs of the Times," in *The Coming and Kingdom of Christ: A Stenographic Report of the Prophetic Bible Conference Held at the Moody Bible Institute of Chicago, February 24–27, 1914,* ed. James M. Gray (Chicago: Bible Institute Association, 1914), 103.

59. Albert E. Thompson, "The Capture of Jerusalem," in *Light on Prophecy: A Coordinated, Constructive Teaching Being the Proceedings and Addresses at the Philadelphia Prophetic Conference, May 28–30, 1918,* ed. William L. Pettingill, J. R. Schafler, and J. D. Adams (New York: Christian Herald Bible House, 1918), 144, 142–53.

60. Pettingill, Schafler, and Adams, *Light on Prophecy,* 12.

61. Arno C. Gaebelein, "The Capture of Jerusalem and the Glorious Future of that City," in *Christ and Glory: Addresses Delivered at the New York Prophetic Conference, Carnegie Hall, November 25-28, 1918* (New York, 1919[?]), 157.

62. Frank E. Gaebelein, *The Story of the Scofield Reference Bible* (New York: Oxford University Press, 1959).

63. Arno C. Gaebelein, "Fulfilled Prophecy, a Potent Argument for the Bible," in *The Fundamentals: A Testimony to the Truth,* 12 vols., ed. Amzi C. Dixon, Louis Meyer, and Reuben A. Torrey (Chicago: Testimony, 1910–15), 11:57, 60.

64. See Reuben A. Torrey, *Bible Doctrines, First Course* (Chicago: Moody Bible Institute, 1901), 203–4, 208–11; Reuben A. Torrey, *Practical and Perplexing Questions Answered* (Chicago: Fleming H. Revell, 1908), 86; Reuben A. Torrey, "Jesus Christ: Notes on Lectures Delivered by R. A. Torrey," *Institute Tie* 2 (1893): 48–49.

65. Torrey, Bible *Doctrines, First Course,* 203–4, 208–11.

66. Reuben A. Torrey, *The Return of the Lord Jesus* (Los Angeles: Bible Institute of Los Angeles, 1913), 68, 69–79.

67. James M. Gray, "God's Covenant with Abraham, or Why He Chose Israel," in *A Textbook on Prophecy* (New York: Fleming H. Revell, 1918), 18–26.

68. James M. Gray, "The War and the Jews," *Christian Workers Magazine* 16 (1916): 347–48.

69. James M. Gray, "The Capture of Jerusalem," *Christian Workers Magazine* 18 (1918): 447; James M. Gray, "Israel Restored and Renewed" and "Jerusalem's Capture in the Light of Prophecy," in *Textbook on Prophecy,* 41–47, 200–206.

70. James M. Gray, *Great Epochs of Sacred History* (New York: Fleming H. Revell, 1910), 107.

71. James M. Gray, "The Jewish Protocols," *Moody Bible Institute Monthly* 22 (1921): 598.

72. William L. Pettingill, *Israel: Jehovah's Covenant People* (Harrisburg, PA: Fred Kelker, 1905), repr. in *Loving His Appearing and Other Prophetic Studies* (Findlay, OH: Fundamental Truth Publishers, 1943), 90–145.

73. William L. Pettingill, *God's Prophecies for Plain People* (Philadelphia: Philadelphia School of the Bible, 1923), 81; William L. Pettingill, *Nearing the End* (Chicago: Van Kampen Press, 1948), 50.

74. On Blackstone's life, see "William E. Blackstone—The Friend of Israel," *Jewish Era* 1 (1892): 7–76; Cutler B. Whitwell, "The Life Story of William E. Blackstone and of 'Jesus Is Coming,'" *Sunday School Times,* January 11, 1936, repr. in *Jewish Era* 46 (1936): 64–67; "Their Works Do Follow Them," *Alliance Weekly,* January 18, 1936; Beth M. Lindberg, *A God Filled Life: The Story of William E. Blackstone* (Chicago: n.p., n.d.); Sandy Keck, "W. E. Blackstone, Champion of Zion" (series of eleven articles), *American Messianic Fellowship Monthly* 78–79 (1973–74); Jonathan David Moorhead, "Jesus Is Coming: The Life and Works of William E. Blackstone, 1841–1935" (PhD diss., Dallas Theological Seminary, 2008), ch. 1, http://gradworks.umi.com/33/18/3318932.html.

75. On Blackstone's thought concerning the Jews, see also Moorhead, "Jesus Is Coming," chs. 3–4.

76. See, e.g., Blackstone, *Jesus Is Coming,* 3rd ed. (Los Angeles: Bible House, 1908), 162–76.

77. William E. Blackstone, *The Heart of the Jewish Problem* (Chicago: Chicago Hebrew Mission, 1905), 16.

78. Blackstone, *Jesus Is Coming,* 84.

79. Ibid., 222

80. Ibid., 236–41.

81. See, e.g., William E. Blackstone, "The Jews," *Jewish Era* 33 (1924): 87.

82. See, e.g., William E. Blackstone, "Jerusalem," *Jewish Era* 1 (1892): 70–71.

83. William E. Blackstone, "Missions," in *Prophetic Studies of the International Prophetic Conference, Chicago, November 1886* (Chicago: Fleming H. Revell, 1886, 194–202; William E. Blackstone, *Satan, His Kingdom and Its Overthrow* (Chicago: Fleming H. Revell, 1900), 36.

84. "From Los Angeles, California," *Jewish Era,* 17 (1918): 80–82; William Blackstone to President Woodrow Wilson, November 4, 1914, and William Blackstone, telegram to President Warren Harding, December 30, 1920, copies of both in Blackstone Personal Papers, Billy Graham Center, Wheaton, IL.

85. See John Hagee's website, www.JohnHagee.com.

86. Blackstone, *Jesus Is Coming,* 65.

4. EVANGELICALS AND JEWISH RESTORATION

1. Anthony Ashley Cooper, 7th Earl of Shaftesbury, "Restoration of the Jews," advertisement, *Times* (London), 4 November 1840; Anthony Ashley Cooper, 7th Earl of Shaftesbury, to Lord Palmerston, March 1841, letter accompanying the petition, in *History of Zionism, 1600-1918,* ed. Nahum Sokolow (London: Longmans, Green, 1919), 2:408 (Addenda). See also Barbara W. Tuchman, *Bible and Sword: England and Palestine from the Bronze Age to Balfour* (London: Macmillan, 1983),175–207; Donald M. Lewis, *The Origins of Christian Zionism: Lord Shaftesbury and Evangelical Support for a Jewish Homeland* (Cambridge: Cambridge University Press, 2010), 107–212; Jill Hamilton, *God, Guns and Israel: Britain, the First World War and the Jews in the Holy City* (Stroud: Sutton, 2004), 63–75.

2. Anthony Ashley Cooper, 7th Earl of Shaftesbury, draft dispatch No. 33 to Lord Ponsonby, Foreign Office, 17 February 1841, regarding the expediency of the provision of Turkish security for the Jews in Palestine, in *Minorities in the Middle East: Jewish Communities in Arab Countries, 1841-1974,* ed. Beitullah Destani ([Slough]: Archive Editions, 2005), vol. 1, document 1.

3. Franz Kobler, *The Vision Was There: A History of the British Movement for the Restoration of the Jews to Palestine* (London: Lincolns-Prager, 1956); Ernest Sandeen, *The Roots of Fundamentalism: British and American Millenarianism, 1800-1930,* (Grand Rapids, MI: Baker Book House, 1978); Lewis, *Origins of Christian Zionism,* 36–103; Stephen Sizer, *Christian Zionism: Road Map to Armaggedon* (Leicester: Intervarsity Press, 2004), 30–55.

4. Abigail Green, "Rethinking Sir Moses Montefiore: Religion, Nationhood, and International Philanthropy in the Nineteenth Century," *American Historical Review* 110, no. 3 (2005): 631–58.

5. On Gawler and Montefiore and their impact on Jewish restoration, see Reed M. Holmes, *Dreamers of Zion: Joseph Smith and George J. Adams, Conviction,*

Leadership and Israel's Renewal (Brighton: Sussex Academic Press, 2003), 21; Abigail Green, *Moses Montefiore: Jewish Liberator, Imperial Hero* (Cambridge, MA: Harvard University Press, 2010), 214–16.

6. Yaakov Ariel, *On Behalf of Israel: American Fundamentalist Attitudes towards Jews, Judaism and Zionism* (New York: Carlson, 1991), 55–96; Jonathan David Moorhead, "Jesus Is Coming: The Life and Works of William E. Blackstone, 1841–1935" (PhD diss., Dallas Theological Seminary, 2008).

7. William Blackstone, *Jesus Is Coming*, 3rd ed. (Los Angeles: Bible House, 1908), 211–13, 236–41.

8. Moshe Davis, "American Christian Devotees in the Holy Land," in *America and the Holy Land: With Eyes toward Zion—IV* (Jerusalem: International Center for the University Teaching of Jewish Civilization, 1995).

9. Blackstone quoted in Lewis, *Origins of Christian Zionism*, 151; Shaftesbury quote from Edwin Hodder, *The Life and Work of the Seventh Earl of Shaftesbury, K.G.* (London: Cassel, 1887), 2:478.

10. George F. Magoun, "The Chicago Jewish-Christian Conference," *Our Day* 7 (1890): 266–71.

11. William E. Blackstone, "Blackstone Memorial." A copy of the original typed petition is preserved in Blackstone Personal Papers, Billy Graham Center, Wheaton, IL (hereafter BPP/BGC).

12. Cyrus Adler and Aaron M. Margalith, *With Firmness in the Right: American Diplomatic Action Affecting Jews, 1840–1945* (New York: American Jewish Committee, 1946).

13. See Shalom Goldman, *Zeal for Zion: Christians, Jews, and he Idea of the Promised Land* (Chapel Hill: University of North Carolina Press, 2009), 1–41.

14. Marnin Feinstein, *American Zionism, 1884–1904* (New York: Herzl Press, 1965).

15. A. J. G. Lesser, *In the Last Days* (Chicago: N. Gonsior, 1897), preface.

16. "Return to Zion: Our Hope and the Hope of Righteous Christians," *Ha Pisga* 3 (May 8, 1891): 1 [in Hebrew].

17. On Selah Merrill and his attitudes toward the Jewish settlement in Palestine, as well as toward evangelical settlers in the country, see Frank Edward Manuel, *The Realities of American Palestine Relations* (Washington, DC: Public Affairs Press, 1949), 68–75; Ron Bartour, "Episodes in the Relations of the American Consulate in Jerusalem with the Jewish Community in the 19th Century, 1856-1906," *Cathedra* 5 (1977): 127, 128, 131–32; Ruth Kark, "Annual Reports of the United States Consuls in the Holy Land as a Source for the Study of 19th Century Eretz Israel," in *With Eyes toward Zion—II*, ed. Moshe Davis (New York: Praeger, 1986), 147–48.

18. Adler and Margalith, *With Firmness in the Right*, 225.

19. James D. Richardson, *A Compilation of the Messages and Papers of the Presidents* (Washington, DC: Government Printing Office, 1817–92), 9:188.

20. Claude Duvernoy, *The Prince and the Prophet* (Paradise, CA: Land of Promise, 1973).

21. Leonard Stein, *The Balfour Declaration* (London: Valentine, Mitchell, 1961); Isaiah Friedman, *The Question of Palestine, 1914–1918: British-Jewish-Arab Relations* (London: Routledge and K. Paul, 1973); Tuchman, *Bible and Sword*; Jonathan Schneer, *The Balfour Declaration: The Origins of the Arab-Israeli Conflict* (New York: Random House, 2010).

22. Yaakov Ariel, "William Blackstone and the Petition of 1916: A Neglected Chapter in the History of Christian Zionism in America," *Studies in Contemporary Jewry* 7 (1991): 68–85.

23. Ibid.

24. In a letter to President Wilson on November 16, 1917, Blackstone wrote: "It would have been possible to have secured any number of signatures of the most representative character to the Memorial, but this was so evident that it was not necessary. The endorsement of the Presbyterian General Assembly, the Ministers' Meetings of the Methodists and Baptists, and many representative individuals and officials, evidence the general approval which the Memorial receives from our entire population," in BPP/BGC.

25. *Minutes of the General Assembly of the Presbyterian Church in the United States of America,* vol. 16 (Philadelphia: Office of the General Assembly, 1916), 185–86; Rev. W. H. Roberts to John W. Baer, president of Occidental College, L.A., August 28, 1916, in BPP, BGC.

26. In BPP/BGC.

27. See Blackstone's correspondence with Bishop Bashford in BPP/BGC, e.g., their exchange of letters on July 2 and 3, 1917.

28. See Wise to Blackstone, June 30, 1917, and September 27, 1918; Nathan Straus to Blackstone, May 16, 1916; Jacob de Haas to Blackstone, December 26, 1916; and Louis D. Brandeis to Blackstone, February 21, 1917, all in BPP/BGC. See also Louis D. Brandeis to Jacob de Haas, May 8, 1917, June 7, 1917, and December 6, 1917, in Melvin I. Urofsky and David W. Levy, eds., *Letters of Louis D. Brandeis* (Albany: State University of New York Press, 1971-78), 4:289, 296, 327.

29. Stephen Wise had shown it to the president "in an unofficial manner" twice, in June 1917 and September 1918. See Wise to Blackstone, June 30, 1917, and September 17, 1918, in BPP/BGC. Blackstone sent a copy of the petition to Wilson in May 1916.

30. Historians who have not gone through Blackstone's personal papers have mistakenly thought that Blackstone submitted the petition. See, e.g., Anita Libman-Lebeson, "Zionism Comes to Chicago," in *Early History of Zionism in America: Papers Presented at the Conference on the Early History of Zionism in America,* ed. Isidore Solomon Meyer (New York: American Jewish Historical Society and Theodor Herzl Foundation 1958), 163; Yona Malachy, *American Fundamentalism and Israel* (Jerusalem: Hebrew University Press, 1978), 139; Lawrence J. Epstein, *Zion's Call: Christian Contributions to the Origins and Development of Israel* (Lanham, MD: University Press of America, 1984), 112.

31. See a copy of his letter to Stephen Wise, July 9, 1917, in BPP/BGC.

32. In his letter to Blackstone on 30 June 1917, Stephen Wise wrote: "I had the honor of presenting in informal fashion to the President at the White House yesterday a copy of your petition. The President accepted it, but he felt that this was not the best time for the public or private presentation thereof. I think I have the right to say that the President is prepared to leave to Justice Brandeis the decision with respect to the most opportune time in which formally to present the petition to him." In BPP/BGC. Bashford, one of the people to whom Blackstone entrusted the presentation of the petition, wrote to Blackstone two days afterward and told him, "The whole matter of a public hearing depends upon President Wilson. At times he seems to want the public hearing and at other times he requests it to be postponed." In BPP/BGC.

33. See Robert Speer to Blackstone, May 23, 1917, and Bashford to Blackstone, June 1, 1917, both in BPP/BGC. Wilson discussed his suggestions for changes with Brandeis. His specific request was to drop the suggestion to put the future Jewish commonwealth in Palestine under "international control" and to leave the control "undesignated." Brandeis was in favor of the same changes. See Brandeis to Jacob de Haas, May 8, 1917, in Urofsky and Levy, *Letters of Louis D. Brandeis,* 4:289. Brandeis obviously discussed the petition in detail with Wilson.

34. At one point Wilson sent an emissary, Henry J. Morganthau, to the Middle East to try to persuade Turkey to sign a separate peace treaty with the Entente Powers. The British, who were eager to conquer Turkish territories, sent Chaim Weizmann to persuade Morgenthau to abandon his mission. Wilson was aware of Britain's attempt to use her promise to build a Jewish home in Palestine as a means of taking control of Palestine. Although he favored the Zionist idea, Wilson hesitated at first to give his approval to the issuing of the Balfour Declaration. See Stein, *Balfour Declaration,* 529; Peter Grose, *Israel in the Mind of America* (New York: Knopf, 1983), 61–62.

35. See Grose, *Israel in the Mind,* 60–63; Stein, *Balfour Declaration,* 30.

36. See Ben Halpern, *A Clash of Heroes: Brandeis, Weizmann, and American Zionism* (New York: Oxford University Press, 1987), 168.

37. "He never once mentioned the second coming, and he always said that we need not worry about heaven—that would take care of itself—but he had to be concerned about the problems of this world." Arthur S. Link, Wilson's biographer and editor of his papers, to Yaakov Ariel, July 18, 1984.

38. Stephen P. Wise, *Challenging Years* (New York: G. P. Putnam and Sons, 1949), 186–87.

39. Joseph L. Grabill, *Protestant Diplomacy and the Near East: Missionary Influence on American Policy, 1810–1927* (Minneapolis: University of Minnesota Press, 1971).

40. See, e.g., George T. B. Davis, *Fulfilled Prophecies That Prove the Bible* (Philadelphia: Million Testaments Campaign, 1931); and Keith L. Brooks, *The Jews and the Passion for Palestine in Light of Prophecy* (Los Angeles: Brooks Publications, 1937).

41. James Gray, "Editorial," *Moody Bible Institute Monthly* 31 (1931): 346; Arno C. Gaebelein, "The Jewish Population in Palestine," *Our Hope* 43 (1937): 552; "Will Britain White Paper Keep the Jews out of Palestine?" *Our Hope* 46 (1939): 179.

42. Bernard Wasserstein, *Wyndham Deedes in Palestine* (London: Anglo-Israel Association, 1973).

43. Christopher Sykes, *Orde Wingate: A Biography* (Cleveland, OH: World Publishing, 1959); John Bierman and Colin Smith, *Fire in the Night: Wingate of Burma, Ethiopia and Zion* (New York: Random House, 1999).

44. See, e.g., "Observations and Experiences," *Our Hope* 44 (1938): 686; David A. Rausch, "Our Hope: An American Fundamentalist Journal and the Holocaust, 1937–1945," *Fides et Historia* 12 (1980): 83–103.

45. Yaakov Ariel, "Eschatology, Evangelism, and Dialogue: The Presbyterian Mission to the Jews, 1920–1960," *Journal of Presbyterian History* 75, no. 1 (1997): 29–42.

46. Caitlin Carenen, "The American Christian Palestine Committee, the Holocaust, and Mainstream Protestant Zionism, 1938–1948," *Holocaust and Genocide Studies* 24, no. 2 (2010): 273–96.

47. See Herzel Fishman, *American Protestantism and the Jewish State* (Detroit: Wayne State University Press, 1975).

48. Donald E. Wagner, *Dying in the Land of Promise: Palestine and Palestinian Christianity from Pentecost to 2000* (London: Melisende, 2003); Sizer, *Christian Zionism;* Jimmy Carter, *Palestine: Peace Not Apartheid* (New York: Simon and Schuster, 2006).

5. EVANGELICALS AND JEWS IN THE HOLY LAND

1. On McCaul's premillennialist thought, see Jorge Quiñónez, "The Doyen of 19th Century British Jewish Missions," *Mishkan* 43 (2005): 43–75.

2. Elizabeth Anne Finn, *Reminiscences of Mrs. Finn* (London: Marshall, Morgan, and Scott, 1929).

3. Donald M. Lewis, *The Origins of Christian Zionism: Lord Shaftesbury and the Evangelical Support for a Jewish Homeland* (New York: Cambridge University Press, 2010), 125–45.

4. Gay Daly, *Pre-Raphaelites in Love* (New York: Quality Paperback Bookclub, 2002), 2–3, 48, 109–11, 128–30, 156–57, 223–25, 231–38.

5. Kelvin Crombie, *For the Love of Zion: Christian Witness and the Restoration of Israel* (London: Hodder and Stoughton, 1991).

6. On the Jerusalem syndrome, see Robert Stone, *Damascus Gate* (New York: Houghton Mifflin, 1998).

7. Ada Goodrich-Freer, *Inner Jerusalem* (New York: Dutton, 1904), 80.

8. Yaakov Ariel, "Expecting the Messiah: Christian and Jewish Expectations in the Late Ottoman Period," in *The History of Jerusalem: The Late Ottoman Period (1800-1917)*, ed. Israel Bartal and Haim Goren (Jerusalem: Yad Izhak Ben-Zvi, 2010), 83-96 [in Hebrew].

9. Yaakov Ariel and Ruth Kark, "Messianism, Holiness, Charisma, and Community: A History of the American-Swedish Colony in Jerusalem, 1881–1933," *Church History* 65, no. 4 (1996): 641–57. The most detailed history of the American Colony is that of Helga Dudman and Ruth Kark, *The American Colony: Scenes from a Jerusalem Saga* (Jerusalem: Carta Jerusalem, 1998). On the American Colony from a cultural studies, postcolonialist perspective, see Milette Shamir, "Our Jerusalem: Americans in the Holy Land and Protestant Narratives of National Entitlement," *American Studies* 55, no. 1 (2003): 29–60.

10. Bertha Spafford Vester, *Our Jerusalem* (Garden City, NY: Doubleday, 1950), 1–61.

11. Donald W. Dayton, *Theological Roots of Pentecostalism* (Grand Rapids, MI: Francis Asbury, 1987), 101–6.

12. Vester, *Our Jerusalem*, 45–46; Alfred B. Smith, comp., *Inspiring Hymns* (Grand Rapids, MI: Singspiration, 1951), no. 271.

13. Anna Spafford to Hannah Whitall Smith and others, January 25, 1883, in Hannah Whitall Smith Archive, Asbury Theological Seminary, Wilmore, KY.

14. Vester, *Our Jerusalem*, 54–61, 156–58, .

15. Vester, *Our Jerusalem*, 55–61; Spafford to Smith, January 25, 1883, and January 17, 1900, in Smith Archive, and *Chicago Daily News*, May 14–15, 1895.

16. "Life in the City of Zion," *Chicago Daily News*, May 14, 1895, 2; "Holy City Their Home," *Chicago Daily News*, May 15, 1895, 12.

17. Dudman and Kark, *American Colony*, 35–62.

18. Goodrich-Freer, *Inner Jerusalem*, 48.

19. Spafford to Smith, January 25, 1883, in Smith Archive. A copy of the Mi SheBe'rach blessing composed by Yemenite Jews in honor of Spafford has been on display in a historical exhibition organized by the American Colony Hotel, Jerusalem.

20. See the description of Mrs. Gordon in Selma Lagerlöf's novel *Jerusalem* (1905), trans. Velma Swanston Howard (Garden City, NY: Doubleday, 1915), as well as Jane Geniese's *American Priestess: The Extraordinary Story of Anna Spafford and the American Colony in Jerusalem* (New York: Doubleday, 2008). The latter is more critical of Anna Spafford's personality.

21. Elmer T. Clark, *The Small Sects in America*, rev. ed. (New York: Abingdon-Cokesbury Press, 1949), 11–24; Yaacov Oved, *Two Hundred Years of American Communes* (New York: Oxford University Press, 1988), 369–77; Ruth Kark, "William H. Rudy and His Route from Chicago to the American-Swedish Colony in Jerusalem" [in Hebrew], *Ariel* 100 (1994): 33–43.

22. Ariel and Kark, "Messianism, Holiness."

23. Alexander H. Ford, "Our American Colony," *Appleton's Magazine* 8, no. 6 (1906): 643-55.

24. Paul Elmen, "The American-Swedish Kibbutz," *Swedish Pioneer Historical Quarterly* 32 (1981): 205–18.

25. Edith Larsson, *Dalafolk i Heligt Land* (Stockholm: Natur och Kultur, 1957), 20–27, 33–34, quoted in Ariel and Kark, "Messianism, Holiness." I owe thanks to Ruth

Kark, who in 1996 initiated a joint paper on the group and conducted large parts of the research.

26. Dudman and Kark, *American Colony*, 111-12.

27. Dov Gavish, "The American Colony and Its Photographers," in *Zev Vilnay's Jubilee Volume*, ed. Ely Schiller (Jerusalem: Ariel, 1984), 127–44 [in Hebrew].

28. Lagerlof, *Jerusalem*; Selma Lagerlof, *Address to the Universal Christian Conference in Stockholm* (Stockholm: n.p., 1925), 1–4, in Bertha Spafford Vester, "Scrapbook of Articles about the American Colony, and Loose Enclosures," Library of Congress, Manuscript Division, www.loc.gov/item/mamcol000130.

29. Ariel and Kark, "Messianism, Holiness."

30. Lester I. Vogel, *To See a Promised Land* (University Park: Pennsylvania State University Press, 1993), 152–59.

31. Quoted in Vivian D. Lipman, *Americans and the Holy Land through British Eyes, 1820– 1917: A Documentary History* (London: published by author, 1989), 153–57.

32. See, e.g., *Hymns of the Christian Life* (Harrisburg, PA: Christian Publications, 1936), 125.

33. Anne Grace Lind, interview by Yaakov Ariel, December 28, 1993, Jerusalem; Ariel and Kark, "Messianism, Holiness."

34. This is apparent from a chapter (32) that Vester added to her book *Our Jerusalem* ([Beirut]: Middle East Export Press, 1950).

35. Rosabeth Moss Kanter, *Commitment and Community: Communes and Utopias in Sociological Perspective* (Cambridge, MA: Harvard University Press, 1977), 138–45; Robert S. Fogarty, *All Things New: American Communes and Utopian Movements, 1860–1914* (Lanham, MD: Lexington Books, 2003).

36. See, e.g., Elizabeth Summer, "A Different Kind of Freedom? Order and Discipline among the Moravian Brethren in Germany and Salem, North Carolina, 1771–1801," *Church History* 63 (1994): 221–34.

6. INSTRUCTING CHRISTIANS AND JEWS

1. Albert E. Thompson, *A Century of Jewish Missions* (Old Tappan, NJ: Fleming H. Revell, 1905).

2. Le Roy E. Froom, *The Prophetic Faith of Our Fathers,* 4 vols. (Washington, DC: Review and Herald, 1946–54), 3:415–33; Kelvin Crombie, *For the Love of Zion: Christian Witness and the Restoration of Israel* (London: Hodder and Stoughton, 1991).

3. Thompson, *Century of Jewish Missions*, 93–106, 279–80.

4. Samuel Freuder, *My Return to Judaism,* 2nd, enl. ed. (New York: B. Zuckerman, 1922); Joseph Hoffman Cohn, *I Have Fought a Good Fight: The Story of Jewish Mission Pioneering in America* (New York: American Board of Missions to the Jews, 1953).

5. See Yaakov Ariel, "Counterculture and Missions: Jews for Jesus and the Vietnam Era Missionary Campaigns," *Religion and American Culture.* 9, no. 2 (1999): 233–57.

6. See Jonathan Sarna, "The American Jewish Response to Nineteenth-Century Christian Missions," *Journal of American History* 68 (1981): 35-51.

7. See George L. Berlin, *Defending the Faith: Nineteenth-Century American Jewish Writings on Christianity and Jesus* (Albany: State University of New York Press, 1989), 31-51.

8. "Working against the Missions," *American Hebrew* 91 (September 27, 1912): 617.

9. Rose Cohen, *Out of the Shadow: A Russian Jewish Girlhood on the Lower East Side* (New York: George H. Doran, 1918), 160.

10. "Working against the Missions," 617.

11. William R. Hutchison, *Between the Times: The Travail of Protestant Establishment in America, 1900-1960* (New York: Cambridge University Press, 1989); Bradley J. Longfield, *The Presbyterian Controversy: Fundamentalists, Modernists and Moderates* (New York: Oxford University Press, 1991).

12. *Minutes of the General Assembly of the Presbyterian Church in the U.S.A,* vol. 16 (Philadelphia: Office of the General Assembly, 1916), 185-86.

13. John Stuart Conning, *Our Jewish Neighbors: An Essay in Understanding* (New York: Fleming H. Revell, 1927).

14. Ibid., esp. 40-50.

15. Home Mission Reports to the General Assembly of the Presbyterian Church in the U.S.A., *Minutes of the General Assembly of the Presbyterian Church in the U.S.A* (Philadelphia: Office of the General Assembly, 1920-60).

16. This comes out strongly in Esther Bronstein's biography: Janet Hoover Thoma, *Esther* (Elgin, IL: D. C. Cook, [1978?]).

17. Ibid.

18. See, e.g., Conrad Hoffman, "Jewry in Distress! What of It?," *Missionary Review of the World* 61 (June 1938): 261-62.

19. Haim Genizi, *American Apathy: The Plight of Christian Refugees from Nazism* (Ramat Gan: Bar-Ilan University Press, 1983).

20. Harold A. Sevener, *A Rabbi's Vision* (Charlotte, NC: Chosen People Ministry, 1994), 188-219.

21. Robert W. Ross, "Perverse Witness to the Holocaust: Christian Missions and Missionaries," *Holocaust Studies Annual* 2 (1986): 127-39.

22. See correspondence with directors of the missionary centers at the Presbyterian Historical Society, Philadelphia, group 27, box 15, folder 4.

23. *Minutes of the General Assembly of the Presbyterian Church in the U.S.A*, 3rd set., vol. 19 (Philadelphia: Office of the General Assembly, 1931), pt. 2, 47.

24. David Bronstein, *Peniel Portrait* (Chicago: D. C. Peck, 1943); Thoma, *Esther*, 94-95, 133.

25. See Elias Newman, "Looking Back Twenty-Five Years," *Hebrew Christian Alliance Quarterly* 25 (1940): 24.

26. Bronstein, *Peniel Portrait.*

27. Bronstein, *The Jewish Passover and the Christian Communion* (Chicago: published by the author, 1941).

28. Benny Kraut, "Towards the Establishment of the National Conference of Christian and Jews: The Tenuous Road to Religious Goodwill in the 1920s," *American Jewish History* 77, no. 3 (1988): 388–412; Benny Kraut, "A Wary Collaboration: Jews, Catholics, and the Protestant Goodwill Movement," in *Between the Times: The Travail of the Protestant Establishment in America, 1900–1960,* ed. William R. Hutchison (Cambridge: Cambridge University Press, 1990): 193–230.

29. See John S. Conway, "Protestant Missions to the Jews: Ecclesiastical Imperialism or Theological Aberration?" *Holocaust and Genocide Studies* 1 (1986): 127–46, esp. 134–44.

30. Ibid.

31. Daniel F. Rice, "Reinhold Niebuhr and Judaism," *Journal of the American Academy of Religion* 45, no. 1, suppl. (1977): 101–46; Egal Feldman, "Reinhold Niebuhr and the Jews," *Jewish Social Studies* 46, nos. 3–4 (1984): 293–302.

32. See yearly reports of the Missions Department in the yearly *Minutes of the General Assembly of the Presbyterian Church in the U.S.A.* (Philadelphia: Office of the General Assembly, 1946–60).

33. On the ecumenical-evangelical debate, see William Hutchison, *Errand to the World: American Protestant Thought and Foreign Missions* (Chicago: University of Chicago Press, 1987), 177–83.

34. See "A Theological Understanding of the Relationship between Christians and Jews," adopted by the General Assembly of the Presbyterian Church in the U.S.A. in June 1987, in *The Theology of the Churches and the Jewish People: Statements by the World Council of Churches and Its Member Churches,* ed. Allan R. Brockway and the World Council of Churches (Geneva: WCC Publications, 1988), 105–20.

35. Marvin Hier and Abraham Cooper, "Presbyterians against Israel: Liberal Protestants Are Engaging in Historical Revisionism Concerning Jews and the Holy Land," *Wall Street Journal*, Friday, December 3, 2010.

7. EVANGELICAL YIDDISH

1. See Benjamin Harshav, *The Meaning of Yiddish* (Stanford: Stanford University Press, 1990); Leonard Jay Greenspoon, ed., *Yiddish Language and Culture: Then and Now* (Omaha: Creighton University Press, 1998), which includes a much welcomed essay on Bible societies in Britain and their efforts to translate the Bible into Yiddish; and Miriam Weinstein, *Yiddish: A Nation of Words* (New York: Ballantine Books, 2001).

2. See Karl Pruter, *Jewish Christians in the United States: A Bibliography* (New York: Garland, 1987).

3. Arno C. Gaebelein, *Half a Century: The Autobiography of a Servant* (New York: Our Hope, 1930), 30.

4. On the program at the Moody Bible Institute, see Yaakov Ariel, *Evangelizing the Chosen People: Missions to the Jews in America, 1880–2000* (Chapel Hill: University of North Carolina Press, 2000), 93–100.

5. In the latter decades of the journal's existence, the mission published *Roe Yisroel* in two languages, English and Yiddish.

6. See the pages of *The Shepherd of Israel*, in the archives of the Chosen People Ministries, New York.

7. Robert I. Winer, *The Calling: The Hebrew Christian Alliance* (Philadelphia: Hebrew Christian Alliance, 1990).

8. See, e.g., *Der Vekhter* (*The Watchman*) 2, no. 1 (January 1918).

9. Yaʾel (Joseph Immanuel Landsman), *Der Tolui* (Newark, NJ: Light Bearers Publication Society, 1926). I owe thanks to Leonard Prager, who brought the booklet to my attention, and to Mr. Jorge Quiñónez, for sending me a copy.

10. Arn-Yude [Aaron] Kligerman, *Der Got-Mentsh — Ver iz Er?* (Chicago: Book Store, n.d.).

11. Khanokh K. Bregman, *Rosheshone* (Toronto: Beys Dorshey Emes, n.d.).

12. Harold A. Sevener, *A Rabbi's Vision: A Century of Proclaiming Messiah; A History of Chosen People Ministries, Inc.* (Charlotte, NC: Chosen People Ministries, 1994), 182–83.

13. William E. Blackstone, *Dos tsveyte Kumen fun dem Meshiekh* (Chicago: Fleming H. Revell, 1917), 152–53. I owe thanks to Mr. Wes Taber, who very kindly sent me a copy of the Yiddish version of the book.

14. Ibid., 10–18.

15. Henry Einspruch, "Literature for the Christian Approach to the Jews," in *Christians and Jews: Report of the Atlantic City Conference on the Christian Approach to the Jews* (New York: International Missionary Council, 1931), 97–102.

16. On Einspruch's life, see Henry Einspruch, *The Man with the Book* (Baltimore: Lederer Foundation, 1976).

17. Ibid.

18. See William F. Smalley, *Translation as Mission: Bible Translation in the Modern Missionary Movement* (Macon, GA: Mercer University Press, 1991), 16, 39–40.

19. On the Tsenerene, see Weinstein, *Yiddish*, 23.

20. Harry M. Orlinsky, "Yehoash's Yiddish Translation of the Bible," in *Essays in Biblical Culture and Bible Translation* (New York: Ktav, 1974), 418–22.

21. See Einspruch, *Man and the Book*, 83–132.

22. Yiddish readers in America who have read Einspruch's translation tend to agree with Ravitsh's assessment of its beauty. Peter Heineg expressed this opinion to me in a letter of June 23, 2002.

23. Leonard Prager, *Yiddish Culture in Britain* (Frankfurt: Peter Lang, 1990), 383–84.

24. The American Board of Missions to the Jews would not distribute Einspruch's translation even before Krelenbaum's translation came out. Instead, in 1947 they used "a translation made and published by the British and Foreign Bible Society of London, England, in 1901 and now reprinted with their approval." The American Board called the 1947 reprint the "Leopold Cohn Memorial Edition" in honor of its founder and first director.

25. See, e.g., the column "In the Little Shtetl of Vaysechvoos," in the journal *Issues: A Messianic Jewish Perspective*.

8. EVANGELICAL CHRISTIANS AND ANTI-JEWISH CONSPIRACY THEORIES

1. Arno C. Gaebelein, *The Conflict of the Ages, the Mystery of Lawlessness: Its Origin, Historic Development and Coming Defeat* (New York: Publication Office, "Our Hope," 1933).

2. David Rausch, *Arno C. Gaebelein: Irenic Fundamentalist and Scholar* (New York: Edwin Mellen Press, 1983).

3. Gaebelein, *Conflict of the Ages*. On *Protocols of the Elders of Zion,* see Norman Cohn, *Warrant for Genocide: The Myth of the Jewish World-Conspiracy and the Protocols of the Elders of Zion* (London: Eyre and Spottiswoode, 1967); Esther Webman, ed., *The Global Impact of "The Protocols of the Elders of Zion"* (London: Routledge, 2011).

4. William V. Trollinger, *God's Empire: William Bell Riley and Midwestern Fundamentalism* (Madison: University of Wisconsin Press, 1990), esp. 80; James M. Gray, "The Jewish Protocols," *Moody Bible Institute Monthly* 22 (1921): 598.

5. Timothy P. Weber, *On the Road to Armageddon* (Grand Rapids, MI: Baker Academic Press, 2004), 129–54.

6. Glen Jeansonne, *Gerald L. K. Smith: Minister of Hate* (New Haven: Yale University Press, 1988).

7. Ralph L. Roy, *Apostles of Discord* (Boston: Beacon Press, 1953).

8. George M. Marsden, *Reforming Fundamentalism: Fuller Seminary and the New Evangelicalism* (Grand Rapids, MI: Eerdmans, 1987), 39.

9. George M. Marsden, *Fundamentalism and American Culture: The Shaping of Twentieth-Century Evangelicalism, 1870–1925* (New York: Oxford University Press, 1980); Martin E. Marty, *Modern American Religion*, vol. 1, *The Irony of It All, 1893–1919* (Chicago: University of Chicago Press, 1986), 208–50.

10. Yaakov Ariel, "The Growth of American Fundamentalism: 1865–1925," *Zmanim* 38 (Summer 1991): 92–93.

11. Shanny Luft, "The Devil's Church: Conservative Protestantism and the Movies, 1915–1955" (PhD diss., University of North Carolina, Chapel Hill, 2009).

12. Timothy P. Weber, *Living in the Shadow of the Second Coming* (Chicago: University of Chicago Press, 1988).

13. Gaebelein, *Half a Century*, 35.

14. Arno C. Gaebelein, "The Middle Wall of Partition," *Our Hope* 34 (June 1928): 750.

15. Weber, *Living in the Shadow,* 156–57.

16. Gaebelein, *Conflict of the Ages,* 147.

17. Arno C. Gaebelein, "Aspects of Jewish Power in the United States," *Our Hope* 29 (1922): 103.

18. Charles C. Cook, "The International Jew," *King's Business* 12 (November 1921): 1087.

19. Arno C. Gaebelein, "Isaiah Chapter XIX, the Conversion of Egypt," *Our Hope* 27 (1921): 601.
20. Neil Baldwin, *Henry Ford and the Jews: The Mass Production of Hate* (New York: Public Affairs, 2001).
21. Robert Sugerman, "The American Career of The Protocols of the Elders of Zion," *American Jewish History* 1 (September 1981): 48–78.
22. Marsden, *Fundamentalism and American Culture*, 176–95.
23. Weber, *Living in the Shadow*; Weber, *On the Road*, esp. 45–66.
24. William B. Riley, *Protocols and Communism* (Minneapolis: L. W. Camp, 1934). See also Leonard Dinnerstein, *Antisemitism in America* (New York: Oxford University Press, 1994); Egal Feldman, *Dual Destinies: The Jewish Encounter with Protestant America* (Urbana: University of Illinois Press, 1990), 175–88.
25. "Unmasking the 'Hidden Hand'—A World Conspiracy," *Defender* 7 (February 1933): 3; "Protocols Confirmed," *Defender* 8 (November 1933): 15; Luft, "Devil's Church."
26. Gaebelein, *Conflict of the Ages*, 95–100.
27. Elias Newman, *The Fundamentalist Resuscitation of the Antisemitic Protocol Forgery* (Minneapolis: Augsburg Publishing House, 1934).
28. William B. Riley, "Cohn vs. Riley," *Pilot* 15 (May 1935): 218; William B. Riley, "Joseph Cohn Again," *Pilot* 15 (June 1935): 249–50; Gerald B. Winrod, "Editor Winrod Answers Editor Cohn," *Defender* 8 (June 1933): 60; see also Joseph Hoffman Cohn, *I Have Fought a Good Fight: The Story of Jewish Mission Pioneering in America* (New York: American Board of Missions to the Jews, 1953).
29. William Vance Trollinger, *God's Empire: William Bell Riley and Midwestern Fundamentalism* (Madison: University of Wisconsin Press, 1990), 76.
30. Ibid., 76–77.
31. David Rausch, "Our Hope: An American Fundamentalist Journal and the Holocaust, 1937–1945," *Fides et Historia* 12 (1980): 89–103.
32. George T. B. Davis, *Adventures in Soul-Winning* (Philadelphia: Million Testaments Campaign, 1942), 76–77.
33. William B. Riley, *Wanted—A World Leader!* (Minneapolis: published by the author, 1939), 41–51, 71–72.
34. Martin E. Marty, *Modern American Religion*, vol. 3, *Under God Indivisible, 1941–1960* (Chicago: University of Chicago Press, 1996).
35. Will Herberg, *Protestant, Catholic, Jew: An Essay in American Religious Sociology* (New York: Anchor Books, 1960).
36. Jeansonne, *Gerald L. K. Smith*.
37. Marsden, *Reforming Fundamentalism*.
38. See, e.g., Jay Rawlings and Meridel Rawlings, *Gates of Brass: The Voice of Russian Jews Denied Exit Visas to Israel* (Chichester: New Wine Press, 1985).

9. THE EVANGELICAL UNDERSTANDING OF THE HOLOCAUST

1. Peter Novick, *The Holocaust in American Life* (New York: Houghton Mifflin, 1999); David Cesarani, ed., *After Eichmann: Collective Memory and the Holocaust since 1961* (New York: Routledge, 2005); Edward T. Linenthal, *Preserving Memory: The Struggle to Create America's Holocaust Museum* (New York: Penguin, 1995); Hasia Diner, *We Remember with Reverence and Love: American Jews and the Myth of Silence after the Holocaust, 1945–1962* (New York: New York University Press, 2008).

2. Carol Rittner, Stephen D. Smith, and Irena Steinfeldt, eds., *The Holocaust and the Christian World,* ed. (New York: Continuum, 2000); Friedrich Zipfel, *Kirchenkampf in Deutschland, 1933–1945* (Berlin: De Gruyter, 1965); Robert P. Ericksen and Susannah Heschel, eds., *Betrayal: German Churches and the Holocaust* (Minneapolis: Fortress Press, 1999); Richard Steigman-Gall, *The Holy Reich* (Cambridge: Cambridge University Press, 2003).

3. Corrie ten Boom, *A Prisoner and Yet* (London: Christian Literature Crusade, 1954).

4. Corrie ten Boom, with John and Elizabeth Sherrill, *The Hiding Place* (Washington Depot, CT: Chosen Books, 1971). The 1975 movie of the same name was directed by James F. Collier.

5. Joseph Michman, "Some Reflections on the Dutch Churches and the Jews," in *Judaism and Christianity under the Impact of National Socialism,* ed. Otto Dov Kulka and Paul Mendes-Flohr (Jerusalem: Zalman Shazar Center, 1987), 349–52.

6. ten Boom, *Hiding Place,* 123–24. Subsequent page citations to this work are given parenthetically in the text.

7. See, e.g., Irmgard A. Hunt's *On Hitler's Mountain: Overcoming the Legacy of a Nazi Childhood* (New York: HarperCollins, 2005) and the anonymous *A Woman in Berlin* (New York: Picador, 2006).

8. Maria A. Hirschmann, *Hansi: The Girl Who Loved the Swastika* (Wheaton, IL: Tyndale House, 1970); Maria A. Hirschmann, *Hansi's New Life* (Old Tappan, NJ: Fleming H. Revell, 1980).

9. Hirschmann, *Hansi's New Life,* 106. Subsequent page citations to this work are given parenthetically in the text.

10. Johanna-Ruth Dobschiner, *Selected to Live* (London: Pickering and Inglis, 1976). Subsequent page citations to this work are given parenthetically in the text.

11. Vera Schlamm and B. Friedman, *Pursued* (San Francisco: Hineni Ministries, 1972).

12. John G. Cawelti, *Adventure, Mystery, and Romance: Formula Stories as Art and Popular Culture* (Chicago: University of Chicago Press, 1976); Gary L. Comstock with C. Wayne Marshall, *Religious Autobiographies* (Belmont, CA: Wadsworth, 2004), 2–22.

13. Rose Warmer, *12 Months in the Concentration Camp* (Columbus, OH: Bible Literature International, s.d. [ca. 1960]).

14. Myrna Grant, *The Journey* (London: Hodder and Stoughton, 1978). Subsequent page citations to this work are given parenthetically in the text.

15. Jan Markell, *Angels in the Camp: A Remarkable Story of Peace in the Midst of the Holocaust* (Wheaton, IL: Tyndale House, 1979). Subsequent page citations to this work are given parenthetically in the text.

16. Hal Lindsey, *The Late Great Planet Earth* (Grand Rapids, MI: Zondervan, 1970).

17. Lynn S. Neal, *Romancing God: Evangelical Women and Inspirational Fiction* (Chapel Hill: University of North Carolina Press, 2007).

18. Efrain Sicher, *The Holocaust Novel* (New York: Routledge, 2005).

19. Leon Uris, *Exodus* (Garden City, NY: Doubleday, 1958).

20. See Deborah Dash-Moore, *To the Golden Cities* (New York: Free Press, 1994), 243, 248–60.

21. See the Thoenes' page "Shiloh Light Foundation" at www.thoenebooks.com/foundation.asp.

22. Bodie Thoene and Brock Thoene, *The Zion Covenant, Book 4: Jerusalem Interlude* (Wheaton, IL: Tyndale House, 2005), 422.

23. See, e.g., Bodie Thoene and Brock Thoene, *The Zion Covenant* (Wheaton, IL: Tyndale House, 2005). The series was originally published by Bethany House, Grand Rapids, MI.

24. Thoene and Thoene, *Jerusalem Interlude*.

25. See, e.g., ibid., 410–13.

26. See, e.g., Bodie Thoene and Brock Thoene, *Thunder from Jerusalem: A Novel of the Struggle for Jerusalem* (New York: Penguin Putman, 2001).

10. EVANGELICALS AND THE BIRTH OF THE JEWISH STATE

1. See, e.g., George T. B. Davis, *Fulfilled Prophecies That Prove the Bible* (Philadelphia: Million Testaments, 1931); Keith L. Brooks, *The Jews and the Passion for Palestine in Light of Prophecy* (Grand Rapids, MI: Zondervan, 1937).

2. Dwight Wilson, *Armageddon Now! The Premillenarian Response to Russia and Israel since 1917* (Grand Rapids, MI: Baker Book House, 1977).

3. Gershon Nerel, "Operation Mercy on the Eve of the Establishment of the State of Israel," *Mishkan* 61 (2009): 21–32.

4. Louis T. Talbot and William W. Orr, *The New Nation of Israel and the Word of God* (Los Angeles: Bible Institute of Los Angeles, 1948); M. R. DeHaan, *The Jew and Palestine in Prophecy* (Grand Rapids, MI: Zondervan, 1954); Arthur Kac, *The Rebirth of the State of Israel: Is It of God or Men?* (Chicago: Moody Press, 1958); George T. B. Davis, *God's Guiding Hand* (Philadelphia: Million Testaments Campaign, 1962).

5. Uri Avneri, *Milhemet HuYom Hashvii [The Seventh Day War]* (Tel Aviv: Yam Suf, 1968), 145–80.

6. Zvi Rin to Yaakov Ariel, July 30, 1996.

7. A copy in Yaakov Ariel's collection of Robert Lindsey's personal papers.

8. Robert Lindsey, "The Jews and Christian Hope," unpublished typewritten manuscript, in Yaakov Ariel's collection.

9. David Ohana, *The Origins of Israeli Mythology: Neither Canaanites nor Crusaders* (New York: Cambridge University Press, 2012).

10. John Walvoord, *Israel in Prophecy* (Grand Rapids, MI: Zondervan, 1962), 19.

11. Gershon Nerel, *Anti-Zionism in the "Electronic Church" of Palestinian Christianity* (Jerusalem: Hebrew University Press, 2006).

12. L. Nelson Bell, "Unfolding Destiny," *Christianity Today* (1967): 1044–45; John F. Walvoord, "The Amazing Rise of Israel," *Moody Monthly* 68 (October 1967): 22-25. Nelson Bell, an evangelical leader in his own right, was Billy Graham's father-in-law.

13. Peter L. Williams and Peter L. Benson, *Religion on Capitol Hill: Myth and Realities* (New York: Oxford University Press, 1986); Allen D. Hertzke, *Representing God in Washington* (Knoxville: University of Tennessee Press, 1988); Mark Silk, *Spiritual Politics* (New York: Touchstone, 1989); and Michael Lienesch, *Redeeming America: Piety and Politics in the New Christian Right* (Chapel Hill: University of North Carolina Press, 1993).

14. See John Hagee, *Final Dawn over Jerusalem* (Nashville, TN: T. Nelson, 1998).

15. Thomas McCall and Zola Levitt, *The Coming Russian Invasion of Israel* (Chicago: Moody Press, 1974).

16. Billy Graham, *World Aflame* (Surrey: Word's Work, 1965); Wilson, *Armageddon Now!*; A. G. Mojtabai, *Blessed Assurance: At Home with the Bomb in Amarillo, Texas* (Boston: Houghton Mifflin, 1986); Angela M. Lahr, *Millennial Dreams and Apocalyptic Nightmares: The Cold War Origins of Political Evangelicalism* (New York: Oxford University Press, 2007).

17. Jay Rawlings and Meridel Rawlings, *Gates of Brass: The Voice of Russian Jews Denied Exit Visas to Israel* (Chichester: New Wine Press, 1985).

18. Melani McAlister, *Epic Encounters: Culture, Media, and U.S. Interests in the Middle East, 1945–2000* (Berkeley: University of California Press, 2001), 197.

19. Warren Bass, *Support Any Friend: Kennedy's Middle East and the Making of the U.S.-Israel Alliance* (New York: Oxford University Press, 2003).

20. Paul Merkley, *American Presidents, Religion and Israel: The Heirs of Cyrus* (Westport, CT: Praeger, 2004), 54–61.

21. Michael Oren, *Six Days of War: June 1967 and the Making of the Modern Middle East* (New York: Presidio Press, 2002).

22. Peter Grose, *Israel in the Mind of America* (New York: Knopf, 1983).

23. Merkley, *American Presidents*, 162–80.

24. Jimmy Carter, *Palestine, Peace, Not Apartheid* (New York: Simon and Schuster, 2006). Carter's book resembles that of other progressive evangelicals.

25. Martin Gardner, "Giving God a Hand," *New York Review of Books*, August 13, 1987, 22; Timothy P. Weber, *On the Road to Armageddon* (Grand Rapids, MI: Baker Academic Press, 2004), 201.

26. Mark Silk, *Spiritual Politics* (New York: Touchstone, 1989); Lienesch, *Redeeming America*; Stephen Spector, *Evangelicals and Israel: The Story of American Christian Zionism* (New York: Oxford University Press, 2009).

27. Victoria Clark, *Allies for Armageddon: The Rise of Christian Zionism* (New Haven: Yale University Press, 2007), 273–77; Merkley, *American Presidents*, 213–28.

28. Spector, *Evangelicals and Israel*, 234.

29. Irvine H. Anderson, *Biblical Interpretation and Middle East Policy: The Promised Land, America and Israel, 1917–2002* (Gainesville: University Press of Florida, 2005).

30. Jackie Feldman, "Constructing a Shared Bible Land: Jewish Israeli Guiding Performances for Protestant Pilgrims," *American Ethnologist* 34 (2007): 349–72.

31. Stephen Sizer, *Christian Zionism: Road Map to Armaggedon* (Leicester: Intervarsity Press, 2004), 216–19.

32. Kai Kjaer-Hansen and Bodil F. Skjott, *Facts and Myths about the Messianic Congregations in Israel* (Jerusalem: United Christian Council in Israel in Cooperation with the Caspari Center, 1999).

33. Paul C. Merkley, *Christian Attitudes towards the State of Israel* (Montreal: McGill-Queens, 2001), 170–80; Weber, *On the Road,* 213–34.

34. Merkley, *Christian Attitudes,* 176–83; Clark, *Allies for Armageddon*, 201–30.

35. Jan Willem van der Hoeven, *If I Forget Thee O Jerusalem,* brochure (Jerusalem: International Christian Embassy, 1984), 4.

36. Arlynn Nellhaus, "Go Tell It on the Mountain," *Jerusalem Post Magazine*, October 1992, 6–7.

37. A social worker who wished to remain anonymous, interview by author, Jerusalem, December 2009.

38. "US Gives Tax Breaks for Donation to Aid Settlements in the West Bank," *New York Times,* July 6, 2010, A1, A10, A11.

39. Weber, *On the Road,* 230.

40. *Washington for Israel Summit* (Jerusalem: International Christian Embassy, Jerusalem, 1992).

41. Jan van der Hoeven, *Babylon or Jerusalem* (Shippensburg, PA: Destiny Image, 1993).

42. *Le Maan Tzion Lo Echeshe* (Jerusalem: International Christian Embassy, 1990), 13.

43. Van der Hoeven, *Babylon or Jerusalem*, esp. 47–71, 131–46, 169–78.

44. Thomas S. Kidd, *American Christians and Islam: Evangelical Culture from the Colonial Period to the Age of Terrorism* (Princeton: Princeton University Press, 2009); Spector, *Evangelicals and Israel*, 50–110.

45. John F. Walvoord, *Israel in Prophecy* (Grand Rapids, MI: Zondervan, 1962); Billy Graham, *World Aflame* (Garden City, NY: Doubleday, 1965); Hal Lindsey, *The Late Great Planet Earth* (Grand Rapids, MI: Zondervan, 1970); Derek Prince,

Promised Land: God's Word and the Nation of Israel (Charlotte, NC: Derek Prince Ministries, 2006).

46. Elishua Davidson, *Islam, Israel, and the Last Days* (Eugene, OR: Harvest House, 1991); Randall Price, *Unholy War: America, Israel and Radical Islam* (Eugene, OR: Harvest House, 2001).

47. Spector, *Evangelicals and Israel*, 76–110.

48. Hal Lindsey, *The Everlasting Hatred: The Roots of Jihad* (Murieta, CA: Oracle, 2002).

49. Spector, *Evangelicals and Israel*, 150; Michael Krupp, "Falsche Propheten in Jerusalem," October 3, 1988, an unpublished essay sent to Protestant religious journals in Germany, a copy in Ariel's possession.

50. On the MECC and Israel, see Merkley, *Christian Attitudes*, 184–86.

51. *Signs of Hope: 1988 Annual Report of the Middle East Council of Churches*, Cyprus, July 1989.

52. *What Is Western Fundamentalist Christian Zionism?* (Limosol, Cyprus: Middle East Council of Churches, April 1988; rev. ed., August 1988). The revised edition is somewhat more moderate than the first.

53. *Mishkan*, no. 12 (1990).

54. See, e.g., Michael Pragai's book *Faith and Fulfillment* (London: Valentine Mitchell, 1985). The author, who served as the head of the Department for Christian Churches and Organizations in the Israeli Ministry of Foreign Affairs, demonstrated a complete lack of knowledge of the nature of the evangelical support of Zionism and of the differences between conservative and mainline/liberal churches.

55. Uri Bialer, *Cross on the Star of David* (Bloomington: Indiana University Press, 2005).

56. Yona Malachy, *American Fundamentalism and Israel* (Jerusalem: Hebrew University Press, 1978).

57. Ibid., 106–11.

58. David E. Harrel, *Oral Roberts: An American Life* (Bloomington: Indiana University Press, 1985), 137.

59. See, e.g., Robert L. Lindsey, *Israel in Christendom* (Tel Aviv: Dugit, 1961).

60. Per Osterlye, *The Church in Israel* (Lund: Gleerup, 1970).

61. "Israel Looks on U.S. Evangelical Christian as Potent Allies," *Washington Post*, March 23, 1981, A11.

62. For a photograph of such a gathering, see Tzipora Luria, "Lelo Tasbichim: Notztim Mechuiavim LeYesha" [Without Inhibitions: Christians Committed to Judea and Samaria], *Nekuda*, no. 128, March 17, 1989, 31.

63. Yael Eshkenazi, "HaKesher HaNotzri Shel Moledet" [The Christian Connection with Moledet], *Kol HaIr*, November 1, 1991, 30.

64. Luria, "LeLo Tasbichim," 30–34.

65. Daniel Ben Simon, "Doing Something for Judaism," *Haaretz*, December 18, 1997, English ed., 1–2.

66. From a letter circulated on the Internet by Noam Hendren, Baruch Maoz, and Marvin Dramer, March 1997, https://groups.google.com/ forum/?fromgroups=#!topic/alt.christnet.evangelical/ed3NrNqOUEg.

67. I am thankful to the Ray Gannon, who discussed the opposition to the law with me during a visit to Chapel Hill in 1996.

68. Kai Kjaer-Hansen, "Editorial: Mission and Evangelization in Israel, 1948–1998," *Mishkan* 28 (1998): 1.

69. Merkley, *Christian Attitudes,* 21–22.

11. EVANGELICAL CHRISTIANS AND THE BUILDING OF THE TEMPLE

1. Dennis Michael Rohan, criminal file 69/173, Jerusalem District Court, Archive.

2. Sara Japhet, "From the King's Sanctuary to the Chosen City," in *Jerusalem: Its Sanctity and Centrality to Judaism Christianity and Islam*, ed. Lee I. Levine (New York: Continuum, 1999), 3–15.

3. Abraham Joshua Heschel, *The Sabbath* (New York: Farrar, Strauss and Giroux, 1951).

4. Yaron Z. Eliav, *The Temple Mount in Time, Place, and Memory* (Baltimore: Johns Hopkins University Press, 2005).

5. Stefan C. Reif, "Jerusalem in Jewish Liturgy," in Levine, *Jerusalem*, 424–37.

6. Mishnah, Kelim 1, 8; "Har Ha Bayit," in *HaEncyclopedia HaTalmudit*, 10:575–92.

7. Michael Oren, *Six Days of War: June 1967 and the Making of the Modern Middle East* (New York: Presidio Press, 2002), 245.

8. Gideon Aran, "From Religious Zionism to Zionist Religion: The Roots of Gush Emunim," *Studies in Contemporary Jewry* 2 (1986): 118.

9. Shmuel Berkovitz, *The Temple Mount and the Western Wall in Israeli Law* (Jerusalem: Jerusalem Institute for Israeli Studies, 2001).

10. Ehud Sprinzak, *The Ascendance of Israel's Radical Right* (Oxford: Oxford University Press, 1991), 279–88.

11. Dennis Michael Rohan, criminal file 69/173, Jerusalem District Court, Archive.

12. Motti Inbari, "The Oslo Accords and the Temple Mount, a Case Study: The Movement for the Establishment of the Temple," *Hebrew Union College Annual* 74 (2005): 1–45.

13. Benjamin Beit-Hallahmi, *Despair and Deliverance: Private Salvation in Contemporary Israel* (Albany: State University of New York Press), 69–70.

14. Gideon Aran, "The Father, the Son and the Holy Land," in *Spokesmen for the Despised*, ed. Scott Appleby (Chicago: Chicago University Press, 1996).

15. See Avi Sagi and Yedidia Stern, "The Gap between the Halacha and Reality Had Never Been So Large," *Haaretz,* December 12, 2005.

16. Sprinzak, *Ascendance of Israel's Radical Right.*

17. Motti Inbari, *Jewish Fundamentalism and the Temple Mount* (Albany: State University of New York Press, 2008).

18. Inbari, "Oslo Accords."

19. I am thankful to the late Pnina Pely, a veteran of a number of the groups, for sharing her collection of documents with me.

20. On the Jewish groups aiming at building the Temple during the 1970s and 1980s, see Sprinzak, *Ascendance of Israel's Radical Right*, 264–69, 279–88.

21. Joel Bin-Nun, *The Day the Temple of the Lord Is Built* (Jerusalem: Jerusalem First College, n.d).

22. See *Ibane HaMikdash* (Let the Temple Be Built), a monthly journal of the Movement for the Building of the Temple, and hand-typed circulation letters of the Unto the Mount of the Lord movement. I am indebted to Pnina Pely for providing me with copies of the publications. On the scope and variety of the Jewish Temple builders, see also Nadav Shragai, "To Bring God Home," *Haaretz*, September 17, 1998, B2.

23. See Mel Gibson's movie *The Passion of the Christ* (2003).

24. Norman Cohn, *In Pursuit of the Millennium* (New York: Oxford University Press, 1970).

25. Raymond L. Cox, "Time for the Temple?," *Eternity* 19 (January 1968), 17–18; Malcolm Couch, "When Will the Jews Rebuild the Temple?," *Moody Monthly* 74 (December 1973): 34–35, 86.

26. Hal Lindsey, *The Late Great Planet Earth* (Grand Rapids, MI: Zondervan, 1970), 32–47.

27. See Grant R. Jeffrey, *Armageddon: Appointment with Destiny* (New York: Bantam Books, 1990), esp. 108–50.

28. See, e.g., Don Stewart and Chuck Missler, *The Coming Temple: Center Stage for the Final Countdown* (Orange, CA: Dart Press, 1991), 157–70.

29. Stanley Goldfoot, interview by author, Jerusalem, November 12, 1990. See also the brochure *Jerusalem Temple Foundation* (Jerusalem: Jerusalem Temple Foundation, n.d.).

30. Motti Inbari, *Jewish Fundamentalism and the Temple Mount: Who Will Build the Third Temple?* (Albany: State University of New York Press, 2009), 181.

31. See Lambert Dolphin's website, www.Ldolphin.org. Copies of tracts that the Californian physicist has published are in Yaakov Ariel's collection.

32. Stewart and Missler, *Coming Temple*, 157–70.

33. See Yisrayl Hawkins, *A Peaceful Solution to Building the Next Temple in Yerusalem* (Abilene: House of Yahweh, 1989).

34. See, e.g., Doug Wead, David Lewis, and Hal Donaldson, *Where Is the Lost Ark?* (Minneapolis: Bethany House, n.d.).

35. Lawrence Wright, "Forcing the End," *New Yorker*, July 20, 1998, 42–53; "Breeding Red Heifers," Jewish Telegraph Agency, September 2, 1999, /www.jta.org/sep99/02-cows.htm.

36. See, e.g., C. W. Sleming, *These Are the Garments* (Fort Washington, PA: Christian Literature Crusade, n.d.); Wead, Lewis, and Donaldson, *Where Is the Lost Ark?*; Don Stewart and Chuck Missler, *In Search of the Lost Ark* (Orange, CA: Dart Press, 1991); Thomas Ice and Randall Price, *Ready to Rebuild: The Imminent Plan*

to Rebuild the Last Days Temple (Eugene, OR: Harvest House, 1992); John W. Schmitt and J. Carl Laney, *Messiah's Coming Temple* (Grand Rapids, MI: Kregal, 1997).

37. See, e.g., Tim LaHaye and Jerry R. Jenkins, *Left Behind* (Wheaton: Tyndale House, IL, 1995), 415, *Nicolae: The Rise of Antichrist* (Wheaton, IL: Tyndale House, 1997), 369, and *Tribulation Force: The Continuing Drama of Those Left Behind* (Wheaton, IL: Tyndale House, 1996), 208.

38. LaHaye and Jenkins, *Tribulation Force*, 277.

39. Quoted in Robert I. Friedman, *Zealots for Zion* (New York: Random House, 1992), 144.

40. Ibid., 144–45.

41. Ice and Price, *Ready to Rebuild*.

42. On the Noahide movement, see Jeffrey Kaplan, *Radical Religion in America* (Syracuse: Syracuse University Press, 1997) 100–126; Kimberly Hanke, *Turning to Torah: The Emerging Noachide Movement* (Northvale, NJ: Jason Aronson, 1995).

43. See the Temple Mount Faithful's website at www.templemountfaithful.org and their newsletter the *Voice of the Temple Mount*.

44. Jan Willem van der Hoeven, *Babylon or Jerusalem?* (Shippensburg, PA: Destiny Image, 1993), 131–46, 170–71. See also Peter A. Michas, *What Is Islam?* (Poway, CA: Christian Mid-East Conference, n.d.); Randall Price, *Unholy War: America, Israel and Radical Islam* (Eugene, OR: Harvest House, 2001); Elishua Davidson, *Islam, Israel and the Last Days* (Eugene, OR: Harvest House, 1991).

45. John Elson, "Apocalypse Now?," *Time*, February 11, 1991, 64.

46. See the advertisement in the Israeli daily *Haaretz*, "Holiday of Freedom, Passover 1983," signed by Terry Risenhoover, James Deloach, and Doug Krieger. A copy is in Yaakov Ariel's possession.

47. See Yiftah Zilberman, "The Struggle over Mosque/Temple in Jerusalem and Ayodhya," in *Sovereignty of God and Man: Sanctity and Political Centrality on the Temple Mount*, ed. Yitzhak Reiter (Jerusalem: Jerusalem Institute for Israel Studies, 2001); Jeffrey Goldberg, "Israel's Y2K Problem," *New York Times Magazine*, October 3, 1999; Gershom Gorenberg, "The Heart of the Matter," *Jerusalem Report*, August 14, 2000, 14–17.

48. Bernard Wasserstein, *Jerusalem Divided* (New Haven: Yale University Press, 2001), 226, 317–44; Yitzhak Reiter, "Third in Sanctity, First in Politics: The Haram al-Sharif for Muslims," in Reiter, *Sovereignty of God and Man*, 155–80.

49. Avi Dichter, head of Israeli General Security Service, speech at Herzliya College, December 16, 2003, quoted in Inbari, "Oslo Accords," 3.

50. Barbara Ledeen and Michael Ledeen, "The Temple Mount Plot," *New Republic*, June 18, 1984, 20–23.

51. David Landau, *Piety and Power: The World of Jewish Fundamentalism*, 160; Nadav Shragai, *The Contested Mountain: The Struggle over the Temple Mount, Jews, Muslims, Religion and Politics since 1967* (Jerusalem: Keter, 1995), 340–63 [in Hebrew].

52. Eli Ishai, "Epokalipsa Kimat Achshav" [Apocalypse Almost Now], *Makor Rishon, Yoman Shevue,* May 22, 1999, 10–11; Boaz Gaon, "Mekhakim LaMashiach" [Waiting for the Messiah], *Sofshavua,* May 22, 1999, 14–18, 78.

53. Gershom Gorenberg, "Israel Pushes Out 'Elijah' for Promising to Bring the Redemption," *Jerusalem Report,* September 27, 1999.

54. See Jerusalem Connection, www.thejerusalemconnection.us.

55. This is evident in the series Left Behind, published during the late 1990s and 2000s.

12. EVANGELICAL JEWS

1. David Eichhorn, *Evangelizing the American Jew* (Middle Village, NY: Jonathan David, 1978), 45–140.

2. Robert I. Winer, *The Calling: The Hebrew Christian Alliance* (Philadelphia: Hebrew Christian Alliance, 1990).

3. Kai Kjaer-Hansen, *Joseph Rabinowitz and the Messianic Movement* (Grand Rapids, MI: Eerdmans, 1995).

4. David Rausch, *Arno C. Gaebelein: Irenic Fundamentalist and Scholar* (New York: Edwin Mellen Press, 1983), 19–52.

5. Elias Newman, "Looking Back Twenty-Five Years," *Hebrew Christian Alliance Quarterly* 25 (1940): 24.

6. S. B. Rohold, "Messianic Judaism," *Prayer and Work for Israel,* January 1918, 8–11; Rausch, *Messianic Judaism: Its History, Theology, and Polity* (New York: Mellen, 1982), 32–43.

7. Robert L. Lindsey, ed., *Christian Terms in Hebrew* (Jerusalem: United Christian Council in Israel, 1976).

8. This comes across in the writings of Messianic Jews who emphasize the independent spirit of their movement: see, e.g., Michael Schiffman, *Return of the Remnant: The Rebirth of Messianic Judaism* (Baltimore: Lederer Publications, 1992).

9. Louis Goldberg, *Turbulence over the Middle East: Israel and the Nations in Confrontation and the Coming Kingdom of Peace on Earth* (Neptune, NJ: Loizeaux Brothers, 1982).

10. Yaakov Ariel, "Hasidism in the Age of Aquarius: The House of Love and Prayer," *Religion and American Culture* 13, no. 2 (2003): 139–65.

11. Elliot Klayman, "Messianic Zionism: God's Plan for Israel," *Messianic Outreach* 7, no. 4 (1998): 3–8.

12. David A. Rausch, "Hebrew Christian Renaissance and Early Conflict with Messianic Judaism," *Fides et Historia* 15, no. 2 (1983): 67–79.

13. See, e.g., Edward F. Plowman, "Turning On to Jeshua," *Christianity Today,* December 17, 1971, 34–39; Carl F. Henry, "Jews Find the Messiah," *Christianity Today,* April 13, 1973, 28–29. I am thankful to Professor Terry Muck of Asbury Theological Seminary for speaking with me about his experience in initiating such conversations when he was the editor of *Christianity Today.*

14. Abe Cohen et al., "More Jewish Than Ever—We've Found the Messiah," *Christianity Today,* February 1, 1974, 11–17.

15. Louis Goldberg, "The Messianic Jew," *Christianity Today,* February 1, 1974, 6–11.

16. James Hutchens, "A Case for Messianic Judaism" (PhD diss., Fuller Theological Seminary, 1974), preface.

17. William Willoughby, "A Breakthrough for Messianic Judaism?," *Moody Monthly,* March 1972, 16-19.

18. Rausch, *Messianic Judaism.*

19. Rausch, "The Messianic Jewish Congregational Movement," *Christian Century,* September 15–22, 1982, 928–29.

20. See, e.g., World Council of Churches, *The Theology of the Churches and the Jewish People* (Geneva: WCC Publications, 1988).

21. See James K. Wellman, *Evangelical vs. Liberal: The Clash of Christian Cultures in the Pacific Northwest* (New York: Oxford University Press, 2008).

22. Jeffrey Goldberg, "Some of Their Best Friends Are Jews," *New York Times Magazine,* March 16, 1997, 42–44.

23. Harold A. Sevener, *A Rabbi's Vision: A Century of Proclaiming Messiah; A History of Chosen People Ministries, Inc.* (Charlotte, NC: Chosen People Ministries, 1994), 420–21, 453–56.

24. Ibid., 454.

25. Randall Balmer, *Mine Eyes Have Seen the Glory* (New York: Oxford University Press, 1989), 17; Elaine Eckland, *Korean American Evangelicals: New Models for Civic Life* (New York: Oxford University Press, 2006).

26. See, e.g., the website of Jews on First! at www.jewsonfirst.org. The motto of the group is: "Defending the First Amendment against the Christian Right . . . because if Jews don't speak out, they'll think we don't mind."

27. See Sean McCloud, *Making the American Religious Fringe: Exotics, Subversives, and Journalists, 1955–1993* (Chapel Hill: University of North Carolina Press, 2003); Harvey Cox, "Deep Structures in the Study of Religions," in *Understanding the New Religions,* ed. Jacob Needleman and George Baker (New York: Seabury Press, 1978), 122–30.

28. David Max Eichhorn, *Evangelizing the American Jew* (Middle Village, NY: Jonathan David, 1978); "Jews for Jesus Is New Freak Group," *Jewish Post and Opinion,* May 14, 1971.

29. Ronald Gittelsohn, "Jews for Jesus: Are They Real?" (1979), repr. in *Smashing the Idols: A Jewish Inquiry into the Cult Phenomenon,* ed. Gary D. Eisenberg (Northvale, NJ: Jason Aronson, 1988), 171.

30. Ibid., 172.

31. Yaakov Ariel, "From New Hasidism to Outreach Yeshirot: The Origins of the Movement of Renewal and Return to Tradition," in *Kabbalah and Contemporary Spiritual Revival,* ed. Boaz Huss (Beer Sheva: Ben Gurion University Press, 2011), 1-21 [in Hebrew].

32. On the ongoing programs of the group, see the websites http://jews4judaism.org/jewsforjudaism/ and http://jewsforjudaism.org.

33. On the activities of Yad L'Achim, see www.yadlachimusa.org.il.

34. Copy in the possession of Yaakov Ariel.

35. Lawrence M. Silverman, *What to Say When the Missionary Comes to Your Door* (Plymouth, MA: Plymouth Lodge, B'nai Brith, n.d.).

36. Benjamin J. Segal, ed., *The Missionary at the Door—Our Uniqueness* (New York: Youth Commission, United Synagogue of America, 1972), quote on 18. See also Gerald Sigal, *The Jew and the Christian Missionary: A Jewish Response to Missionary Christianity* (New York: Ktav, 1981).

37. See, e.g., Zion Messianic Fellowship, *Magnify and Sanctify His Name* (Vancouver, BC: Zion Messianic Fellowship, 1987); Peniel Fellowship, *Messianic Congregation Peniel, Songbook* (Tiberias: Peniel Fellowship, n.d.).

38. David Loden, "Messianic Music in Modern Israel," *Mishkan* 46 (2006): 32–38.

39. John Fischer and David Bronstein, *Siddur for Messianic Jews* (Palm Harbor, FL: Menorah Ministries, 1988).

40. See, e.g., Eric Peter Lipson, *Passover Haggadah: A Messianic Celebration* (San Francisco: JFJ Publications, 1986); Ron Tavalin, *Kol Hesed Messianic Haggadah* (Woodville, TX: Dogwood Press, 1993); Harold A. Sevener, ed., *Passover Haggadah for Biblical Jews and Christians* (Orangeburg, NY: Chosen People Publications, n.d.).

41. Lipson, *Passover Haggadah*, 66.

42. Ibid., 23.

43. Jews for Jesus, *Invite Jews for Jesus,* brochure, ca. 2005. See also Robert L. Pressler and William E. Currie, *100 Years of Blessings, 1887–1987: The Centennial History of the American Messianic Fellowship* (Lansing, IL: American Messianic Fellowship, 1987), 31.

44. See, e.g., Brad H. Young, *Jesus and His Jewish Parables: Rediscovering the Roots of Jesus' Teaching* (New York: Paulist Press, 1989).

45. Schiffman, *Return of the Remnant.*

46. Ibid., 126; see also Sidney Goldstein, "Profile of American Jewry: Insights from the 1990 National Jewish Population Survey," *American Jewish Year Book* 92 (1992): 124–28.

47. Kai Kjaer-Hansen and Bodil F. Skjott, "Facts and Myths about the Messianic Congregation in Israel, 1998–1999," *Mishkan* 30/31 (1999): 71.

48. On non-Jews versus Jews in Messianic congregations, see Shoshanah Feher, *Passing over Easter: Constructing the Boundaries of Messianic Judaism* (Walnut Creek, CA: AltaMira Press, 1998).

49. See, e.g., Rausch, *Messianic Judaism*, 145–62; Jews for Jesus, *Jewish Believers Survey: Demographic Social and Spiritual Profiles of Jews who Believe in Jesus, a Statistical Report,* Jews for Jesus, August 1983, in Jews for Jesus Archives, San Francisco.

50. "Do Messianic Jews Proselytize?" *IRC Report* 4, no. 1 (1993): 68–69.

51. See Manny Brotman, *A Training Manual on How to Share the Messiah* (Bethesda, MD: Messianic Jewish Movement International, 1977).

52. See Susan F. Harding, "Convinced by the Holy Spirit: The Rhetoric of Fundamental Baptist Conversion," *American Ethnologist* 14 (1987): 167–81. For a discussion of the role of language in the process of conversion, see also Peter G. Stromberg, *Language and Self-Transformation: A Study of the Christian Conversion Narrative* (Cambridge: Cambridge University Press, 1993).

53. See Nancy Tatom Ammerman, *Bible Believers: Fundamentalists in the Modern World* (New Brunswick: Rutgers University Press, 1997).

54. On such tours, see the video *Kol Simcha, Sound of Joy: First Time in the Land!* (Philadelphia: Kol Simcha, 1991).

55. Benjamin Beit-Hallahmi, *Despair and Deliverance: Private Salvation in Contemporary Israel* (Albany: State University of New York Press).

56. Ibid.

57. Dahaf Research Institute, *Dahaf Report on Israeli Public Opinion Concerning Messianic Jewish Aliyah* (Jerusalem: David Stern, 1988).

58. See, e.g., David Zeidan's *Messiah Now! Ten True Stories from Modern-Day Israel of Men and Women Who Met Yeshua* (Carlisle, OM Publishing, 1992); Ben Hoekendijk's *Twelve Jews Discover Messiah* (1992; repr., Chichester: New Wine Press, 1997); Jacob Damkani's *Why Me?* (Tel Aviv: Kochav Hayom, 1993); Sid Roth, *They Thought for Themselves: Ten Amazing Jews* (Shippenburg, PA: Destiny Image, 2009).

59. See Christian Smith, *American Evangelicalism: Embattled and Thriving* (Chicago: University of Chicago Press, 1998).

60. Menahem Benhayim, "Messianic Movement in Israel—A Personal Perspective," *Mishkan* 28 (1998): 30.

61. See Catherine Wanner, *Communities of the Converted: Ukrainians and Global Evangelism* (Ithaca: Cornell University Press, 2007).

62. Serge Ruzer, "Jewish Christianity in Russia after the Six-Day War: Israeli Factor, Eschatology and *Nostra Aetate*," *Revue des Études Juives* 168 (2009): 547–61.

63. David H. Stern, *Jewish New Testament* (Jerusalem: Jewish New Testament Publications, 1990), 295.

64. Arnold G. Fruchtenbaum, *Hebrew Christianity: Its Theology, History and Philosophy* (Grand Rapids, MI: Baker Book House, 1974).

65. Ibid., 88.

66. "An Interchange on Hebrew Christian/Messianic Jewish Congregation," Appendix 3, in Arnold G. Fruchtenbaum, *Israelology: The Missing Link in Systematic Theology* (Tustin, CA: Ariel Ministries, 1983), 917–49.

67. David H. Stern, *Messianic Jewish Manifesto* (Jerusalem: Jewish New Testament Publications, 1988), 12.

68. David Brickner, *Future Hope: A Jewish Christian Look at the End of the World* (San Francisco: Purple Pomegranate Publications, 1999).

69. Stern, *Messianic Jewish Manifesto*, 4.

70. I am thankful to Gershon Nerel for sharing his thoughts with me. On Nerel's ideas, see Richard Harvey, "A Typology of Messianic Jewish Theology," *Mishkan* 57 (2008): 15–16.

71. Gershon Nerel, *Anti-Zionism in the "Electronic Church" of Palestinian Christianity*, ACTA 27 (Jerusalem: Hebrew University, 2006).

72. Tsvi Sadan, *A Flesh of Their Flesh: Jesus in Zionist Thought* (Jerusalem: Carmel, 2008). I am thankful to Tsvi Sadan for sharing his ideas with me.

73. See, for example, Tsvi Sadan, "Leper Messiah," in *Messianic Jewish Musings*, www.derekleman.com/musings/category/tsvi-sadan/; Derek Leman, review of *The Concealed Light*, by Tsvi Sadan, www.derekleman.com/musings/2012/03/14/review-the-concealed-light-by-tsvi-sadan/.

74. See Mark Kinzer, *Post-Missionary Messianic Judaism: Redefining Christian Engagement with the Jewish People* (Grand Rapids, MI: Brazos, 2005).

75. Toward the end of his life, Louis Goldberg, a moderate, middle-of-the-road Jewish Christian thinker, expressed such views. *God, Torah, Messiah; The Messianic Jewish Theology of Dr. Louis Goldberg*, ed. Dr. Richard A. Robinson (San Francisco: Purple Pomegranate Productions, 2009).

76. The group's website is www.hashivenu.org.

77. See Darrel L. Bock, "Response to Mark Kinzer's Finding Our Way through Nicaea: The Deity of Yeshua, Bilateral Ecclesiology, and Redemptive Encounter with the Living God," paper presented at the Hashivenu Forum, 2010, Los Angeles.

78. Messianic Jewish Theological Institute, Studium Catholicum, "Helsinki Conference on Jewish Continuity in the Church Unites and Challenges," press release, June 23, 2010.

79. See Gershon Nerel, "Nostra Aetate: Between Hebrew Catholics and Messianic Jews," *Mishkan* 46 (2006).

80. See Joel Robins and Matthew Engelke, "Introduction," *South Atlantic Quarterly* 109, no. 4 (2010): 623–31.

CONCLUSION

1. A. James Rudin and Marvin R. Wilson, *A Time to Speak: The Evangelical-Jewish Encounter* (Grand Rapids, MI: Eerdmans, 1987).

2. Gerald Strober, *Portrait of the Elder Brother* (New York: American Jewish Committee and the National Conference of Christians and Jews, 1972).

3. Caitlin Carenen, *The Fervent Embrace: Liberal Protestants, Evangelicals, and Israel* (New York: New York University Press, 2012).

4. Some have attempted to educate Jews on evangelical culture, opinions, and institutions. See, e.g., Mark I. Pinsky, *A Jew among the Evangelicals: A Guide for the Perplexed* (Louisville, KY: Westminster John Knox Press, 2006).

5. Charles Y. Glock and Rodney Stark, *Christian Beliefs and Antisemitism* (New York: Harper Torchbooks, 1966).

6. L. Lanniello, press release, Anti-Defamation League, New York, January 8, 1986.

7. See Regina Sherif, *Non-Jewish Zionism: Its Roots in Western History* (London: Zed Books, 1983).

8. See Thomas F. Stransky, "A Catholic Views Zionism and the State of Israel," John Osterreicher Memorial Lecture, November 9, 1997, *Holy Land*, no. 1 (1999), www. christusrex.org/www1/ofm/mag/TSmgenA0.html, which highlights the positions and complaints of local Palestinian Christians. See also David Klinghoffer, *Enemies or Allies? Why American Jews Should Learn to Stop Worrying and Love Conservative Christians* (Mercer Island, WA, n.d.).

nineteenth century and, 36–37, 83, 101, 102, 111, 112–13, 124, 138, 215, 276n24; Jewish Christians as missionaries, 121, 134–39, 159–60, 162–63, 215–16; Jewish reaction to, 7–8, 117–19, 123, 132, 137, 138, 193, 250; keeping Jewish symbols, 70, 215, 216; Messianic Jews as, 234–35; missionary reaction to Messianic Judaism, 117, 221–23, 224–25; Moody Bible Institute and, 75–77; pietists and, 18–19, 24–29, 112, 113, 215; post-World War II, 123, 124–25; premillennialist faith and, 66, 67, 77, 79, 111–14; Presbyterians and, 119–24; toning down, building ties with Israel, 188, 192. *See also* Yiddish evangelical literature

Evangelical Christians' interest in Jews: anti-Jewish conspiracy theories and, 142–44, 146–49, 150, 151; apostate Jews and, 145–46; Arab-Israeli War (1967), effects on, 6, 55, 151, 178–84, 188, 196–97, 247, 250; defending Jews, 3, 19, 60, 66, 71; educating Christians about Jews and, 26, 85, 111, 114–15, 116; evangelical communities settled in Palestine and, 12, 100–110, 172; evangelical novels and portrayal of Jews, 13, 47–49, 51–52, 53, 54–57, 165–68; expecting Jews to convert to Christianity, 3, 6, 19, 23, 24, 33, 36–37, 66, 68–69, 77, 111, 170, 177, 246; Holocaust and, 13, 153–64, 165–68; Israel support and, 1, 6–7, 9, 10, 11, 13, 47, 151, 171, 179–89, 197, 245, 248, 252; Jewish immigration to Israel and, 151, 171, 173, 179, 188, 246; Jewish immigration to Palestine and, 6, 12, 45, 76, 85, 86, 97–98, 109; Jewish role in history and, 12–13, 15, 20, 36, 76–77, 86, 88, 91, 119, 153, 163, 170, 191, 251; Jews as rejecters of Christ, 18–19, 20, 41, 56, 64–65, 66, 68, 70, 76, 78, 143, 144–45, 191, 246; Jews as God's chosen people and, 31, 37, 66–67, 70, 76, 80–81, 144, 146, 152, 157, 170, 177, 191, 245–46; Jews as heirs of children of Israel and, 5–6, 17, 19, 21, 23, 40, 42, 60, 78, 83, 101; learning Yiddish, 26, 127–28, 140; Messianic Judaism and,

221–23; mixed ideas about Jews, 2–3, 28, 33, 46, 65–66, 76, 77, 79, 150, 180; stereotyping Jews and, 1, 2, 16, 28, 54, 61–62, 64–65, 78, 143–44, 146, 152, 246; suffering of Jews and, 37, 55–56, 60, 69, 77, 78, 169–70, 251; support of Jews, 3, 6–7, 8, 141, 246, 249–50; support of Jews, in Israel, 187–88, 194, 196; support of Jews, in Palestine, 84, 101, 102, 105, 108, 109, 272n19; tourism to Israel and, 6, 183–84, 187, 188, 194, 204, 251; translating New Testament into Hebrew, 173–74; visiting Palestine and, 85, 100, 102, 105, 106, 107, 108, 110, 171. *See also* Dispensationalism; End Times; Israel; Jews returning to Palestine; Messianic faith; Palestine; Pietists; Premillennialist messianic faith; Prophecy in the Bible; Temple in Jerusalem; Zionism

Evangelical-Jewish relations, 4, 8–9, 10–11; Arab-Israeli War (1967), effects on, 6, 188, 247, 250; in recent times, 11–12, 246–52. *See also* Israel; Protestants; Temple in Jerusalem; Zionism

Exodus (Uris), 53, 166, 167
Exodus, Book of, 40, 232, 233
Expulsion Act of 1290 (England), 23

Falwell, Jerry, 5, 47, 194
Feher, Shoshanah, 10
Fellowship of Christian Testimonies to the Jews, 221
Felsenthal, Bernhard, 89
Finch, Henry, 22
Finn, Elizabeth Anne, 100–101
Finn, James, 100, 101
First Great Awakening, 24
Fischer, John, 232, 239
Fleming H. Revell, 136
Fletcher, Giles, 22
Flinkman, Marilou, 55
Flusser, David, 174
Ford, Henry, Sr., 146, 149
Four Square Gospel, 109
France, 182, 187
French Revolution era, 29–30, 36

ABOUT THE AUTHOR

Yaakov Ariel is Professor of Religious Studies at the University of North Carolina at Chapel Hill and obtained his PhD from the University of Chicago. His research focuses on Christian-Jewish relations in the late modern era and on Jewish responses to modernity and postmodernity. He has published numerous articles and books on various aspects of Protestant-Jewish relations. His book *Evangelizing the Chosen People* was awarded the Albert C. Outler Prize by the American Society of Church History.

DATE DUE

DEC 2 0 2010			
		PRINTED IN U.S.A.	